KING LEOPOLD'S LEGACY

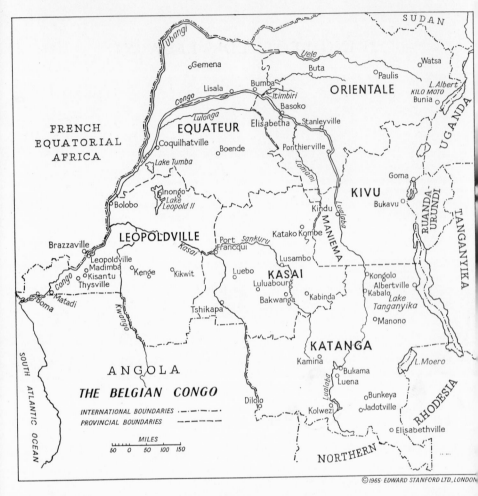

Map of the Belgian Congo

KING LEOPOLD'S LEGACY

THE CONGO UNDER BELGIAN RULE
1908-1960

ROGER ANSTEY

Issued under the auspices of the
Institute of Race Relations, London

OXFORD UNIVERSITY PRESS

LONDON   NEW YORK   IBADAN

1966

Oxford University Press, Ely House, London W. 1.

GLASGOW   NEW YORK   TORONTO   MELBOURNE   WELLINGTON
BOMBAY   CALCUTTA   MADRAS   KARACHI   LAHORE   DACCA
KUALA LUMPUR   HONG KONG   CAPE TOWN   SALISBURY
IBADAN   NAIROBI   LUSAKA   ADDIS ABABA

The Institute of Race Relations is an unofficial and non-political body, founded in 1959 to encourage and facilitate the study of the relations between races. The Institute is precluded by the Memorandum and Articles of its incorporation from expressing a corporate view. The opinions expressed in this work are those of the author.

*Printed in Great Britain by
The Camelot Press Ltd., London and Southampton*

To
Avril

CONTENTS

ILLUSTRATIONS

NOTE ON CURRENCY

When the sources give currency in Belgian/Congolese francs I have normally converted the figures into sterling at the 'par of exchange' prevailing at the end of the year in question. It should be noticed that in most of the inter-war period the market rate of exchange was appreciably different. For instance, at the end of 1934, when the par rate was FB 175 to the pound, the market rate was 105·5.

NOTE ON QUOTATIONS

When the originals are in French, quotations have normally been translated.

FOREWORD

I wish gratefully to acknowledge very varied forms of help given me during the writing of this book. It is not simply a question of expressing appreciation of help given by others working in related fields, or by colleagues in such matters as difficult points of translation, but of acknowledging the insights and information which I gained from talking to a wide range of people in England, Belgium and in the Congo. Beyond this, when travelling in the Congo, even in the relatively tranquil conditions of 1962–3, I was heavily dependent on people's hospitality and kindness, and on the facilities which various bodies made available. In particular I should like to thank the following: the authorities of the B.C.K. railway, especially MM. Denoeseux and André Baken; the Union Minière du Haut-Katanga and especially MM. Paret, J. Sohier, Robert Derriks and Bouchat; Plantations Lever and especially MM. J. Jonniaux and Vanneck, together with my hosts at the Elisabetha plantation in May 1962; the Baptist Missionary Society and in particular the Rev. Clifford Parsons and the Rev. and Mrs. H. F. Drake; the Librarian and staffs of the Library of the Ministry of African Affairs, Brussels, and of the Bibliothèque Royale, Mr. L. Allen, M. W. Bal, Father F. Bontinck, Dr. C. Bowers, Mr. Richard Brain, the late M. Georges Brausch, the Rev. Dr. and Mrs. John Carrington, Mr. and Mrs. H. Casebow, Mlle Centner (CEPSI), Mr. L. Collis, M. and Mme. R. Devers, Dr. G. Dumont, Mr. and Mrs. Denzil Dunnett, Mr. and Mrs. J. Gale, Messrs. B. G. Garnham, Robert Gardiner and N. Gaydon, Professor A. Gérard, Dr. A. Gille, Mr. Douglas Graham, the Rev. Mr. Hawksley, Mr. and Mrs. Lewis Hoffacker, Miss Catherine Hoskyns, the Abbé L. Jadin, the Rev. Marcus James, Miss Dorrie Jenks, M. Mathieu Kalenda, the Rev. Ephraim Kayumba, Maître de la Kethulle de Ryhove, Mr. and Mrs. A. Le Jeune, Mr. and Mrs. Charles Le Jeune, the Rev. A. Larsen, M. David Léonard, Dr. Wm. R. Louis, MM. Philibert Luyeye, L. M. Monassé and Mpase, the Rev. and Mrs. Angus Macneil,

Mrs. H. Marsden-Smedley, Mr. F. W. Meanwell, the Rev. Mr. and Mrs. Nock, Pastor L. Nkosi, M. G. Nève de Mevergnie, Professor Roland Oliver, Father P. Pascal, the Rev. and Mrs. R. Robinson, Dr. Helen Roseveare, Mr. and Mrs. John Sacker, Father P. Schwartzenbreck, Professor Silvestre, M. A. Sita, Dr. Ruth Slade, Professor J. Stengers, Dr. Grace Thornton, M. Tamba (OTRACO), Father Th. Theuws, M. Tchaly, His Excellency M. Moise Tshombe, M. Jean Van Lierde, Professor and Mrs. A. Verbruggen, Professor B. Verhaegen, Miss Audrey Weller, the Rev. L. West, Dr. and Mrs. E. H. Wyatt, Dr. P. Whittaker, the Rev. Mr. Woodcock, M. F Mankwe.

I also have pleasure in acknowledging the sabbatical term which the University of Durham awarded me in 1962 and the invaluable financial help made available for this project by the Rockefeller Foundation through the Institute of Race Relations. To Mr. Philip Mason, the Director, to Mr. Christopher Hill, Miss Janet Evanson and the editorial assistants I owe a very great debt of gratitude.

ROGER ANSTEY
University of Durham,
20 February 1965

ABBREVIATIONS

Among the more important abbreviations used in the text or the footnotes are the following:

A.B.A.K.O.	*Alliance des Ba-Kongo*
A.B.I.R.	Anglo-Belgian India Rubber Company
ADAPES	Association of former pupils of the *Pères de Scheut*
A.P.I.C.	*Association du Personnel Indigène de la Colonie*
A.R.S.C.	*Académie Royale des Sciences Coloniales*
A.R.S.O.M.	*Académie Royale des Sciences d'Outre-Mer*
BALUBAKAT	*Association des Ba-Luba du Katanga*
B.C.K.	*Compagnie du Chemin de Fer du Bas-Congo au Katanga*
B.M.S.	Baptist Missionary Society
C.E.C.	*Centre Extra-Coutumier*
C.E.P.S.I.	*Centre d'Étude des Problèmes Sociaux Indigènes*
C.E.R.E.A.	*Centre de Regroupement Africain*
C.O.A.K.A.	*Coalition Kasaienne*
CONAKAT	*Confédération des Associations tribales du Katanga*
COTONCO	*Compagnie Cotonnière Congolaise*
C.P.I.	*Commission Permanente pour la Protection des Indigènes*
C.R.A.	Congo Reform Association
C.R.I.S.P.	*Centre de Recherche et d'Information Socio-Politiques*
FÉDACOL	*Fédération des Associations des Colons du Congo Belge et du Ruanda-Urundi*
FORÉAMI	*Fonds Reine Élisabeth pour l'Assistance Médicale aux Indigènes*
FORMINIÈRE	*Société Internationale Forestière et Minière du Congo*
H.C.B.	*Huileries du Congo Belge*
I.R.C.B.	*Institut Royal Colonial Belge*

L.U.K.A.	*Union Kwangolaise pour l'Indépendance et la Liberté*
M.N.C.	*Mouvement National Congolais*
M.N.C.—K.	*Mouvement National Congolais—Kalonji*
M.N.C.—L.	*Mouvement National Congolais—Lumumba*
OTRACO	*Office des Transports Coloniaux*
P.N.P.	*Parti National du Progrès*
P.S.A.	*Parti Solidaire Africain*

ACKNOWLEDGEMENTS

For permission to make certain quotations, grateful acknowledgments are due to: Dr. J. S. Cookey (in respect of 'Great Britain and the Congo Question', unpublished Ph.D. thesis of the University of London, 1964); the Baptist Missionary Society (for permission to quote from the correspondence of the Rev. A. E. Scrivener); the Oxford University Press (Lord Hailey, *An African Survey*, 1957); Établissements Émile Bruylant (G. Van der Kerken, *Les Sociétés bantoues du Congo belge*, 1920); the Académie Royale des Sciences d'Outre-Mer, Brussels (F. Grévisse, *La Grande pitié des juridictions indigènes*, 1949); Colin Turnbull Esq. and Messrs Chatto and Windus (C. Turnbull, *The Lonely African*, 1963); the Rev. Efraim Andersson (*Messianic Popular Movements in the Lower Congo*, 1958); the Yale University Press (B. Malinowski, *The Dynamics of Culture Change*, 1961); UNESCO (Daryll Forde (ed.), *Social Implications of Industrialization and Urbanization in Africa South of the Sahara*, 1956); the Northwestern University Press (A. P. Merriam, *Congo: Background of Conflict*, 1961); and Father J. Van Wing ('Une évolution de la coutume Bakongo'; see Appendix).

Grateful acknowledgment is also made to the following for permission to reproduce illustrations: the Centre de Recherche et d'Information Socio-Politiques, Brussels (the P.S.A. poster: from H. Weiss and B. Verhaegen (eds.), *Parti Solidaire Africain*, 1963); William Fagg Esq. and Studio Vista (the Batawba figures: from W. Fagg and M. Plass, *African Sculpture*, 1964); the Compagnie du Chemin de Fer du Bas-Congo au Katanga (the *Cité des Travailleurs*); the Oxford University Press (Leopold II: from R. Slade, *King Leopold's Congo*, 1962); *Le Dossier de mois* (Patrice Lumumba: from *Le Dossier*, IV, 4, 1964); the Académie Royale des Sciences d'Outre-Mer (Leopoldville: from J. Denis, *Le Phénomène urbain en Afrique centrale*, 1958); Messrs Chapman and Hall (River Congo: from G. Martelli, *Leopold to Lumumba*, 1962); the Baptist Missionary Society (photograph showing a child at school); and the Librairie des Éclaireurs Unionistes, Brussels (Church of Christ Congo Mission at Coquilhatville: from E. M. Braekman, *Histoire de protestantisme au Congo*, 1961).

I

BELGIUM TAKES OVER THE CONGO

THE Belgian Congo was the creation of King Leopold II. Less than two decades after he had ascended the Belgian throne in 1865, his *Association Internationale du Congo* was recognized by the European powers as an independent state; a quarter of a century after that recognition, Leopold made over the Congo to Belgium.

Sovereign of a small European state which scarcely provided him with sufficient outlets for his energy, talents and enthusiasm, Leopold had interested himself in various overseas projects from 1855, when he was still heir to the throne, onwards. Words which Leopold uttered in a speech made in 1888 may serve as a text for his political life. 'If the Fatherland remains our headquarters, the world ought to be our objective . . . There are no small nations, there are only small minds.'[1] In the years 1861–5 he considered no less than five overseas schemes, including plans for the purchase of Sarawak and of an Argentine province. The latter, at least, had Leopold acquired it, would have been made over to Belgium. But shortly after he ascended the throne in 1865, Leopold became convinced of the national lukewarmness to the idea of colonies and by December 1866 was thinking in different terms—of an international company, but one with its headquarters in Brussels, which would gradually become for China what the East India Company had been for India. But nothing came of this scheme, nor of attempts to acquire concessions in Mozambique and the Philippines. By 1875 Leopold's hopes had, if only in disappointment, become centred on Africa. He considered first the possibilities of the unstable and near-bankrupt Transvaal, but his main attention soon became fixed on the

[1] Quoted in Pierre Daye, *Léopold II* (Paris, Fayard, 1934), p. 309.

opening up of Central Africa.[1] The years 1876–84 witnessed the birth and early development by Leopold, behind an international façade, of his Congo design. In 1884 Leopold achieved for the Congo that rare consummation of the private enterprise empire-builder—international recognition as an independent state. Of that state—in his personal capacity and not as King of Belgium—Leopold was king.

The Congo Independent State lasted for twenty-four years. They were years of epic achievement. The period saw the exploration of the Upper Congo, the campaign against the Arabs and the Arab slave trade, the attempt to establish the Congo State on the Upper Nile, the occupation of Katanga, the establishment of some sort of European administration in many areas, the opening-up of lines of communication, the extension of Christian missionary operations: the period also witnessed, in the rubber-bearing regions of the forest, the subordination of sound administration to the obtaining of the maximum possible quantity of wild rubber. This came to involve atrocities on a large scale, atrocities which led to the inception of the Congo Reform campaign, and this was the principal immediate reason why Belgium took over the Congo in 1908.[2] Paradoxically it had probably always been Leopold's intention that Belgium should ultimately do so: what he did not intend was that the transfer should be at a time of others' forcing.

Leopold's intention that the Congo should eventually fall to Belgium was made explicit in the publication of a Will and Testament in 1890. The choice of instrument tells its own story: cession was to take place on Leopold's death.[3] Not-

[1] This summary of Leopold's thinking on overseas projects before 1876 is based on A. Roeykens, *Léopold II et l'Afrique, 1855–1880* (Brussels, Académie Royale des Sciences Coloniales, 1958), pp. 13–39, 55–56, though it does not always share its conclusions. For a recent English biography of Leopold, see N. Ascherson, *The King Incorporated* (London, Allen and Unwin, 1963).

[2] For the history of the Congo Independent State see the companion volume of this book: Dr. Ruth Slade, *King Leopold's Congo* (London, Oxford University Press, for the Institute of Race Relations, 1962). In writing of the Belgian take-over it is difficult to avoid some duplication of the concluding chapter of Dr. Slade's book. What it is here sought to do is to provide an account of the take-over for those who come fresh to the subject and to point out certain factors in the process, and in the history of the Congo Independent State, which were important in the development of the Belgian Congo. Sources which have become available since 1962 will also be used.

[3] A. Stenmans, *La Reprise du Congo par la Belgique* (Brussels, Éditions Techniques et Scientifiques, 1949), pp. 114–15.

withstanding, Leopold formally agreed at the same time that Belgium could exercise an option to annexe the Congo State in 1901,[1] whilst in 1895 he was prepared to make an immediate cession.[2] But Leopold's abnegation should not be taken as entirely voluntary. There seems little doubt that he agreed to the 1890 arrangement as a condition of obtaining a desperately needed loan from a Belgium which was experiencing some stirrings of colonial interest and which therefore sought to establish a firm lien on her sovereign's colony.[3] Even clearer is the reluctance with which he accepted his Cabinet's demand in 1895 for an immediate cession. On this occasion Leopold, for a number of reasons, had made himself vulnerable in the eyes of the Belgian Government. There was, first, the policy of direct Congo State participation in economic exploitation, formally adopted in 1891; there was also the discovery of a dubious financial arrangement which Leopold had concluded with Browne de Tiège of Antwerp, aimed at giving him relief in his continuing financial difficulties in the Congo; and there was, finally, the embarrassment which Leopold had caused his ministers by the Congo State's Nile policy which brought complications with Britain, France and Germany. He agreed to cession only because he had no other choice and was saved from this necessity only by the refusal of the Belgian Parliament, now opposed to colonial ventures—not least because of the block of Socialist deputies and senators who had appeared with the constitutional reforms of 1893—to endorse the ministry's action.[4] When, in 1901, under the terms of the 1890 arrangement, Belgium might have exercised her option to annexe the Congo, there was no sufficiently strong and determined body of opinion either in the Cabinet or in Parliament to insist on this course, whilst Leopold publicly worked against immediate annexation.[5] Although by 1901, Leopold was less insistent that the cession of the Congo must wait for his death, he continued firmly to hold that the timing must be his.[6] However, Leopold was able to maintain this line only as long as solely domestic pressures were involved. These, on their own, were never sufficiently strong or determined to make Leopold

[1] A. Stenmans, *La Reprise du Congo par la Belgique*, p. 113.
[2] Ibid., p. 179.   [3] Ibid., pp. 126–7.   [4] Ibid., pp. 164–205.
[5] Ibid., pp. 237–52. Jean Stengers. *Belgique et Congo: l'élaboration de la charte coloniale* (Brussels, La Renaissance du Livre, 1963), pp. 47–50.
[6] Stenmans, *Reprise*, p. 242.

yield. It was with the mounting of an international agitation that Leopold had to give way. Why did such an agitation arise?

From the later 1880's the task of ruling a territory eighty times the size of Belgium threatened to break Leopold financially. Not only this; Leopold was as far away as can be imagined from making a profit out of the Congo, a right which he unhesitatingly believed to be his in virtue of his initiative in the creation of the Congo Independent State. Thus, with the immediate need to raise more money to meet the expenses of administration, and the long-term hope of making a profit, Leopold initiated a system whereby exploitation of the vacant lands of the Congo was reserved either to the State or to concessionary companies nominated by it. The products for which it was eminently worth while to take such measures were wild rubber, now much in demand in Europe, and, to a lesser extent, ivory. The basis of the Leopoldine system was a state Ordinance of 1885 which declared that vacant lands (that is, lands not occupied by Africans or anyone else) belonged to the State. This principle, common amongst colonial governments, was applied in a distinctive way. A decree of September 1891, put into execution by a number of local administrative circulars, empowered administrative officers in much of the vast region north of the Congo river between Coquilhatville and Stanleyville to take all necessary measures to see that wild rubber and ivory should henceforth be offered to the State authorities alone. The next step was a near-comprehensive application of the principle that all vacant lands belonged to the State. From 1892 onwards nearly the whole of the Congo was apportioned into two categories. In the *Domaine Privé* (of the State) the State authorities began the direct exploitation of natural products, private traders being completely excluded. At the same time concessions for the exclusive exploitation of stipulated areas were made, on conditions, to a number of companies or individuals. It appears that Leopold, through nominees of the Congo State, had holdings in many or all of these companies, whilst a large area round Lakes Leopold II and Tumba was first ceded to the 'Duke of Saxe-Coburg-Gotha', then, in 1896, after it had been much extended, its true nature was acknowledged, and it was re-christened the *Domaine de la couronne*. The existence of the *Domaine* was not officially acknowledged until 1901.

The second string to the rubber policy was the requirement, normal enough in itself, that the Congolese should pay taxes. But in King Leopold's Congo there was until 1903 no legislation of any kind determining the amount of tax to be paid, and, since there was no currency, taxation could only be levied in labour or in kind.

As Leopold's own Commission of Inquiry, which he was eventually obliged to set up, put it:

Each *chef de poste* or of a trading post, without asking himself too much on what basis, demanded from the natives the performance of services of the most diverse kind in labour or in kind, maybe to provide for his own needs and those of the post, maybe to exploit the riches of the *Domaine.*

Logically there was no need for the State or the concession companies to have paid a farthing for any of the produce collected by Congolese, but in practice arbitrary payments of brass rods or cloth were sometimes made. Since the monopoly either of the State or of a concessionary company was inevitable, there could be no possibility that one buyer, or 'buyer', would have to compete against another. The absence of any legislation on taxation—or, after the legalization of a labour tax of forty hours per month by a decree of 18 November 1903, of adequate legislation—made it easier for State officials and company agents to inflict what punishments they liked in case of default on amounts fixed for each village, and it appears that the infliction of a penalty for any excess of zeal, though this did happen, was so infrequent as to constitute no significant check on the arbitrary exercise of authority. A final and important component of the system was that administrators and company agents received, until 1896, premiums on the amount of produce which they collected, and from that year, bonuses payable at the end of their Congo service which were in practice related to the success of their produce collection.[1]

In such a context it is scarcely surprising that rubber collection came to dominate the activities of officials and agents in

[1] This outline of the nature and operation of the rubber policy is mainly derived from S. J. S. Cookey, 'Great Britain and the Congo Question, 1892–1913' (unpublished Ph.D. thesis, University of London, 1964), pp. 9–22. But see also the Report of the Congo State Commission of Inquiry in *Bulletin officiel*, September–October 1905, pp. 135–285 (the quotation is on p. 164), and F. Cattier, *Étude sur la situation de l'état indépendant du Congo* (Brussels, F. Larcier, 1906), *passim.*

the rubber districts. As the Rev. A. E. Scrivener, a Baptist missionary, said of a State post for whose commandant he had nothing but *praise*,

Everything was on a military basis, but so far as I could see the one and only reason for it all was RUBBER. It was the theme of nearly every conversation and it was evident that the only way to please one's superiors was to increase the output somehow.[1]

From this it was only a step to abuse, abuse which had a varying intensity. In 1899 a State official told a British consular officer his method of rubber collection in the Ubangi region.

His method of procedure was to arrive in canoes at a village, the inhabitants of which invariably bolted on their arrival; the soldiers were then landed, and commenced looting, taking all the chickens, grain, etc., out of the houses; after this they attacked the natives until able to seize their women; these women were kept as hostages until the Chief of the district brought in the required number of kilogrammes of rubber.

The rubber having been brought, the women were sold back to their owners for a couple of goats a-piece, and so he continued from village to village until the requisite amount of rubber had been collected.[2]

Sometimes methods were even less agreeable. Alfred Parminter, an Englishman who had worked on the Congo, told Reuters in an interview of how

On one occasion, at Bopoto, having dined with Lieutenant Blochter . . . I was smoking with him on the bank. It was late in the evening when suddenly a force of his troops returned from an expedition on which he had sent them in the morning. The sergeant held up triumphantly a number of ears fastened together on a string. . . . The soldiers were praised for their success, and ordered to return next day and capture the chief.[3]

The cutting-off of ears and other forms of mutilation sometimes formed a part of a macabre system of accounting. In 1899 a State official in the Momboyo river region of the

[1] B.M.S. Archives, Scrivener Box. Rev. A. E. Scrivener, 'Notes on a Journey to Lake Leopold II', August 1903. Scrivener's Notes are to be found in edited form in the *West African Mail*, Liverpool, 8 January 1904, pp. 1042–5.

[2] F.O. 10/731, Pulteney to F.O., 15 September 1899, quoted in Cookey, 'Great Britain and the Congo Question', p. 63, n.

[3] *The Standard*, 8 September 1896, quoted in Cookey, 'Great Britain and the Congo Question', p. 50.

Domaine de la couronne, mistaking the identity of his interlocutor, told an American missionary, who noted the conversation in his diary, that:

> Each time the corporal goes out to get rubber, cartridges are given to him. He must bring back all not used; and for every one used, he must bring back a right hand! . . . As to the extent to which this is carried on, he informed me that in six months they, the State, on the Momboyo River had used 6,000 cartridges, which means that 6,000 people are killed or mutilated. It means more than 6,000, for the people have told me repeatedly that soldiers kill children with the butt of their guns.[1]

If, as these testimonies indicate, the atrocities were for the most part carried out by Congolese soldiers or 'forest-guards', it is evident that they acted under orders. It is also the case that white officials or agents of companies sometimes took a direct part. Scrivener brought to light the case of the notorious 'Malu Malu', to give the European in question his native name, who was stationed in the Lake Leopold II region from 1898 to 1900. On a number of occasions men who had failed to produce their quota of rubber were shot dead by him on the spot, whilst he is also known to have placed a group of such men in file behind each other and used one bullet to kill them all.[2] It was interesting to observe, on a recent visit to the region, that there is in Bolobo a nearly universal folk-memory of Malu Malu. In conversations about the rubber period his name was constantly brought up or else seized upon with characteristic, positive recognition. My clear impression was that, though Malu Malu lacked the technical equipment of a Heydrich or an Eichmann, he was in precisely the same category of bestiality. It was also apparent that a strong strand of local, oral tradition holds the rubber policy to have been a greater cause of death and depopulation than either the scourge of sleeping-sickness or the periodic ravages of smallpox.[3] That the operation of the rubber policy did ravage whole areas was emphatically

[1] Quoted in F.O. 10/806, Casement to Lansdowne, 11 December 1903, pp. 20–21. This is the famed 'Casement Report', which, with certain excisions, was published as Africa No. 1, 1904, Cd. 1933 (1904, lxii, p. 357). See also Clark to Casement, 3 August 1903, p. 49 of the Report.

[2] B.M.S. Archives. Scrivener, 'Notes on a Journey to Lake Leopold II', Scrivener to Casement, 22 September 1903, printed in 'Casement Report', pp. 39–41.

[3] Personal information.

claimed by Casement: 'Perhaps the most striking change observed during my journey into the interior was the great reduction observable everywhere in native life' (he had had earlier experience of the Congo)—whilst he went on to give specific instances,[1] as did Scrivener in his report. Scrivener, for example, estimated that the population of Ngongo, within a quarter-mile radius of the *Domaine de la couronne* rubber post, dropped from two thousand to two hundred between 1898 and 1903.[2] Leopold's own Commission of Inquiry, it should be said, regarded smallpox and sleeping-sickness as the primary causes of depopulation.[3]

None the less there is no doubt that the operation of the Leopoldine rubber policy was in essence as Casement portrayed it. It is not that we are dependent solely on Casement's impressions—his later career might suggest that the instability that then manifested itself could have distorted his judgement in 1903; there is, simply, an abundance of corroborative evidence, the nature of which has been indicated. That evidence includes (as will be seen later) the substantial endorsement of Casement's findings which was made by Leopold's own Commission of Inquiry and which was perhaps epitomized in its president's admission to Mackie, a British consul in the Congo, that 'the evidence collected agrees in all essential details with Mr. Casement's reports on the subject'.[4] Pickersgill, an earlier consul, clearly indicated how such a system was bound to involve cruelty, and it is important to realize that no action against abuses could be effective whilst the system lasted— though, with a somewhat anachronistic regard for the social stratification of colonial life, the Administration was sometimes prepared to act against the agents of the concessionary com-

---

[1] 'Casement Report', pp. 1, 6–7, 47. This last page, quoting Rev. J. Clark to Casement, 3 August 1903, gives population estimates, founded on personal knowledge over the previous ten years, for a number of villages in the Lake Tumba area.

[2] B.M.S. Archives, Scrivener, 'Notes on a Journey to Lake Leopold II'.

[3] Report of Commission of Inquiry, *Bulletin officiel*, September–October 1905, pp. 236–40.

[4] F.O. 10/813 Mackie to Villiers, 'Private', 20 February 1905, quoted in Cookey, 'Great Britain and the Congo Question', p. 164. See also Van Eetvelde's admissions to the British minister in Brussels (F.O. 10/642, Plunkett to F.O., 20 October 1895, 'Very Confidential', and F.O. 403/304, Plunkett to F.O., 26 September 1896, 'Very Confidential', cited in Cookey, 'Great Britain and the Congo Question', p. 51).

panies, A.B.I.R. (the Anglo-Belgian India Rubber Company), the Lulunga Company, and the rest.[1]

In such a country and such a climate put a rough-grained Belgian army officer, unaccustomed to the management of coloured races and untrained to civil government; give him absolute power over the native population, and orders to raise revenue to the utmost of his ability; above him place a military autocrat as governor, as sternly determined to be obeyed as if he were at the head of a regiment; and, higher still, appoint a resolute Minister, desirous above all things of proving his royal master's enterprise to be commercially sound, and the train is fully laid for exactions enforced by cruelty. The Minister fires the Governor, and the Governor fires the *Commissaire*, and the whole force of the explosion falls upon the wretched aborigines.[2]

Or, as the Commission of Inquiry put it, the system was worth what the men who operated it were worth. If a man was reasonable and farsighted he would attempt to reconcile the interests of the State or private company with those of the Africans, and sometimes he would obtain a great deal without recourse to violence. 'But a good number of agents only thought of obtaining the maximum possible in the minimum possible time, and their demands were often excessive.'[3]

It should be added that Leopold had great difficulty in recruiting suitable men in a country with no tradition of colonial service. The Belgian army was the largest single source of agents but it could not always provide men of the requisite character and ability. The shortage was partly made good by other Belgians and by foreigners. The question which, at the time, was frequently asked in Belgium about anyone who took up service in the Congo, 'Why? What has he done?', suggests that many of the Congo State's agents were unlikely to be over-scrupulous.

In Belgium there had been protests at the policy of direct

---

[1] F.O. 10/731. Remarks by Mr. Pickersgill, 'Confidential', 1 June 1897. The British interest in A.B.I.R. was more apparent than real. Though founded by a Colonel North, in 1892, and although most of the capital was held in his name, he was a 'dummy' for Leopold himself (H. Waltz, *Das Konzessionswesen im Belgischen Kongo*, Jena, 1917), I, pp. 40, 54.

[2] F.O. 10/731. Remarks by Mr. Pickersgill, 'Confidential', 1 June 1897.

[3] Report of Commission of Inquiry. *Bulletin officiel*, September–October 1905, p. 164.

economic exploitation[1] at the time of its inception. The
Governor-General himself had resigned and both Baron
Lambermont and Émile Banning, each of whom had done so
much for Leopold's Congo venture in its early stages, protested
strongly against the new policy—and were henceforth to be
strong advocates of the making-over of the Congo to Belgium.
As the nineties progressed periodic reports of abuses were
received and in Press and Parliament Belgian voices began to
be raised in protest, especially that of the radical liberal, G.
Lorand, who, in a 1900 parliamentary interpellation gained
the support both of the Socialist leader, E. Vandervelde, and
a Catholic deputy, M. Colfs.[2] If at this stage, and subsequently,
the most vociferous opposition to Leopold's Congo régime
came from the Socialists and the radical Liberals, it should be
remembered that they had a natural function of opposition to
a Catholic and royalist ministry. It was no less to be expected
that opposition to Leopold should be slower to emerge from the
benches of the governing party. The most weighty and penetrating criticism of policy came from a Belgian authority on
Colonial Law, Professor F. Cattier, in his book, *Droit et administration de l'état indépendant du Congo*, published in 1898.[3]

British protests had originated even earlier. During the early
and middle nineties isolated protests were made, whilst from
the end of 1896 the Aborigines Protection Society, under its
crusading if ageing secretary, H. R. Fox-Bourne, seriously
entered the lists. It was as part of its campaign that in April
1897 Sir Charles Dilke moved in the House of Commons that
the Government should consider taking international action
to secure 'equitable treatment of the natives of Africa', by
which was particularly meant the Congo State. In the event
neither these pressures nor the periodic reports of maladministration which the Foreign Office received from consuls
were sufficient to compel it to take action, but the turn of the
century, significantly for the future, saw the beginnings of
collaboration between E. D. Morel and John Holt. Holt,
wealthy and influential as an African merchant and of genuine
humanitarian zeal withal, gave over the years invaluable support to the former shipping clerk who had become convinced

---

[1] The term is not here used pejoratively.

[2] Cookey, 'Great Britain and the Congo Question', pp. 58–60; Stenmans, *Reprise*,
pp. 219–20, 223–4.

[3] See Cookey, 'Great Britain and the Congo Question', p. 60.

that the formation of the Congo State was one enormous fraud at the expense of its peoples. By May 1902, that essential ingredient of the British humanitarian campaign, a Mansion House meeting, could be called and this was followed a year later by a major debate in the Commons in which strong feeling was expressed and unanimous support was obtained for a resolution in the name of Herbert Samuel that 'this House requests His Majesty's Government to confer with the other Powers . . . in order that measures may be adopted to abate the evils prevalent in that State [the Congo]'.[1]

The response of the British Government was to appeal to the Powers who had signed the Berlin Act of 1885 to assist her in working out a solution to the Congo question. Partly because the note was conceived in rather vague terms, and also because it offered little hard evidence of atrocities, and because the grounds for any international intervention were indefinite and controversial, the British approach brought no response; Leopold contributed to this result by the use which he made of Belgian diplomats in Europe's capitals.[2] But a second action of the British Government, the dispatch of their recently appointed Congo consul, Roger Casement, on a fact-finding mission (on which in any case he was about to embark of his own accord) was to prove of momentous importance.

Starting from Leopoldville, his tour lasted eleven weeks, during which time he visited several points on the banks of the Congo as far up as the confluence with the Lulonga river, ascended that river and its principal feeder, the Lopori, as far as Bongandanga, and made a circuit of Lake Tumba. He came back with a whole inventory of atrocity and abuse, his information having been gleaned from Protestant missionaries, from certain of the white agents of the State and of A.B.I.R., and from the Congolese themselves. In the published version of Casement's report many of the names of persons and of places were suppressed, but the narrative of constant and excessive demands for rubber, the taking of hostages, the mutilations and killings carried out by the so-called forest guards, the more occasional excesses of European agents, the depopulation, was compulsive. In Morel's words, as he heard from Casement's own lips of his experiences,

---

[1] Cookey, 'Great Britain and the Congo Question', pp. 44–103, *passim*.
[2] Ibid., pp. 103–12.

the scenes so vividly described seemed to fashion themselves out of the shadows before my eyes. The daily agony of an entire people unrolled itself in all the repulsive terrifying details. I verily believe I *saw* those hunted women clutching their children and flying panic-stricken to the bush; the blood flowing from those quivering black bodies as the hippopotamus-hide whip struck and struck again; the savage soldiery rushing hither and thither amid burning villages; the ghastly tally of severed hands.[1]

Morel, it should be said, was already a violent opponent of the rubber policy; but in an age which had recently been horrified by the Armenian atrocities his reaction was probably typical.

The publication of the Casement report was of decisive importance in at least three ways. First, it produced a profound and widespread feeling in Britain that the administrative system of the Congo Independent State must be reformed: 'Nothing, indeed, is more remarkable in the movement for the reform of the Congo administration than the absolute unanimity with which the demand is advanced and supported by every section of public opinion', wrote the *Morning Post*.[2] Secondly, the report gave birth to the vital engine of reform, the Congo Reform Association. Finally, the report impelled Leopold to action which was itself fraught with further consequences, the appointment of his own Commission of Inquiry.

Specifically, the foundation of the Congo Reform Association resulted from the discussions between Casement and Morel at the time of the appearance of Casement's report. They decided, quite simply, 'to unite in one body the various influences at work against Leopoldianism . . . to appeal to a wide public on a single issue'.[3] Edmund Dene Morel was a crusader born. One feels that he would have conducted a campaign against the purveyors of poor-quality baby-food whilst yet in the cradle! In 1904 he had for four or five years believed that the Leopoldine system was viciously oppressive and must be

---

[1] Morel Papers: E. D. Morel, unpublished 'History of the Congo Reform Association', quoted in W. R. Louis, 'Roger Casement and the Congo', *Journal of African History*, V, 1, 1964, p. 114.

[2] *Morning Post*, 10 June 1904, quoted in W. Roger Louis, 'The Triumph of the Movement for Reform in the Congo, 1905-1908'. At the time of going to press this article had not been published. Dr. Louis very kindly allowed me to consult his article in typescript.

[3] Unpublished C.R.A. history quoted in Louis, 'Roger Casement and the Congo', p. 115.

changed, and had been able to initiate a persistent newspaper campaign to this end in the pages of the *West African Mail*, which he founded in April 1903. But only with the appearance of Casement's report did the existence of widespread abuses come to be accepted; only with the foundation of the Congo Reform Association did a vehicle for a really effective campaign come into existence. Within a few months of its creation in February 1904 the Association counted an influential member-ship—ten peers and over forty M.P.s[1]—and for five years, particularly, it exerted a constant and effective pressure on the British Government.

The reply to the Casement report which the Congo State Government made was in the long run important not because of its denials and defences but because the Congo Government undertook to carry out an inquiry into the alleged atrocities. However little Leopold may have intended by this concession, the fact that it was made was used by the British and Belgian opponents of the Congo State to press—successfully—for the appointment of an impartial commission with adequate powers. Quite apart from its important Belgian consequences, the sub-stantial confirmation that the system was producing abuses enabled the British Government to press its intervention farther and, from April 1906 onwards, to work for Belgian annexation as the best solution. This solution had earlier been advocated in various quarters, notably in 1905 by Sir Harry Johnston, the former African administrator and traveller, and, before that, perhaps hinted at by Grey himself when speaking for the Opposition in a parliamentary debate of June 1904. It was logical for the Foreign Office to take up advocacy of the Belgian solution since, from 1900 onwards, the office had never believed that the Berlin Act, 1885, by which the Congo Free Trade Zone was set up, and in the context of which the Congo Independent State had its birth, gave any effective right of international intervention.[2] Amongst the Congo Reformers Belgian annexa-tion was a solution which some were loath to espouse, but to which there was no effective alternative.

The British Government did have an axe to grind in its

[1] Louis, 'Triumph of Congo Reform'.

[2] The development of the British diplomatic offensive is based, broadly on Cookey, 'Great Britain and the Congo Question', pp. 134ff. but see also Louis, 'Roger Casement and the Congo', p. 100; Louis, 'Triumph of Congo Reform'; and *Hansard*, cxxxv, H.C., 9 June 1904, 1288.

demand for the demise of the Congo State. As long as the Foreign Office was obliged to make representations about events in the Congo, it incurred the ill-will of Belgium, a client state, and this could upset the European alliance pattern.[1] Secondly Britain was, in the early twentieth century, still concerned to maintain the sway of Free Trade—and under the Independent State there was no free trade in the Congo.[2] The axe which Belgian opinion thought Britain was grinding —the desire to acquire the Congo for herself—was a paper one indeed. Rather did Sir Edward Grey, the Foreign Secretary, go so far as to suggest to the French in 1907 that France might partition the Congo State with Germany[3]—a proposal which was certainly sinister enough from the Belgian point of view, but which was not self-interested in a crude sense. It is clear that Grey and his predecessor, Lord Lansdowne, had become genuinely appalled by what they believed was going on in the Congo, resolved—in the case of Grey, at least—to do something about it and were kept to the resolve by the pertinacity of the Congo Reformers. Here was the major spring of British official action.[4]

In December 1906 the United States Government aligned itself with Britain in pressing for reforms in the Congo. The United States, like Britain, had had its Congo reform campaign (Morel himself had crossed the Atlantic in the autumn of 1904) and the effect of that campaign on the Administration had been more rapidly felt than in Britain.[5] In December 1906 also, France displayed a distinctly cool attitude towards Leopold. Never enthusiastic about international action towards the Congo State, principally because an essentially similar Concessions system operated in the French Congo,[6] France nevertheless had her obligations to the Anglo-French *entente* to consider. When, therefore, the Belgian minister in Paris sought in December to enlist French sympathy for the Congo State in face of the British attacks upon it and upon Belgium, he was simply told that the *entente* of 1904 was a reality.[7]

[1] Louis, 'Triumph of Congo Reform'.

[2] See the British position as cited in Stenmans, *Reprise*, p. 445.

[3] Louis, 'Triumph of Congo Reform'.

[4] Ibid., *passim*; Cookey, 'Great Britain and the Congo Question', *passim*.

[5] Louis, 'Triumph of Congo Reform'; Cookey, 'Great Britain and the Congo Question', pp. 207–12.

[6] Ibid., pp. 108, 227.

[7] Stengers, *Belgique et Congo*, pp. 81–82.

It was on 13 December that Leopold asked his ministers to take in hand the task of making over the Congo to Belgium.[1] It appears that it was international pressure which was primarily responsible for Leopold's surrender.[2] None the less an epic debate on the whole question of the Congo was taking place in the Belgian Chamber of Deputies at the very time of Leopold's message to his ministers, and that debate was itself by no means the first manifestation of a domestic, Belgian criticism of the Congo Independent State and most of its works. Early Belgian misgivings about the Congo have already been noticed (p. 10). But only at the turn of 1905–6 did an important section of Belgian opinion begin to be seriously worried. The occasion was the publication in November 1905 of the report of Leopold's own commission of inquiry, whose very origin was due to the necessity of countering the Casement report, and the appearance in February 1906 of Félicien Cattier's '*Étude sur la situation de l'état indépendant du Congo*'. Only one member of the commission had any direct connexion with the Congo and any remaining doubts that the commissioners might be mere conformists were stilled when they produced a document which, though polite and in some places even laudatory, made it clear that abuses were widespread in the Congo State and that the administrative system itself was the cause of those abuses.[3] However, the report was couched in general and unsensational terms, with the result that its impact on public opinion generally was as slight as its effect upon lawyers, politicians and those who knew how to read such a document was considerable.[4]

The book by Cattier, an acknowledged specialist in colonial law, was much more trenchant and much less inhibited; its effect was consequently great. The principal immediate outcome

---

[1] Ibid., p. 82.

[2] Ibid.; J. Stengers, 'Quand Léopold II s'est-il rallié à l'annexion du Congo par la Belgique?', *Bulletin de l'Institut Royal Colonial Belge*, XXIII, 1952, pp. 783–824; Stenmans, *Reprise*, p. 376.

[3] The report is published in the *Bulletin officiel*, September–October 1905, pp. 135–285, and summarized in the slightly more accessible book of Stenmans, already cited, pp. 297–306. When confronted with an adverse report, Leopold tried to blunt its effect—by, for instance, supplying the British Press with a pre-publication 'summary' put out by the 'West African Missionary Association', an improbable group of Irishmen resident in Brussels: see R. Slade, *English-Speaking Missions in the Congo Independent State* (Brussels, A.R.S.C., 1959), pp. 296–7.

[4] Stengers, *Belgique et Congo*, pp. 67–9; Stenmans, *Reprise*, pp. 307–8.

of the two publications was a parliamentary debate whose concluding resolution, of 2 March 1906, demonstrated that opinion in favour of a Belgian take-over of the Congo was hardening, for the Chamber resolved to take in hand without delay the consideration of 'the project of law . . . on the government of the colonial possessions of Belgium'. Of course, this was something less than a decision to annexe, but the resolution was clearly a portent.[1] Then in the spring of that year a Jesuit, Father Vermeersch, published *La Question congolaise*, strongly criticizing Congo administration, and in this way did from a Catholic perspective what Cattier's book had done from a Liberal one, and may have done much to persuade hitherto unpersuaded Belgian Catholics that criticisms of the Congo régime were justified. A little later, in June, the king made matters worse from his own point of view by making public a long letter, and codicil to his will, in which his opposition to annexation was made clear and couched, withal, in somewhat haughty terms.[2] This *démarche* by the king led in turn to a further parliamentary debate spanning the period 28 November to 14 December. Its outcome was a large majority for a resolution asserting that Belgium had the right to take over the Congo; that it was exclusively for the Belgian Parliament to determine the form of government to be enjoyed by the Congo in such a case; that the consideration of the colonial charter by the parliamentary sub-committee, the Commission of XVII, should be hastened; and that the decision on the question of the take-over should be made as quickly as possible.[3]

If Belgian political opinion was by December 1906 settling firmly in favour of annexation, it has been seen that Leopold had made the crucial decision to yield up the Congo by 13 December and that it was international rather than domestic pressure which had brought him to that point. This does not mean that domestic pressure should be regarded as unimportant, for several reasons. To the extent that Belgian ministries were loth to go against Leopold's wishes in Congo matters (and this was generally the case with the De Smets de Naeyer and De Trooz ministries), foreign pressure needed the secondary mediatory pressure of a domestic opposition. Secondly,

[1] Stengers, *Belgique et Congo*, pp. 69–72; Stenmans, *Reprise*, pp. 313–19.
[2] Stenmans, *Reprise*, pp. 330–40.
[3] Ibid., pp. 346–69; Stengers, *Belgique et Congo*, pp. 83–86.

only in so far as some general feeling against the Congo abuses and atrocities was aroused in Belgium, could Belgium generate any sort of resolve to adopt 'the Belgian solution'. Thirdly, though few Belgian parliamentarians, once they had faced up to the necessity of a Belgian take-over, were oblivious of the continued admonitory gaze of Britain and the United States, it was they, and only they, who could draw up the actual legislation concerning the take-over and the régime which the future colony was to enjoy. This broad twofold pattern of foreign and domestic pressure upon Leopold, with his ministers occupying an unenviable sandwich position, was even more apparent after December 1906 than before.

From that time onwards the British position, seconded by the United States, was that she was prepared to allow Belgium a certain time to arrange for a Belgian take-over but that she would not wait indefinitely, and would closely scrutinize the terms of cession.[1]

'I think it is only right and fair to say,' said Grey in the House of Commons on 15 May 1907, 'that now that that Government has lost no time in declaring its intention to annex we should wait for a reasonable time to see what progress is made, and what the conditions of annexation will be. That is my attitude at the present moment. But I would repeat again what I said in the House last year, that I do not think anyone can wait indefinitely upon this question.'[2]

Annexation must be 'a reality and not a sham' he said forcefully in February 1908,[3] whilst it is probable that on one important, particular point, that of the continued existence of the *Fondation de la couronne*, which was financed by the *Domaine de la couronne*, Anglo-American intervention in January 1908 was decisive (though no overt reference was made to the *Fondation*) in thwarting Leopold's ardent wish to return personal control of the *Fondation*.[4] Against this background of sustained international pressure, the conflict on the Belgian parliamentary stage centred on the terms on which Belgium would take over

---

[1] Cookey, 'Great Britain and the Congo Question', pp. 220–94; Louis, 'Triumph of Congo Reform', and Stenmans, *Reprise*, pp. 369–71, 373–6, 382, 391–7, 444–7, 456–7.

[2] *Hansard*, clxxiv, H.C., 15 May 1907, 1014; Stenmans, *Reprise*, p. 376.

[3] Louis, 'Triumph of Congo Reform', citing *The Times* quotation of 28 February 1908.

[4] Stengers, *Belgique et Congo*, pp. 169–70.

C

the Congo and on the provisions of the colonial law which was to govern the new colony. In the conflict over the terms of transfer, attention focused particularly on whether the king should retain personal control of the *Domaine de la couronne* in order that his beloved *Fondation de la couronne*, through which he had begun to embellish Belgium with parks, monuments and bathing places, might continue to be sustained.

The handling of the take-over was in conservative hands, those of the governing Catholic party. At first sight this would seem to suggest that the terms of the cession might be more favourable to the king, might endorse a continuing element of royal absolutism in the new colony, as a result of the innate sympathy for monarchism of a conservative party. In fact the ministries both of De Smets de Naeyer and of De Trooz did take the predictably unpopular stand of supporting the continued existence of the *Fondation de la couronne* with its corollary of the continued autonomy within the Congo of the *Domaine de la couronne*.[1] But when the De Trooz ministry, in November 1907, actually signed a treaty of cession which undertook to 'respect existing foundations in the Congo' such a political storm arose that, when De Trooz died suddenly on the last day of the year, the king was obliged to call upon a known opponent of the *Fondation*, Schollaert, to form a ministry.[2] If, as has been seen, it was probably Anglo-American intervention that made Leopold eventually yield over the *Fondation*, domestic opposition had played an important part.

The question of the future of the *Fondation* indeed dominated the whole of the Belgian discussion of the take-over after the publication of the treaty of cession in November 1907. Was a territory variously estimated as between one-sixth and one-eighth of the area of the Congo to be subtracted from effective Belgian rule? Was a region which had suffered some of the worst of the abuses to continue to be subject to them? Professor Stengers makes the point that, from the signature of the Treaty of Cession in November 1907 onwards, such was the over-shadowing importance of this question that the yet more important matter of how Belgium's new colony was to be governed was left to be thrashed out in the obscurity of a parliamentary committee.[3] One may also reasonably ask if,

[1] Stengers, *Belgique et Congo*, pp. 92, 158.   [2] Ibid., pp. 159–73.
[3] Ibid., pp. 179–80, 201.

on the analogy of the Catholic ministries' endorsement of the continued existence of the *Fondation de la couronne*, they may also positively have initiated an authoritarian constitution for the Congo. Certainly, when the question was first seriously broached in January 1907, the draft of a colonial constitution submitted to the committee by the De Smets de Naeyer ministry was authoritarian to a degree. But in fact it was a draft which Leopold himself had fashioned six years previously,[1] which suggests that the Catholic party was the prisoner of royal wishes in the matter of the constitution no less than it had initially been in the question of the *Fondation*.

Prisoner the ministry may originally have been, but for a number of reasons the document which finally issued from the committee as the draft *Charte coloniale* was significantly different from that which had been placed before it in January 1907. In the first place, following Belgian parliamentary custom, the parliamentary committee included members of the opposition parties as well as supporters of the Government. Not unnaturally the party in power was most strongly represented— indeed more so than it deserved to be on a proportional basis[2] —but this advantage was partially nullified by the fact that some of its representatives, especially a trio led by the veteran Auguste Beernaert, displayed a singular (and liberal) independence of mind.[3] Furthermore, the ministry itself became more liberal in Congo matters, following the reconstruction by Schollaert in the New Year of 1908, and in any case was increasingly aware—as, despite himself, was Leopold—that too autocratic a constitution would meet embarrassing and possibly fatal objections from abroad and would not obtain the measure of national support necessary at the inception of a totally new kind of national venture.[4]

The upshot was that the *Charte coloniale* reflected to a remarkable degree the honest quest of men of goodwill for a good colonial constitution.[5] Naturally their conceptions of 'good' were circumscribed. One had once spent eight days in the Congo,[6] four were associated with Congo companies[7]—a quality of experience which may have conditioned their thinking more than it deepened their understanding. More to

---

[1] Ibid., p. 110.   [2] Ibid., p. 90.   [3] Ibid., pp. 95–110.
[4] Ibid., pp. 173–8.   [5] See ibid., pp. 201–4.   [6] De Groote; ibid., p. 108.
[7] Begerem, De Broqueville, Delbeke and Renkin; ibid., pp. 107–8.

the point, the members of the committee had available as their most relevant information and as their criterion of 'good' principally a knowledge of contemporary Belgian political institutions and practice. They can scarcely be criticized for not possessing wider experience. One wonders, indeed, if the *Charte coloniale* would have been any better a constitution if it had been worked out more in the public gaze. Even on the arguable assumption that the constitution should have been more liberal, it is difficult to see how wider discussion would have made it so, because the most radical political groups were opposed to colonial ventures, anyway. Fears that the Belgian conscripts who, under a colonial policy, would have to be sent to the Congo would end their careers in cannibal stewpots—as a Socialist election poster of 1908 suggested—would scarcely conduce to the conferring upon their consumers of the additional armoury of the Rights of Man. It will later be suggested that the *Charte coloniale* suffered from the general circumstances of its birth: the midwives did their work well enough.

The extent of the changes made in the 1901 draft of a colonial charter by the parliamentary committee can be seen in one or two leading comparisons. In the 1901 draft the king could act personally in a wide field of legislative and executive action: in the 1908 draft the term 'le roi' is used in a purely constitutional sense. Personally he could do nothing; in everything the counter-signature of the Minister of the Colonies was required. Again the earlier draft provided for a *Conseil colonial* to whose royally nominated members any matter might be referred for an opinion if the king so wished. In the 1908 draft the king nominated no members of the council in his personal capacity whilst at the same time the drafts of all decrees had to be submitted to the council. Most important of all, whereas by the earlier proposal, 'Legislative and executive powers in the colonial possessions of Belgium belong to the King' (Art. I), by 1908 there was both a categorical assertion of the supremacy of the law (meaning the Belgian legislature) in all matters and the specific stipulation—obviously of crucial importance—that the annual colonial budget should be approved by that same legislature.[1]

The final stages of the general Belgian debate on the annexation of the Congo Independent State occupied the period

[1] See Stengers, *op. cit.*, pp. 13–20 for this, and also for a much fuller comparison.

April–September 1908, during which there was the domestic complication of parliamentary elections in May. The annexation question was the primary issue in the elections. It is significant that the result was a drop from twelve to eight in the slender Catholic majority, and no less significant that the cry, 'Fathers [*pères de famille*], you do not want your children to die on the Congo, vote for the Liberals, vote for the Socialists!'[1] had only a limited effect. There was, all in all, a feeling of disquiet and uncertainty about the whole question[2] and much of the oratory in the parliamentary debates of the spring and summer, as well as at the hustings, was devoted either to assuaging or to deepening this unease. It was entirely natural that the citizens and politicians of a small country set amidst giants should, in their fears, reflect the inconveniences of that position and, in their reassurances, the business tenacity and success which was not the least guarantee of Belgian national independence.

Would not the acquisition of a colony lead to international complications? On the contrary, the European powers positively wanted Belgian annexation. Would not possession of a colony involve Belgium in an expenditure of treasure insupportable by a small nation? No, because the *Charte coloniale* specifically decreed that the Congo would have a distinct legal personality, that the service of its debt would be the responsibility of the colony itself. Moreover, there had never in the history of colonization been a more promising prospect than the Congo, whilst at the same time annexation would enable Belgium, in one view, to continue the humanitarian work of the Congo State's founder or, in another, to atone for the cruelties of his régime.

Such an impressionistic analysis, suggesting that affirmation only just triumphed over negation is nothing more than an attempt to capture the feeling of the parliamentary and public debate in Belgium.[3] But at least it is consistant with the narrow margin by which the Catholic party was victorious in the elections of May 1908 and, perhaps, with the voting and the atmosphere when the question of annexation finally came to be decided in the Chamber—the Senate at this period was little more than a rubber stamp. In the Treaty of Cession eighty-three

[1] Quoted in ibid., p. 188.   [2] Ibid., p. 188.
[3] The parliamentary debates are summarized in Stenmans, *Reprise*, pp. 414–51.

were in favour, fifty-four against, whilst nine abstained. In the subsequent vote on the *Charte coloniale*, the most vital decision having already been taken, ninety voted in favour, forty-eight against, and seven abstained. It is significant both that one of the major parties, the Liberals, remained divided till the end, and that, in the words of an eye-witness, when the vote was taken 'some members of the majority applauded timidly, some Socialists hissed. The applause lacked conviction....'[1] 'Never before', said the *Daily News*, 'was greatness forced by circumstances upon a more reluctant people.'[2]

It was of not a little importance for the future that the Belgian attitude to the take-over was as it was. To a situation precipitated by Leopold, Belgium, spurred on—bullied even—by Britain and America, had responded dutifully but with some reluctance. Her resolve finally to end the cruelties and abuses involved in the domainal and concession policies had perhaps been fortified by the hope of lucrative economic opportunity. But reluctance is not a positive quality. Leopold may have bequeathed a colony: he could not bequeath a considered and purposeful national will to manage it.

[1] Quoted in Stengers, *Belgique et Congo*, p. 199.
[2] *Daily News*, 16 April 1908, quoted in Cookey, 'Great Britain and the Congo Question', p. 279.

II

THE PEOPLES OF THE CONGO ON THE
EVE OF BELGIAN ANNEXATION

THE great majority of the people of the Congo are Bantu. The exceptions are the scattered groups of pygmies, the Sudanese in the north and north-east, and a small number of Nilotics on the Uganda border. The term 'Bantu' is a linguistic rather than a racial definition and primarily implies no more than that the tribes so described speak languages possessing certain common characteristics. The preponderant, Bantu part of the Congo can in fact be divided into four main linguistic groups, but the very limited unity implied in the term 'Bantu' is emphasized by the fact that a vernacular in one of these main language groups differs from a vernacular in another as much as English differs from modern Greek, whilst there can sometimes be sufficient differences between vernaculars within one language group for there to be important barriers to communication.[1]

In social and political groupings there are also common characteristics as well as wide variations. Of basic and general importance is the kinship group or clan, defined as 'a group recognizing descent in one line (whether patrilineal or matrilineal) within which intermarriage is not allowed'.[2] The matrilineal system predominated in the south-west, the patrilineal in the north and east, whilst both customs could be found in Kasai and Katanga.[3]

Almost invariably clans were combined into the large unit

[1] C. G. Seligman, *Races of Africa* (London, Oxford University Press, 1957) (3rd edition), pp. 162–4; D. Biebuyck and Mary Douglas, *Congo Tribes and Parties* (London, Royal Anthropological Institute, 1961), pp. 17, 49.

[2] Seligman, *Races of Africa*, p. 2.

[3] Biebuyck and Douglas, *Congo Tribes and Parties*, p. 26; *Encyclopédie du Congo belge*, Map I, p. 174.

of the tribe.[1] At this level there was wide variation. On the eve of the European occupation, though there were very many groupings of the simple kind in which the chief and elders exercised a varying authority over a group of clans, groupings such as those of the Alur or the Ba-Nyanga are more properly described as petty states. There were also highly centralized systems like those of the Ba-Lunda and confederations like the Ba-Kuba empire as well as states originating more directly in military conquest, with the vanquished admitting the continuing suzerainty of the conqueror.[2] As exceptions there were even groups such as the Ba-Tetela which were organized in chiefless political systems,[3] whilst the most sophisticated political system was probably that of the Ba-Kuba, who lived between the Sankuru and Lulua Rivers. Their system of government consisted of a hierarchy of ministers, presided over by the king, and consisting of the Prime Minister, the minister of war, a representative from each of the four provinces into which the kingdom was divided, and two women, daughters of former kings. Below these dignitaries came descending grades of court officials and representatives of trades, guilds and sub-tribes. Some of the officials also had judicial functions and in addition there were twelve judges. Though the spiritual ascendancy of the king was considerable, his temporal power was strictly limited.[4]

Judicial power certainly, especially amongst the smaller groupings, was restricted. More precisely, the ability to inflict punishment was limited, since the whole concept of law consisted in the restoration of social equilibrium by the bringing of one or both parties, through the unfolding of custom and, possibly, a little coercion, to understand how equilibrium had been disturbed. The emphasis was therefore on compensation rather than punishment, on reconciliation, and it is further implied that customary law, which of course was unwritten law, tended to be static. But it did have a limited capacity to evolve.[5]

It must not, however, be supposed that at the time of the

---

[1] Biebuyck and Douglas, *Congo Tribes and Parties*, p. 2; Lord Hailey, *An African Survey* (London, Oxford University Press, 1957) pp. 30–31, 39.

[2] Biebuyck and Douglas, *Congo Tribes and Parties*, p. 26.   [3] Ibid.

[4] Seligman, *Races of Africa*, pp. 187–8. Ba-Kuba are also known as Bushongo.

[5] See Lord Hailey, *An African Survey*, pp. 590–1.

Belgian annexation traditional institutions always maintained full and inviolate existence. Rather must one assume the reverse, for many of the tribes and kingdoms of the Congo had fallen into serious disarray. In much of the western part of the Congo a long shadow had been left by the Atlantic slave trade, with its consequential raiding and inter-tribal warfare, and this was paralleled in the east and north by the destructive impact on Bantu life, in all its forms, of the Arab slave trade, which had come to the Congo in the later nineteenth century. At the same time, what was probably the strongest indigenous kingdom, Garenganze, was already breaking up at the time of the tyrant Msiri's death in 1891, whilst in the rubber regions African political organization must have taken a severe blow. None the less, in a book in which the contact of cultures is the leading theme it is important to indicate the African categories of political thought, the type of political and social institution which Africans regarded as basic, even at the cost of implying that these categories had a more untarnished existence at the commencement of Belgian rule than in fact they had.

As far as economic life is concerned, the Congo knew much activity. There was considerable excellence in crafts such as the weaving and dyeing of textiles in raffia and palm fronds, in ivory carving and in the design and embellishment of iron tools and weapons.[1] In measure as different regions of the Congo had been drawn into the economic cycle of Europe in the time of the Congo Independent State, these crafts had begun to die out. Even more rapid was the extinction of long-distance trade routes. At a more earthy level there was a varied emphasis on fishing and hunting, according to local opportunity, but almost universal was a subsistence agriculture based on shifting cultivation.

Whatever the variations in African social and political institutions, certain common characteristics do emerge. Right at the centre is a communal rather than an individualistic conception of life. Such a conception is inherent in the African notion of the clan and, only less, of the tribe. Both are means of protection against dangers which in African life were felt never to be far away; both, clearly, make for cohesion. The whole business of sustaining life under primitive conditions likewise conduces to mutual interdependence. But the real sanctions of

[1] Slade, *King Leopold's Congo*, p. 50.

Bantu clan and tribal solidarity are metaphysical rather than physical and stem from a view of life which is very different from Western conceptions. About this view of life there is a degree of agreement. It is accepted that there is a near-universal belief in a Supreme Being, the Creator, albeit usually remote, and, in magic, variously defined; in the continued existence of clan and tribal ancestors and in their ability to influence the fortunes of the group; and in the group's land as possessing a supernaturally endowed integrity. The list might be lengthened.

More controversial are such questions as whether these beliefs ever have sufficient coherence to justify being termed systems or philosophies; whether, as between one part of Bantu Africa and another, they evince such similarities as to warrant the claim that there is a general Bantu pattern of belief and of related institutions and attitudes (or even an African or world-wide pattern of 'primitive' belief). Just such a claim about a general Bantu pattern of belief has been made in recent years and it commands at least conditional accept-ance, if only for the reason that it invests so many things previously known only in isolation, and often only partly understood, with a full and convincing meaning, and because of the persuasive arguments with which the claim is backed. The work in question is that of a Belgian missionary priest, Father Placide Tempels, and it first appeared in 1945–6.[1]

[1] *Bantu Philosophy* first appeared in Flemish and was shortly afterwards trans-lated into French. An English translation, published by *Présence africaine*, Paris, followed in 1959.

There is a useful symposium of views on *Bantu Philosophy* in the journal *Présence africaine*, VII, 1949, pp. 252–78. Reactions have, in fact, varied. There has been forthright rejection; sometimes, evidently, from the conviction that any positive interpretation of Bantu beliefs by a Roman Catholic priest can only be in the mould of Roman Catholic philosophy. Others, by contrast, whilst accepting that Tempels' work is in the strict sense only an hypothesis as far as groups other than the Ba-Luba—on whom Tempels founded his study—are concerned, gave it a more positive welcome. It is not going too far to say that the response of very many ethnographers and anthropologists has been, in effect: 'Not only does *Bantu Philosophy* seem to make a meaningful pattern out of hitherto disparate phenomena, but the beliefs and attitudes which it attributes to the Bantu display striking similarities with those we have begun to discern amongst other Bantu tribes, amongst other African peoples and even amongst "primitive" peoples in other parts of the world. The hypothesis is important enough to demand further testing in other regions.' It is also worth noting that in recent years ethnographers have been more ready to postulate the existence of an essential meaning and unity, a 'theme' (Opler), a 'configuration' (Kluckhohn), in a culture, though the approach exemplified by Professor J. J. Maquet in the *The Premise of Inequality in Ruanda*, whereby the discernment of salient values of a culture is seen as the key to

The key to an understanding of Bantu philosophy, according to Tempels, is the idea of *force vitale*, a term which can be translated only indifferently by the English 'vital force'. To the Bantu, Force is Being, Being is Force—'Being' here signifying the being of a person or of an organism of the natural world, but not in a passive or static sense. The essential quality of being is that it is positive and active. Every being is in psychical relationship to every other. There is, indeed, a hierarchy of forces, originating with the Supreme Being, who is linked through the clan ancestors, regarded as still existing, to the individual Muntu, and extending downwards to the smallest organism. Moreover, Being, the *force vitale*, is subject to change, to strengthening or weakening according to the beneficent or malevolent operation of superior *forces vitales*. Supreme happiness is the possession of the greatest vital force; every illness, wound, suffering and injustice are held to be a diminution of vital force and results from the activity of some external agent who possesses superior vital force. A man, living or deceased, can directly reinforce or diminish the vital force of another man by the use of his own superior *force vitale*; he can, in Tempel's own words, 'directly influence inferior force-beings (animal, vegetable, or mineral) in their being itself'. 'A rational being', defined as a spirit (a spirit of a dead or a living person), can also, Tempels' analysis continues, 'act indirectly upon another rational being by communicating his vital influence to an inferior force (animal, vegetable, or mineral) through the intermediary of which it influences the rational being.'[1] Tempels' interpretation of Bantu thought can be put in another way. In the words of Professor A. D. Ritchie.

Think of the world as a close-knit hierarchy of living forces or centres of energy, with God, as the creative centre, men next, all ordered

the understanding of its inner meaning, is probably more common than the ontological approach of Tempels, that is, an approach relating to the nature of being. (On this last point see J. J. Maquet, 'Conceptions de vie traditionelles', *Livre blanc* (Brussels, A.R.S.O.M., 1962), I, pp. 177–86.) I personally find it striking that a number of educated Congolese with whom I have discussed *Bantu Philosophy* accept the book's argument, and am impressed by the apparent richness and success of a religious movement in Katanga—*Jamaa*—which is an outcome of the presentation of Christianity in the light of Tempels' discernment of basic Bantu beliefs. (See the present writer's 'Christianity and Bantu Philosophy, Observations on the Thought and Work of Placide Tempels', *International Review of Missions*, July 1963, pp. 316–22.)

[1] Tempels, *Bantu Philosophy*, p. 46.

according to their social standing (not excluding those who have died), animals, plants and lifeless things at the lower end. Life-forces are all interrelated and capable of varying in intensity. Unhappiness, disease, death are all a lowering of intensity of different degrees. Happiness is essentially a varying of life-force. There is a natural order or balance of life-forces, and injustice or injury consists in the malevolence of one person lowering the intensity of life-force of another below its proper level. Malevolence may employ a variety of agencies; living men, deceased ancestors, or humble, lifeless tools.[1]

Various specific points, less obvious but important, disengage themselves from this analysis. In particular one begins to understand the metaphysical dimension of community in the Bantu mind. As Tempels himself elaborates this point:

This concept of separate beings, of substance (to use the scholastic term . . .) which find themselves side by side, entirely independent of one another, is foreign to Bantu thought. Bantu hold that created beings preserve a bond one with another, an intimate ontological relationship, comparable with the causal tie which binds creature and Creator. . . . One force will reinforce or weaken another . . . [This is] . . . a metaphysical causal action which flows out of the very nature of a created being.[2]

Or again,

For the Bantu, man never appears in fact as an isolated individual, as an independent entity. Every man, every individual, forms a link in the chain of vital forces, a living link active and passive, joined from above to the ascending line of his ancestry and sustaining below him the line of his descendants. It may be said that among Bantu the individual is necessarily an individual within the clan. This relationship is not regarded as simply juridical dependence, nor one of parenthood. It should be understood in the sense of real ontological dependence.[3]

No less important is it to reiterate the essential point that the Bantu universe is made up of vital forces. But over and beyond these particular points lies the claim that there exists in the Bantu mind a coherent and integrated system of ideas. It does not matter whether we term this system a Bantu philosophy, or argue that that term is inappropriate since its

[1] A. D. Ritchie, review of *La Philosophie bantoue*, in *International Review of Missions*, July 1947, pp. 396-8
[2] Tempels, *Bantu Philosophy*, pp. 39-40.   [3] Ibid., pp. 71-72.

delineation is the work of an outsider.[1] Nor, up to a point, does it matter whether Tempels' discernment is accurate, whether he is quite wrong on this point, whether he exaggerates that, whether he misunderstands another. If Bantu beliefs and attitudes are even remotely as Tempels depicts them, and allowing for serious lapses from pristine purity, one begins to understand not only how different were the ideas of the European colonizer, with his distinctions between mind and matter, his attachment to reason, and his individualism, but also that European ideas did not confront a vacuum. Finally, it is evident that an assault on one aspect of a *Weltanschauung* as tightly integrated as that of the Bantu might have incalculable results upon what remained.

The assault had, of course, begun well before the Belgian annexation. It is appropriate only to make a bare mention of the prolonged contact of the Lower Congo with European influences dating from the coming of the Portuguese at the close of the fifteenth century.[2] The Atlantic slave trade had the Lower and part of the Middle Congo as one of its last catchment areas and the last known export of slaves to the New World was as late as 1865. By that time there was also an increasing legitimate trade between the Lower Congo and adjoining coast and Europe—Britain especially—and the British trade alone had attained the substantial level of two million pounds a year by the early 1880's.[3] Missionary work began in 1878 (excepting the considerable Portuguese missionary effort of the sixteenth century), whilst the establishment of posts of Leopold II's *Association Internationale du Congo* along the course of the Congo River began in 1879 and thus preceded the official birth of the Congo Independent State by five years. Something of the impact of the Congo State on African society may be inferred from the previous chapter, whilst that theme, together with a study of the missionary impact, is considered at length in Dr. Slade's *King Leopold's Congo*. Suffice it here to give a very summary indication of the extent of the European impact in the twenty-five years before Belgium became mistress of the Congo.

[1] Tempels' role is, of course, that of an analyst, an interpreter. He expresses no explicit opinion on the measure of truth or error in Bantu thought.

[2] See Slade, *King Leopold's Congo*, Chapters 1 and 2.

[3] R. Anstey, *Britain and the Congo in the Nineteenth Century* (Oxford, Clarendon Press, 1962), pp. 31–33.

The impact of the rubber policy is in part self-evident. In the *Domaine de la couronne*, to the west of Lake Leopold II, for instance, many of the Ba-Tete, Bo-hia, Ba-Boma and especially Ba-Sengele fled in face of the rubber atrocities. Some died in the forest of starvation and hardship, others of the attacks of the then abundant wild animals; still others had been killed by soldiers or by the notorious Malu Malu in person. It is obvious that such experiences would leave strong feelings; certainly Scrivener, the Baptist missionary, found in 1902, when the events were of recent memory, that he had to cease questioning Ba-Sengele refugees because they became so furious at the recollection of what had been done to them, and lost control of themselves.[1] The fact that the name of Malu Malu still means so much today in Bolobo (*see* p. 7) tells its own story. On the other hand the Africans usually distinguished between good and bad Europeans—Casement's informants at Mpolo, for example, listed the names of good as well as bad,[2] and it was made clear to me, sixty years later, that not all the European administrators of the period were placed in the same category as Malu Malu. None the less it is reasonable to infer that the principal impact of European rule, in those regions affected by the rubber policy, was that of an iron fist. Again the effect on tribal society elsewhere must often have been analogous with what happened in the *Domaine de la couronne*. There, for example, the power of the traditional authorities must have suffered particular damage in measure as superior power was seen to rest in the State and its soldiers; and when traditional chiefs were prepared to act as a sort of 'Quisling', as happened with certain Ba-Sengele chiefs;[3] inter-tribal relations were also affected by the flight of many Ba-Sengele and their re-settlement, with Ba-Tende permission, on Ba-Tende land.[4] The proportion of the Congo which was subject to direct economic exploitation of this kind was one-sixth to one-eighth.

In the notable case of the most powerful African potentate with whom the Independent State had to deal, the European impact was much more clear-cut. Msiri, a Muyeke, was sovereign of the centralized conquest state of Garenganze and exercised despotic rule over the country from the Lualaba

---

[1] F.O. 10/806 (Enclosure 2, in Casement to Lansdowne, 11 December 1903 ('Confidential Print'), p. 38 ['Casement Report'].

[2] 'Casement Report', p. 37.   [3] Personal information.

[4] 'Casement Report', pp. 8–9, 36–39.

River in the west to Lake Moero and the Luapula in the east, and from the Luvua River in the north southwards to the Congo–Zambesi watershed. This is an area broadly equivalent to the central and eastern portion of Katanga province as it was in later Belgian days. After indecisive contact with Plymouth Brethren missionaries who arrived at his court in 1886, and with the first two Congo State missions of Le Marinel and Delcommune, Msiri's power cracked within days of the arrival of its third mission, led by an Englishman, Captain Stairs. The outcome of a violent argument between Captain Bodson, one of Stairs' party, and Msiri, following Msiri's refusal to accept the Congo State flag, was the death of both Bodson and Msiri. The already tottering empire of Msiri was at an end. The peoples of Katanga as a whole had, by the time of the Belgian annexation, experienced no deep penetration of European power, but those subject to Msiri's sway had been delivered from what was undoubtedly, in the dying Bodson's words, 'one of [Africa's] most detestable tyrants'—at the time of Stairs' *coup d'état* some two hundred prisoners were awaiting execution at Bunkeya, Msiri's capital.[1]

The nature of the impact of Congo State power on Katanga was essentially a function of the motive that had dictated the assertion of that power. Cecil Rhodes and the British South Africa Company must be kept out of Katanga by a semblance of effective occupation, and its likely mineral wealth reserved for future exploitation.[2] The establishment of a skeletal administration was therefore necessary.

In about 1840 the Arabs first crossed to the western shore of Lake Tanganyika and in the next forty years extended their authority over the whole country up to the Lomami River. The Bantu could not resist their power—some, indeed, took service as Arab auxillaries—because of the Arab possession of firearms, and although the Arab incursion might incidentally produce such benefits as rich plantations served by well-treated domestic slaves, its basic purpose was the quest for slaves and ivory for export, and its results appalling. In its early days the Congo State had little choice but to compromise with such a powerful section of its population but in the long run there was no place for shared authority:[3]

---

[1] Slade, *King Leopold's Congo*, pp. 119–40.   [2] Ibid., pp. 128–31.
[3] Ibid., pp. 74–102.

In the last resort Arab authority and Arab wealth in central Africa depended on elements incompatible with European administration; on slave labour, on the forcible seizure of ivory from defenceless tribes, and on Bantu auxiliaries who were often cannibals and even more ruthless than their masters. And so long as the Aruwimi-Lomami region was in fact abandoned to Arab authority, the State would never be master there; so long as the economic policy of the Arabs involved the continuous extension of their field of operations, State posts lower down the river would never be secure.[1]

The power of the Congo Arabs was shattered in ruthless campaigns lasting from 1892–5, during which there were notable examples of Belgian heroism.[2] In the period of pacification which followed, the Belgian task was facilitated by the Arab inheritance—flourishing plantations, a system of canoe transport on the Lualaba, and the established acceptance of an external suzerain by the Bantu tribes of the region.[3] But it is likely that, decisive as the European impact had in one sense been, its overall impact in the Arab zone was as superficial as it was in Katanga. In each case the aims of intervention were not such as to necessitate the subsequent establishment of a tight administrative network, and in any event the resources were not available.

Indeed, the establishment of sound administration in the whole of the Congo in the period of the Independent State suffered not only from the sheer size of the territory, but also from the fact that good administration was always subordinate to other aims. In Katanga it was a question of forestalling Britain in the occupation of a region rich in minerals; in the east and north-east the power of the Arabs must be suppressed; in the *Domaine de le couronne* and in the extensive areas given over to the concessionary companies it was the immediate production of wealth that mattered; and in the Lower Congo over the period 1890–8, judging from the strength of Ba-Kongo memories concerning mortality in the labour lines,[4] all must have been subordinate to the provision of labourers to build the Matadi–Leopoldville railway.

When it is viewed in this light, the legislation which made up native policy under the Congo Independent State can be seen

---

[1] Slade, *King Leopold's Congo*, p. 104.   [2] Ibid., pp. 106–14.
[3] Ibid., pp. 116–18.
[4] J. Van Wing, *Études Bakongo, sociologie, religion et magie* (Brussels, Desclée de Brouwer, 1959), p. 82.

to be too much the expression of the good intentions which an administration preoccupied with more immediate matters could well afford to display. Its tenor is evident in a decree of 1891 which provided for the recognition of customary groupings through a specific act of investiture of the chief, and made the chief responsible for the execution of certain officially imposed tasks. A decree of 1906 built upon that of 1891. The chief's rights and duties were more particularly specified and it was laid down that he should receive a salary, and should have limited control over the departure of his people from his jurisdiction. In so far as the policy was more than the expression of good intentions it—and official interpretations of it—made clear that it basically expressed a concern to ensure at the lowest level of administration a means whereby the will of the colonial administration could be carried out, and African participation in the work and expense of government enforced.[1] To sum up, there was neither the manpower nor the single-minded determination to invest native policy with more than this minimum content. There was therefore little that was positive in the impact of that policy beyond the fact that a superior external force had more or less imposed its authority.

The Christian missions, in territorial terms, had made a remarkable impact by 1908. In the thirty years following the beginnings of missionary enterprise on the Lower Congo by the Baptist Missionary Society in 1878, a relatively concentrated work had developed on the Lower Congo whilst stations had been established at major points on the upper river all the way up to Stanley Falls. In addition the penetration of many of the Congo's tributaries—notably the Kwango, Kasai, Ruhi, Lulonga, Lopori, Itimbiri and Lindi rivers—had begun and the first beginnings had been made in Katanga.[2] As a result of the participation of some 'foreign' Protestant missionaries in the Congo Reform Campaign, the Congo State increasingly favoured the less vocal 'national' Roman Catholic Orders in the important matter of granting sites, in the years immediately before its demise,[3] but this did not decisively check the rate of Protestant advance.

---

[1] A. Gille, 'La Politique indigène du Congo belge et du Ruanda-Urundi', *Encyclopédie du Congo belge*, III, pp. 710–13.
[2] Slade, *English-Speaking Missions*, Map 2.   [3] Ibid., pp. 299–301.

D

Missionary methods were an important determinant of the missionary impact on the peoples of the Congo. Roman Catholics and Protestants alike usually found that their preaching made little impression on traditional African society where this continued to exist. The missionary would find that his first hearers were no more than the 'boys' he had brought with him and a varied collection of others: domestic slaves whom he might redeem from their masters, ransomed slave children or, in areas where there had been recent warfare, individuals torn from their homes. But such communities were wont to grow with almost embarrassing speed and the missionary, sometimes reluctantly, would soon find himself in the position of magistrate as well as Man of God. As one of them put it: 'Many a little Protestant Pope in the lonely bush is forced . . . to be prophet, priest and king rolled into one—really a very big duck he, in his own private pond. . . .'[1] This experience came to Protestants and Catholics alike, though they differed somewhat in their response to it. The Protestant missions were more chary of ransoming slaves and slave children because they were afraid of encouraging a continuing supply, because they were sometimes reluctant to undertake the resulting civil responsibility and because they feared this would delay the fulfilment of their primary aim of penetrating tribal society. The Catholic Orders, on the other hand, welcomed slave redemption, and particularly the ransoming of slave children and tutelage of orphans, for here was a means of rapidly establishing a Christian community in the midst of pagan society. It mattered little that Christian profession was at first only superficial because in Catholic thought 'the Church . . . existed over and above the individual converts who were gathered into membership'.[2]

With these differences the initial impact took place in the context of the Catholic *chrétienté* or the community gathered round a Protestant mission station. The impact was necessarily at different levels. The mission provided security and a means of gaining a livelihood either on a plot of land or through acquiring the skill necessary to do one of the various jobs about the station. It also provided a community which, under the necessary paternalism of the missionary, might bear

[1] Slade, *English-Speaking Missions*, p. 164, quoting D. C. Crawford, *Thinking Black* (London, Morgan and Scott, 1912), pp. 324–5.

[2] Ibid., p. 170. This paragraph is based on pp. 164–82 of Slade, *English-Speaking Missions*. The ensuing paragraph also owes something to this same section.

some relation to the paternalism of the better sort of chief. On a different level, the *chrétienté* and the Protestant community provided an introduction to the ways of the West and a measure of initiation into its techniques. The former was done in such simple ways as the everyday observation of the missionary's habits: the latter by, say, the mastery of some operation connected with the mission's printing press. Where children were concerned there was usually the school, the really vital medium of initiation into the culture—including the power—of the West. There was also an impact at the level which most concerned the missionary. The fact that he represented a culture with, at least, infinitely superior te hnological prowess, adding up to a tremendous impression of greater power, did not mean that he was unable to gain a genuine acceptance for the faith which he had come to preach. Moreover, the Christianity which the missionary preached could, and often did, give a decisive release from the perennial fear of sorcery. At the same time, the fact that the missionary normally shared the cultural arrogance of the Europe of his day meant that he often disrupted traditional beliefs more than was necessary.

The Church life which developed round the pioneer missionary could also be a very vital thing, and could demonstrate a missionary impact of the most fruitful kind. At Bolobo, for instance, it seems clear that 'Ekanda', the Rev. A. E. Scrivener, not least because of his unmasking of the rubber atrocities in the area, and because he was therefore regarded as an emancipator by Bolia, Ba-Senegele and Ba-Boma refugees, built up a thriving Church. Evidently it was a Church run on paternalistic lines but partly because of this it was a Church of considerable quality.[1]

That the missions' impact was usually restricted to individuals and fragments of tribes, was not lost upon the missionaries. Whilst the approach through the *chriétienté* or the Protestant community was all that was on offer, the nucleus of customary society would remain untouched. The Catholic response to the challenge of this wider task was the *ferme-chapelle* system. Initiated by a Jesuit, Father Van Hencxthoven, it was an attempt to bring the influence of African converts to bear on customary society whilst preserving them from the dangers of continuous contact. Starting from a centre at

1 Personal information.

Kisantu, in the Lower Congo, groups of young converts, in the charge of a catechist, were sent out to settle, each near an African village. The group built its own huts, grew its own food and gave schooling to abandoned or orphaned children. At the same time the surplus produce was sold in the neighbouring villages and the catechism taught there. The missionary priest would visit as often as he could. In effect a Christian village was established sufficiently close to a pagan village to have a constant influence upon it, and sufficiently distant for the level of contamination to be acceptable.[1] The Protestant answer went further, involving more direct contact. A teacher-evangelist was, with the chief's permission, sent right into the village, where he taught simple Bible stories to all who would listen and the elements of reading and writing to the children of such parents as could be persuaded to send them. The teacher himself would have been picked out as a promising pupil at the mission station, but there was often an element of real spontaneity in the process of carrying the Christian Gospel to the villages. As in the Catholic system, the missionary would visit when he could.[2] By the time of the Belgian annexation the stage had been reached by the Protestant and Roman Catholic missions alike whereby a direct impact was being made on traditional society. The harvest, both of souls and problems, was to be considerable.

[1] Slade, *English-Speaking Missions*, pp. 194-5.   [2] Ibid., pp. 183-94.

III

THE EARLY PERIOD OF
BELGIAN RULE

BELGIUM'S position in 1908, in regard to the Congo, was akin
to that of an heir who inherits an estate with a predominating
sense of duty, rather than in fulfilment of a long-felt wish, who
is very conscious of a number of limiting conditions in the will,
but who is partially reassured by reports of considerable latent
wealth in the property.[1] It is idle, either in regard to 1908
or to any other period of Belgian colonial rule, to look for
explicit and meaningful statements of Belgium's aims in the
Congo. Rather must one turn to a variety of conditioning
factors. It was the response to these factors, the attitudes derived
from them, rather than any proceeding from first principles,
which determined Congo policy.

The sheer size of the new colony was not the least important
of these factors. It can only have been daunting for a power the
size of Belgium to be confronted, on its first colonial exercise,
with a territory eighty times the area of the mother-country.
On the other hand there had slowly come the realization that
the first estimates by explorers of the Congo's population—in
1885 Stanley had published a figure of forty-three million for the
Congo basin[2]—were hopelessly awry. By 1908 it was realized
that this vast territory was very sparsely populated indeed—
and though the population was slowly to increase, its relative
smallness was a continuing factor of the utmost importance.
With the disadvantage of sheer size was therefore linked the

---

[1] See Chapter I above; Stengers, *Belgique et Congo, passim*; and, for further
evidence of this important element of duty and reluctance in the Belgian attitude,
G. Malengreau, 'La Politique coloniale de la Belgique', *Principles and Methods of
Colonial Administration* (London, Butterworths, 1950), pp. 36–37, 49.
[2] H. M. Stanley, *The Congo and the Founding of its Free State* (London, Sampson
Low, 1885), I, p. x.

limitation of a population too small to develop the colony's resources to the degree that Belgium was to want them developed. In the history of the Congo Independent State lay a further series of conditioning factors. The limitations placed by the Berlin Act of 1885 on the level of import duties that might be levied on goods entering the Congo Free Trade area (an area stretching from coast to coast and taking in the greater part of central Africa, and thus more extensive than the boundaries of the Congo State itself) had been only partly eased in 1890 and remained to bind Belgium. As a result this stock source of colonial revenue was partially closed to her, and a reliance upon what had come to be a feature of the Congo State's policy, the attraction of European companies by the offer of substantial land and other concessions, was suggested. By the same token of practice in the Congo State, the grant of administrative functions to private companies, with all the abuses of which A.B.I.R., the *Société Anversoise*, the Lulunga Company and others had been so conspicuously guilty, must be excluded. (Under Article 22 of the *Charte coloniale* a partial exception was made of Katanga which was to continue to be governed by a body called the *Comité Spécial du Katanga*, two of whose six members represented the *Compagnie du Katanga*.) Again, in an age which still had a very restricted conception of the functions of the State, what more natural than that the more directly civilizing role of the colonial power should continue to be seen as falling almost exclusively to the Christian missions, in accordance both with practice in the Congo State and with universally accepted assumptions?

The way in which the Congo was to be governed also owed much to the immediate past; as was described in Chapter I, the firm guide-lines had been laid down in the *Charte coloniale* which, in turn, reflected the circumstances of its elaboration. Analysed more closely, the charter entrusted executive power and a major stream of legislative authority to the king. He was also to appoint members of the judiciary. But the wide powers thus allotted were accorded to the king in his constitutional capacity. In his personal capacity he had no powers at all. The means by which this was made explicit, and at the same time ministerial responsibility for Congo policy was asserted, was Article 9 of the Charter: 'No act of the king can be effective if it is not counter-signed by a minister, who by that action alone makes himself responsible for it.' Belgium being a constitutional monarchy, the circle of ministerial responsibility was completed in the subjection of the minister to the vote of Parliament. But if the king, albeit as constitutional monarch, had very wide powers, there were also certain limits to these powers. First of all, although there was no question of according political rights, liberty of association or liberty of the Press, certain rights which the king could not override were guaranteed to the inhabitants of the Congo—the liberty of the individual, the right to property, freedom of worship, and so forth. A different type of limitation was the severe restriction of the Crown's right to delegate legislative authority (all that was permitted was the delegation to the Governor-General of power to issue ordinances with a validity of six months), whilst executive authority could only be delegated by the king 'to persons and corporate bodies subordinate to him in the colonial hierarchy'. Events in the Congo Independent State were a sufficient warning against the arbitrary devolution of power. In this context, power could be much better controlled if concentrated.

Much more important was the assertion of unqualified parliamentary supremacy in legislation. The legislature had the right of sovereign intervention in any matter. In addition, certain specified matters were subjects not for the decrees by which the king legislated but for Parliament—the annual colonial budget, the audit of the colony's accounts, the guarantee of loan interest or loan capital, to name the more noteworthy. Of these the approval of the budget was clearly the most important. In addition to limitations, there were controls. These rested in the parliamentary right of interpellation (by which a minister could be called upon to defend a policy which he had endorsed, and through which he might be censured), and the obligation upon the Crown to submit the drafts of decrees in a number of important fields—the grant of mineral, railway and major land concessions, for example—to the substantially independent scrutiny of the *Conseil colonial*.[1]

It may be objected that an analysis of the *Charte coloniale*, with a particular emphasis upon its safeguards against personal

---

[1] This summary of the *Charte coloniale* is based on Professor Stengers' analysis in *Belgique et Congo*, pp. 13–17. The text of the charter is printed in pp. 229–36 of the same book.

royal autocracy, is misplaced when it is remembered that
Leopold II died only a year after the annexation of the Congo
by Belgium. But it is relevant to emphasize that the constitution of the Congo took a certain form on account of a
concern to guard against the personal autocracy of the Crown,
and important to realize that the Charter was and substantially
remained what it was regardless of the fact that the threat of
autocratic intervention which so decisively conditioned its
terms so quickly ceased to exist. The *Charte coloniale* was no less
significant for the future on this account.

A factor of a quite different kind which had a vital influence
on the formulation of Belgian aims in the Congo was a national
distrust of theory, which in this context implies aims, and almost
a passion for the practical approach. A marked addiction to
empiricism is indeed a Belgian quality. A Belgian Cabinet
minister could cause a certain amusement amongst his parliamentary colleagues by declaring, in the Chamber of Deputies,
'I act, then I reflect', but he was doing no more than exaggerat-
ing a common national attitude.[1] Again, in 1953, an English
visitor, talking to high officials in Elisabethville, was struck by
their response to his query as to whether their current practice
in a certain field would still be appropriate two years hence.
'But that is two years ahead', was the reply, with the implication that two years was synonymous with eternity and that it
was a waste of time to think so soon of a time so distant.[2]
Belgians, writes a Belgian University teacher, in a passage
quoted by Professor Malengreau in a paragraph concerned to
stress the empirical element in Belgian colonial policy, are

a people without imagination, a people who do not dream, a people
whose thoughts are fixed on reality and do not go beyond it, but who
make reality yield up useful fruits. A people who do not create but
who utilize, who invent little but who make better use of the
inventions of others than the inventors themselves.[3]

Last of the factors conditioning Belgium's aims in the Congo
was that she inherited a concrete situation, a colonial administration of sometimes poor quality, and a series of decrees and

[1] Quoted by Malengreau in *Politique coloniale de la Belgique*, p. 40.
[2] Personal information.
[3] Malengreau, *Politique coloniale de la Belgique*, p. 40. For a reference to empiricism
see also A. Gille, 'La Politique indigène du Congo belge et du Ruanda-Urundi',
Encyclopédie du Congo belge, III, p. 739.

an administrative comportment which together passed for policy. The situation could not change overnight and, more especially, decrees of the Congo State would remain in force until rescinded. In short, Belgium had inherited her colony with some reluctance and partly out of a sense of duty for which she hoped she might be financially compensated in economic opportunities for her children. Of positive theories of colonial government, of any clearly defined Belgian mission in the Congo, there is no evidence. Policy in the first decade of Belgian rule was to be moulded principally by the conditioning factors whose description has been the burden of this chapter so far.

This is not to suggest that the formation of policy was a completely deterministic process. Legislative and executive action are, after all, fields in which a degree of human intervention is commonly regarded as essential! In the matter of governing the Congo it was theoretically possible, for example, for the Belgian Parliament, either of its own volition or impelled by public pressure, to have widely exercised its right of sovereign intervention in legislation; it is not inconceivable, to give a second example, that Albert I (1909–34) might have cherished a positive programme for the Congo which, granted it could only have found constitutional expression, could scarcely have been without impact. The question of the human and institutional springs of early Belgian government in the Congo must certainly be put, and the broad lines of an answer seem reasonably clear. The Belgian Parliament made only one use of its optional right of sovereign intervention, in a matter of any general importance, in the period up to the early twenties (the convention between Belgium and the Kasai Company of 1911),[1] whilst there is no indication whatsoever that positive schemes of Congo policy emanated from the royal palace or from anywhere else. The *Conseil colonial* was certainly an independent body which painstakingly scrutinized the draft decrees which were placed before it in accordance with the *Charte coloniale*. The fact, moreover, that the Council was required to give a reasoned report on all questions submitted to it, together with a statement of minority views, has meant that this independent scrutiny has had a wider impact. But in

---

[1] J. Stengers, 'Note sur trois aspects de l'exercice des pouvoirs au Congo belge (1908–1960)', *Bulletin des Séances de l'Académie Royale des Sciences d'Outre-Mer*, VII, 4, 1961, pp. 562–5.

practice the Council seems to have concentrated on the detail rather than the substance of the draft decrees submitted to it, and does not appear to have made much use of its right to recommend legislative or administrative measures. In short, although the Council had real value in a certain sphere, it was not a policy-initiating body either in the first period of Belgian rule or subsequently.[1] The assumption must be that decisions were the work of Renkin and the officials of the Ministry of the Colonies, save in so far as in the war years, 1914–19, for most of which the Belgian Government operated from Le Havre and was primarily engrossed with the very survival of the nation, more initiatives probably came from Boma, the Congo capital. This development would have been facilitated by the policy of administrative decentralization on Boma and thence on to four Provinces—Congo-Kasai, Equateur, Orientale and Katanga—initiated by Renkin on the very eve of the outbreak of war and carried through during it.[2] But as far as individuals are concerned, throughout the first decade of Belgian rule the key figure was Renkin, first as the Colonial Minister in an autocratically constituted system of government, then as the initiator of the 1914 reforms, and finally as Colonial Minister throughout the war.

The major concern of the Belgian Government, and of Renkin, the first Minister of the Colonies in particular, when they took up their responsibility for the Congo, was that the Congo budget should balance. In this attitude they reflected contemporary European views on government but there were at least two reasons why Belgium should hold this view with particular firmness—during the national debate on annexation ministers had had firmly to assert that the Congo would not become a liability, whilst it is also reasonable to suggest that a nation, much of whose strength rested in the conspicuous ability of her citizens to run their businesses profitably, would lay particular stress on colonial solvency. At the same time the sheer size of the new colony made the implications of failure the more serious, whilst the internationally backed moral

[1] *African Survey*, pp. 346, 348.

[2] *Bulletin officiel 1914*, pp. 859–96, 898–918, Renkin, Report to King, and *Arrêté Royal* on Central Administration, 28 July 1914; Renkin, Report to King and *Arrêté Royal* on Government of the Colony, 28 July 1914.

Conseil colonial, Speech by Franck, 8 March 1919, quoted in A. Delcommune, *L'Avenir du Congo Belge menacé* (Brussels, Lebègue and Co., 1919), p. 21.

compulsion to eschew many of the methods which the Congo State had used made the task more difficult. If this last consideration was the cause of the decision taken in the autumn of 1909 progressively to end the Government or concessionaire monopoly of natural products in the Congo and, *pari passu*, to open hitherto closed regions to Free Trade,[1] a continued reliance upon concessionary companies, if abuses could be avoided, is wholly understandable. Where else was colonial revenue to come from? One has also to remember that the early twentieth century, like the nineteenth, frequently assumed, without any reservations, that the pursuit of private profit necessarily served the public good. Who more likely than the colonial minister himself, who had been a director of the *Chemins de Fer des Grand Lacs*, to believe that (to adapt the words of a former United States Secretary of Defence and industrialist) what was good for the railway entrepreneur was good for the Congo?[2]

Given a natural and general disposition to accept the entire rightness of entrusting economic development to private enterprise, there was also the important fact that Leopold II had, essentially, bequeathed most of the known mineral and allied opportunities to a group of companies. Following confirmation in the years 1900 to 1904 that Katanga possessed immense mineral riches, the *Union Minière du Haut Katanga* had, in 1906, been created to exploit them. Three days later the *Compagnie du Chemin de Fer du Bas-Congo au Katanga* (B.C.K.) was founded in order to provide Katanga with the necessary railway links with the outside world and was at the same time given the exclusive right to mineral exploitation in the Kasai basin. In November of the same year a third company, *La Société Internationale Forestière et Minière du Congo* (FORMINIÈRE) was given similar exclusive mineral rights elsewhere in Easai, as well as in other scattered parts of the Congo. Significant about these companies is that each enjoyed State participation; that, though their financial structure differed, they all were dominated by the powerful Belgian trust, the *Société Générale*, a control symbolized in the fact that the *Société Générale's* Governor was chairman of all three; and that all

---

[1] Cookey, 'Great Britain and the Congo Question', p. 323. One half of the Congo would be opened on 1 July 1910, a further sixth on 1 July 1911, and again on 1 July 1912. No date was fixed for the remaining sixth.

[2] Cf. 'What is good for General Motors is good for the United States' (Charles E. Wilson).

enjoyed foreign participation—the British Tanganyika Concessions Ltd. in the first two cases, a French bank in the second, and
the American Ryan-Guggenheim group in the third. Leopold
had apparently negotiated foreign participation in order to
thwart any really ruthless Belgian take-over of the Congo,
whilst the wealth and influence of the *Société Générale* was such
that no one in Belgium was likely to be able to tilt successfully
at it—not, of course, that any foreseeable Belgian Government
was likely to want to do so.[1]

It is therefore not surprising that the rights of these and other
lesser companies were substantially confirmed at the take-over,
whilst here to hand was a pattern for economic development
generally. This conferring upon large private companies of
immense land and mineral concessions, with the State possessing an important interest in them, was not the least important
of Leopold's legacies to the Congo. Of course some changes had
to be made. In those parts of the Congo where concessionary
companies had enjoyed the notorious monopoly right to buy
forest produce, the monopoly right was exchanged for freehold
rights over a smaller area selected within the boundaries of the
original concession.[2] Elsewhere concessions were made in a
different form. In the succinct words of *An African Survey*:

Under this form the grantee had at the end of a preliminary period
the right to choose blocks of land up to a fixed maximum within an
area from which other claimants had been excluded during this
period, the area to be acquired depending on the fulfilment of
certain development conditions. The most important grant of this
type was that made in 1911 to the *Huileries du Congo Belge*, which was
associated with the Lever interests. This Company obtained the
right to lease a maximum of 1,875,000 acres, divided between five
circles, each with a radius of 60 kilometres, the amount leased in
each circle being dependent on the erection of oil mills of a given
capacity.

In 1945 the company was to become entitled to freehold rights
over the whole or a part of the area, according as to whether
or not it fulfilled certain conditions.[3]

This policy certainly brought results. In 1910 the B.C.K.

[1] This account has been much simplified. See P. Joye and R. Lewin, *Les Trusts au Congo* (Brussels, Société Populaire d'Éditions, 1961), pp. 209–30; Ascherson, *The King Incorporated*, pp. 266–7; Smith Hempstone, *Katanga Report* (London, Faber and Faber, 1962), pp. 48–49, 55.

[2] *African Survey*, p. 751.   [3] Ibid., p. 751.

railway reached Elisabethville from Sakania on the Rhodesian frontier and by 1918 had reached Bukama, 283 miles to the north-west, in its ambitious progress towards the Lower Congo.[1] By 1915 the rail–river link between Stanleyville and Albertville, on Lake Tanganyika, had been completed with the construction of the Kindu–Kongolo section between 1906 and 1910, and with the building of the Kabalo–Albertville section much accelerated by the demands of the East African campaign against Germany.[2] (The railway making the vital link between Matadi on the Lower Congo and Stanley Pool had been completed at great human and financial cost in 1898.[3]) Copper exports from Katanga began as soon as the railway had reached Elisabethville and by 1923, partly under the impulse of World War I, Katanga had become the world's third largest producer of copper.[4] The production of diamonds, tin and other minerals was also expanding rapidly, as was the agricultural production, chiefly palm produce, of companies like the Kasai Company and the *Huileries du Congo Belge* (H.C.B.). The following export figures give an indication of economic growth in this first period of Belgian rule:[5]

EXPORTS FROM THE BELGIAN CONGO

	Thousands of Tonnes	Pounds Sterling
1913	25	2,207,480
1914	32	2,115,000
1914	39	2,879,800
1916	63	5,177,280
1917	82	6,573,080
1918	66	4,478,760
1919	83	8,165,840
1920	86	12,609,800

In land and native policy the legacy of the Congo Independent State and the circumstances of the Belgian annexation were as important as in economic policy. The basic principle of land policy under the Congo State, it has been seen in Chapter II, was that only lands in actual occupation by Congo

---

[1] *Compagnie du Chemin de Fer du Bas-Congo au Katanga, 1906–1956* (privately published, n.d.), end map and *passim*.
[2] *The Belgian Congo* (Geographical Handbook series of the Naval Intelligence Division, 1944), pp. 465–7.
[3] Ibid., pp. 457–65.   [4] Ibid., p. 402.   [5] *Rapport annuel*, 1920, p. 31.

tribes were recognized as theirs in full possession: all other lands were regarded as vacant, as the patrimony of the State. A decree of 3 June 1906 had modified the rigour of this restriction to the extent that it empowered the Governor-General to confer upon a tribe or other grouping three times as much land, or more, as they actually occupied. For two main reasons it was unlikely that Belgium would radically alter this policy. In the first place, no less than 105,860 square miles of land are estimated to have been granted away in freehold tenure by the time of annexation whilst, as has been seen (p. 44), it was proposed to confer, in exchange for the monopoly rights over the yet more extensive tracts of land which the various concessionary companies enjoyed, freehold rights over lesser, but still tremendous stretches of territory.[1] Probably more important, the belief died hard that most of the Congo really was vacant land. European notions of land tenure confronted (as they had done and were to do all too often in Africa) African ideas of communal usage of land, shifting cultivation, and extensive hunting, harvesting and fishing rights. The result was (mutual) incomprehension in the vital initial stages. In a word, the inherited policy was continued. Even if there were doubts, they were not weighty enough to prevail against the generally held conviction that the Congo could be made viable only by the encouragement of large-scale European enterprise. The only modification made was in two decrees of 1910 which recognized hunting, fishing and harvesting (of wild produce) rights in the colony's domain land.[2]

In native policy we have seen that the inheritance was the decree of 3 June 1906 (p. 33). Native custom was respected unless contrary to public order or healthy development; indigenous authority was in principle recognized; the chief was seen as the link between that indigenous authority and the colonial administration.[3] In practice the ignorance of custom, the significant element of fragmentation in tribal institutions, the paucity of good administrators, the size of the Congo and

[1] *African Survey*, p. 751. About two-fifths of the original freehold area eventually reverted to the State.

[2] G. Van der Kerken, *Les Sociétés bantoues du Congo belge* (Brussels, Émile Bruylant, 1919), pp. 149–50. For a well documented but Marxist-type analysis see M. Merlier, *Le Congo de la colonisation belge à l'indépendance* (Paris, Maspero, 1962), pp. 57–71.

[3] Gille, 'Politique indigène', III, p. 713.

the whole economic orientation of the Congo Independent State meant that scarcely anywhere had the foundation of sound administration been laid.

Over and above the element of fragmentation in traditional society, it also appears that the Administration had frequently resorted to the recognition of petty chiefs, or men of their own creation, from a fear that the more powerful chiefs would be less amenable to European authority. The first major Belgian intervention in the field of native administration was a decree of 2 May 1910. It was in the tradition of previous legislation, with the chief seen primarily as the agent of the Administration, but had as a distinctive quality the division of the whole Congo into *chefferies* (chiefdoms), and sometimes, *sous-chefferies*. Renkin's aim was to use these two categories to permit both the reconstitution of large traditional groupings as *chefferies*, and the continued recognition of authorities already recognized by the Independent State by according them the status of *sous-chefferies*. The chief was to be paid a salary according to the size of his *chefferie*, he was given explicit administrative and police powers, and wider criminal jurisdiction in small matters as of right. The chief continued, of course, to be subject to European control and surveillance, and recognition of him continued to be by a positive act of investiture. The boundaries of each *chefferie* were to be determined by the *commissaire de district*, in conformity with custom.[1] Neither in the report on the decree of the Colonial Council,[2] nor in the decree, nor in any other policy pronouncement of the time was there any statement of how customary authorities should develop under European rule. A sentence in the Congo Annual Report for 1917 is, however, significant of how official thinking soon developed. 'In measure as civilization progresses, the former power of the chiefs will pass into the realm of memory and they will become civil servants applying the laws and regulations of the State.'[3]

In the four years after 1910 changes, more of terminology than of practice, were made in the (European) territorial and administrative structure of the colony. The earlier territorial divisions gave place to *provinces*, *districts* and *territories*, whilst the

---

[1] *Bulletin officiel*, 1910, pp. 456–71. The decree is summarized in Gille, 'Politique indigène', III, pp. 714–15. See also G. Brausch, 'Le Paternalisme: une doctrine belge de politique indigène', *Revue de l'Institut de Sociologie*, II, 1957, p. 198.
[2] *Bulletin officiel*, 1910, pp. 442–56.   [3] *Rapport annuel*, 1917, p. 13.

career structure, from the level of the *district* downwards, became *commissaire de district, administrateur territorial* and *agent territorial*. At the two lowest echelons of the non-customary judicial system, the *tribunal de police* and the *tribunal territorial*, administrative officers were usually the magistrates.[1] The matter of native taxation was definitely regulated by a decree of July 1914. By it all able-bodied adult Africans, with certain exceptions, were subject to a capitation tax, and to a supplementary tax in the case of polygamists. The amount of the capitation tax was to be determined by the Administration each year by regions, according to the resources of the population, within the range two to twenty-five francs (25 francs = £1 sterling at that time). Tax collection was to fall to the Administration, who had the option of delegating the work to chiefs.[2] The decree did not specify that tax payments must be in cash but—not surprisingly when one recalls the abuses accompanying taxation in kind under the old régime—cash payment was what was envisaged.[3]

How did Belgium's early land and native policy work out in practice? A report of 1911 of the *Commission pour la Protection des Indigènes*, an independent body created by Leopold as part of his answer to the Congo Reform campaign, was discouraging. The Commission, whose members were drawn from widely scattered parts of the Congo, spoke of some chiefs abusing their power for personal gain, of others as incapable of carrying out the tasks allotted to them. 'In short, we believe that the existing chiefs are, on the whole, incapable of executing the civilizing programme contained in the decree of 2 May 1910', though the Commission went on to add that there was no choice but to maintain the chiefs' authority. Tax apportionment, however —and this was before the definitive legislation of July 1914— was already more equitable.[4] Two years later the Commission could record the beneficial results of the ending throughout the colony of the régime of commercial monopoly,[5] whilst British consular and missionary observers had detected real improve-

---

[1] Van der Kerken, *Sociétés bantoues*, p. 154.

[2] Décret of 17 July 1914, summarized in Van der Kerken, *Sociétés bantoues*, pp. 162–3.

[3] 'Guide à l'usage du personnel chargé de l'application des dispositions du décret du 17 juillet 1914 . . .', quoted in Van der Kerken, *Sociétés bantoues*, p. 165.

[4] 'Rapport de la Commission . . . pour la Protection des Indigènes', *Bulletin officiel*, 1911, pp. 776–82.

[5] Ibid., 1913, pp. 292–3.

ment in the treatment of the Congolese from the autumn of 1910 onwards, shortly after the measures designed to end monopoly had begun to be put into effect.[1] The Commission was not able to meet during the war years and we are therefore deprived of the valuable reports of a body which, at that stage of its existence, spoke its mind.

By the end of the war, however, a clearer picture of the operation and impact of policy had emerged. As far as land policy was concerned, there was an immediate problem only in those areas where European enterprise made immediate and considerable demands on land. Even here, the provision that three times, or more, land than that in actual occupation could be recognized as being in native possession may often have prevented serious difficulties. But one well-informed observer, in particular, was already concerned to point out what would later become accepted truth. There was, he emphasized, no African conception of individual freehold tenure, and to impose European ideas of land tenure on the Africa-wide view of land as the patrimony of the tribe or clan, who alone could enjoy or delegate the *use* of it, was to lay up immense trouble for the future. What Africans dreaded most and what was most likely to disaffect them was alienation of their land. Indeed, such was their feeling about land as in some sense the preserve of the ancestral spirits that alienation could never have that final meaning which purchase or expropriation would give to the European mind. Even at the more utilitarian level, the three-fold provision, already referred to, was quite inadequate for a society based on shifting cultivation, the wide-ranging harvesting of forest produce, and so on, and whose numbers must be expected to increase considerably in measure as European rule brought its vaunted benefits. A thirtyfold rather than a three-fold provision must be the aim.[2]

Misunderstanding of African concepts of land tenure had been an element in the formulation of land policy, and a partial misconception of the political organization of the Congo peoples seems to have influenced the *chefferie* policy and what went with it. It has been seen [pp. 24–25] that the Congo peoples had not always been divided into a multiplicity of independent tribes: the administrator, however, despite Renkin's intention,

[1] Cookey, 'Great Britain and the Congo Question', pp. 336–8, 343–7.
[2] Van der Kerken, *Sociétés bantoues*, pp. 172–96.

E

commonly acted as if this was the case. The Governor-General's report for the year 1917 certainly speaks of the careful investigation which should precede the creation of a *chefferie*: but it attests that the Administration looked kindly on the frequently desired incorporation of hitherto subject peoples into *chefferies* independent of their erstwhile rulers, and clearly regards as proper and desirable the arrest during the year of Chief Kalamba Tshikomo of the Bena-Lulua and Kasongo Niembo of the Ba-Luba. There would certainly seem to have been the feeling that the paramount chiefs of larger groupings, if recognized as such by the Administration, would merely be confirmed in the tyranny which seemed, as exemplified by Msiri, to be their principal occupation.[1] The result might be that the men recognized as chiefs—the highest recognition which the State could confer—were sometimes men who had only a subordinate position in the traditional hierarchy. Even if a chief were recognized, his authority was all too often acknowledged only in respect of one or more of the component clans of his tribe.

'European rule', wrote Van der Kerken, who at the time was a *commissaire de district* in Katanga, 'in the time of the Independent State and after annexation, has generally organized into *chefferies* families [the extended family is of course meant] and clans, on rare occasions tribes, never a people, at least to our knowledge, sometimes even the fragments of a family or clan'.[2] He goes on to cite specific cases from Katanga and to suggest, from the mathematical evidence of two districts of Orientale and Equateur provinces where the average population of each *chefferie* was as low as 350 and 500 respectively, that the same thing was happening elsewhere.[3] Indeed the mathematical evidence over the colony as a whole is interesting. In 1917 there were 6,095 recognized *chefferies* and *sous-chefferies* for a population estimated at just under six million—a little less than 1,000 people to each *chefferie*.[4] The direct evidence for the continued viability of large groupings comes mainly from Katanga, and it may be that, over considerable areas elsewhere, by the time of the Belgian annexation the effective authority was no more than that of the petty chief.[5] Notwithstanding, a policy of

[1] Van der Kerken, *Sociétés bantoues*, pp. 229–30 ; *Rapport annuel*, 1917, pp. 8–13.
[2] Van der Kerken, *Sociétés bantoues*, p. 233.   [3] Ibid., pp. 235, 237–8.
[4] Ibid., p. 234.   [5] *African Survey*, p. 552.

recognition of customary authority only at the *chefferie* level may well have been unsatisfactory where a larger traditional grouping had existed in the recent past, for that larger grouping may well, in African opinion, have continued to be regarded as the proper framework of authority.

An added distortion came from the division of tribes—through the recognition of their component clans as autonomous *chefferies*—amongst different administrative districts. Van der Kerken cites a number of specific cases in Katanga.[1]

Failure to understand the anatomy of customary society was also a factor making for distortion, and one which Van Wing, from his experience in the Lower Congo, particularly stressed.[2] As a result of such ignorance it often happened that an intriguer, or the head of a faction in a clan or tribal dispute, could get himself recognized as a chief, whilst in other cases the true tribal authority, shrinking from association with European authority, would put forward a man of straw to be invested with authority whilst real authority remained in traditional hands. Sometimes, too, an administrator would yield to the temptation to confer power upon someone with some understanding of European ways, a former soldier or 'boy', for instance, despite the fact that he had no traditional position of authority, in the hope, perhaps, either that the administrator's wishes would be more effectively carried out, or that the civilizing process would be quickened.[3] In the words of the 1918 edition of the general instructions to administrative officers:

A number of *chefferies* have been legally recognized although in reality they were only isolated groups of an indigenous community indivisible according to custom. On the other hand unrelated clans have sometimes been gathered together into one *chefferie*. The quarrelsome and the ambitious have seen their intrigues crowned with success and have obtained by official investiture a dignity and advantages to which they could not legally pretend.

And yet again, genuine chiefs have substituted for themselves men of straw, intended to suffer the remonstrances of our administrators, whilst they themselves continued clandestinely the administration of their communities and enjoyed the use of the salary accorded by the State.[4]

[1] Van der Kerken, *Sociétés bantoues*, p. 237.
[2] Van Wing, *Études Bakongo*, p. 129.
[3] Based on Van der Kerken, *Sociétés bantoues*, pp. 159, 243–5.
[4] *Recueil à l'usage des fonctionnaires et des agents du service territorial* (London, 1918), quoted in Van der Kerken, *Sociétés bantoues*, p. 245.

A number of earlier circulars from the Governor-General to administrative officers testify to these and related shortcomings in the application of native policy, whilst the Governor-General's reports during the war years are very frank about the errors committed and the difficulties experienced in applying the *chefferie* policy generally, and even about its shortcomings as a policy.[1]

There was sometimes in the circulars, explicitly or between the lines, criticism of administrative officers for the way in which they executed policy. What was their performance and quality? Their ranks clearly included men of outstanding quality, of whom Van der Kerken (who has been frequently cited in this chapter) and Paul Salkin, who in 1920 published a similar type of book to Van der Kerken's—*Études africaines*[2]—are leading examples. There were also, no doubt, other no less able and devoted men who did not write books! But apart from the fact that able and devoted men armed with the necessary insight and sympathy must almost by definition be rare, the administration was greatly strained, and often distracted from its true function by the First World War. Home leave to, and recruitment from occupied Belgium were out of the question, whilst much time and energy had to be spent in recruiting porters for the campaign in East Africa, in encouraging recruitment for mines and industry rapidly burgeoning under the impulse of war, and in initiating the policy of compulsory cultivation (see p. 82) laid down in 1917. The effect of this must often have been that the African image of the administrator would be confirmed as that of an oppressor, whilst the administrator for his part would be prevented from establishing a *rapport* with the people in his charge. But in the first half-dozen or so years of Belgian rule the internal structure of colonial administration also had something to do with its failures. The very concern of Belgium to prevent the recurrence of abuses in the Congo had, as we have seen, led her to set up a centralized administrative system. The result, at least until Renkin introduced a measure of decentralization from Brussels to Leopoldville in 1914, and possibly after, was

[1] See *Bulletin mensuel*, Circulaires of 12 June 1914, 24 and 31 July 1915, 19 September 1915, and 20 December 1916, cited in Van der Kerken, *Sociétés bantoues*, pp. 158–9; *Rapports annuels*, 1915–18, Chapters I–V.
[2] Brussels, Ferdinand Larcier.

that men on the spot had too little initiative even in small matters, whilst they might have to wait months or even years for decisions on larger questions.[1]

Of great importance was the type of man who occupied the bottom rung of the administrative ladder. Whereas a man who entered the *service territorial* as an *administrateur adjoint* might, as Van der Kerken believed, suffer from inadequate vocational training,[2] at least he was usually a man of some education with a colonial career in mind, who might well bring to his work and conduct the reinforcement which a professional conscience and awareness sometimes engenders. But below the *administrateur* was the *agent territorial*, a man of less education and much less training even than the *administrateur*. Henri Rolin, a Belgian judge and university teacher, who visited Katanga in 1911 had this to say of the *chef de poste*, the administrative position occupied by an *agent*:

All the witnesses whom we heard were unanimous in confirming what we ourselves observed: our *chefs de poste* are too young and incompetent; they are sent out, without knowing the native language, without serious training, without a probationary period, to a distant place where they are usually alone. Isolated, powerless, able only with difficulty to leave their headquarters, they do not travel enough in their district, they do not get to know the villages.

. . . A distinguished administrator depicted to us the truly unenviable role of the *chef de poste*, at the mercy in fact of his African *capita*, who is essential as an intermediary; the same witness, who had known the country for many years, depicted the *chef de poste*, stretched out on his verandah and, when the Africans come to submit their differences to him, harshly sending them off: *Katuka!* Go away!— which is conduct *truly destructive* [in italics] of all influence over the Africans. The training of our *chefs de poste*, an official of long service told us, is '*une petite école moyenne*'. Of ten or twelve *chefs de poste* [Rolin indicates earlier that there were twenty-eight *postes* in the whole of Katanga], an eminent missionary told us, there are not more than two gentlemen. All witnesses agreed that the *chefs de poste* are generally of the 'N.C.O.' type. We do not wish to malign a very deserving category of public servant, but one will recognize that

[1] H. Rolin, 'Les Vices de l'administration du Katanga—les remèdes', *Revue de l'Université de Bruxelles*, December 1911, pp. 200–13. Stengers, *Belgique et Congo*, p. 224.
[2] Van der Kerken, *Sociétés bantoues*, pp. 351–5.

this is not the type of man who will assure the success of our native policy.

Rolin himself had talked with some new arrivals.

A future *chef de poste*, twenty-one years old and about to be sent into the interior, assured us that he did not know the native language. He had been to a Belgian *athénée* [secondary school] and in the matter of how to treat the African, professed 'strong arm' views. 'Why does one come to the Congo?' he said to us, 'unless to make money quickly and get out?' . . . 'Here', we said sadly to ourselves, 'are the men to whom we entrust the supremely delicate task of governing Africans!'[1]

Rolin, it must be said, was writing of a visit made in 1911, but Van der Kerken, on later evidence, was no less scathing. In his experience *agents* were usually badly qualified and quite unsuitable.

Their participation in native policy and economic policy has been such as to do more harm than good to African societies and to European rule. Their abolition, as political agents, would be an advantage.[2]

In some penetrating and important words Van der Kerken goes on to analyse just why the *agents territoriaux* were as a class both inadequate and positively harmful:

In numerous regions, the actions and faults of former *chefs de poste;* their frequent almost total incomprehension of native institutions; their inability to take a general and detached view, taking into account all aspects of the problem; their frequent tendency to follow a policy aimed at personal prestige, to the detriment of the authority of the traditional rulers, to this day weigh heavily on the shoulders of those entrusted with the political and economic development of native societies.[3]

At the official level the Governor-General could in 1916 attribute to the better *commissaires de district* the view that it was not necessary to increase the number of *agents* (though it is not clear whether the term is being used in a strict technical sense) but to improve their quality.[4]

The inadequacies of, and harm done by the *agents territoriaux*

---

[1] Rolin, *Revue de l'Université de Bruxelles*, pp. 192–4.
[2] Van der Kerken, *Sociétés bantoues*, pp. 356–8.   [3] Ibid., pp. 356–7.
[4] *Rapport annuel*, 1916, p. 2.

—there were of course exceptions—have been elaborated at some length and for good reasons. These were the 'men on the ground', the administrators and the Europeans with whom Africans came into closest contact. The *administrateur territorial* and the *commissaire de district* might have all the imaginable virtues of every possible saint: what was of incalculable importance was that native policy at the grass-roots level was in the hands of men of coarser quality, and assessments of the working-out of native policy must be made with this in mind.

As the years went by the more discerning administrators came to see that what may loosely be called feudal structures of authority *did* sometimes exist in African society, that the *chefferie* policy as hitherto applied was in those cases doing violence to that society, and that it was also prejudicing the attainment of the aims of native policy. The view that had first been urgently pressed by Monseigneur de Clercq at the time of the formulation of the decree of 2 May 1910—that an explicit recognition of the role of the clan and tribal elders in the government of customary African society should be written into native policy—also came to be voiced more and more frequently. Traditional authority, it was argued, was rarely autocratic, and not to confer explicit recognition upon the elders and their role was to distort customary authority and to make it possible for the chief to rule oppresively.[1]

Opinion varied, and continued to vary, on this point, but it is clear that after a decade some of the really important aims of what was understandably a pedestrian-enough native policy were far from being generally attained. Certainly inter-tribal war with all its miseries had been brought virtually to an end and naked oppression of the African was much more rare. These were both impressive achievements, bearing in mind the bad old days and the size of the colony. But European authority was still too 'external'; and indeed, resort to police action and punitive military expeditions was still frequent. And because it still rested too much on superior physical power, European authority was in consequence erratic in its effective exercise. The colonizer had scarcely begun to establish a vital relationship, a *rapport* in which the traditional authorities accepted, even of necessity, European supremacy, and on the basis

[1] See Gille, 'Politique indigène', III, pp. 715–16; Van der Kerken, *Sociétés bantoues*, p. 254; *Conseil colonial*, Proceedings, 1910, pp. 503–9.

of which they might advance to a more fruitful dialogue.

The effects of this failure, not the least of whose origins was the failure properly to discern the nature of African traditional authority, were to be seen at various levels and in a number of forms. From the point of view of the administration there were frequent laments—in the annual reports of the Governor-General, for example—at the weakness and inadequacy of the recognized chiefs.[1] Important in itself, this deficiency had many consequences. The help of the chiefs in tax-collection was rarely sought, with the result that administrators were frequently confronted with the flight *en masse* of a village when they came to collect taxes. They were thus reduced to sending out parties of police and 'boys'—an action which resulted in oppression and consequent African ill-will, as well as very incomplete tax collection. It also caused much disturbance to African life and even loss of life, as a result of the hardships attending flight into the bush.[2]

Again, the lack of African respect for many of the recognized chiefs meant that little progress was made in the attempt to establish them as the bottom tier in the administration of justice. Disputes were frequently resolved by the shadow traditional authorities, or might form an increasing burden on administrators, who began to suspect that resort was made to them not least by the party who had been found guilty by customary law and who sought in the administrator's ignorance of custom a reversal of that decision.[3] One of the very virtues of Belgian rule had a certain effect on the authority and prestige of the chiefs. This was the refusal to recognize domestic slavery—which was claimed to be often mild and paternalistic rather than oppressive. As a result chiefs might find that their chattel slaves, an important element in their power, wealth and prestige, fled or occasionally were liberated by an administrator.[4] If this loss were made good by a salary commensurate with the chief's important role in administration, the effects might be minimized, but very often the salary of the chief was lower than that of a clerk or an interpreter, even of a houseboy.[5]

This last point brings home the fact that African society and institutions were beginning to be subjected not only to the

---

[1] *Rapports annuels du Congo belge*, 1915–18, Chapters 1–3 *passim*; Van der Kerken, *Sociétés bantoues*, p. 235.

[2] Van der Kerken, *Sociétés bantoues*, pp. 274–6.   [3] Ibid., p. 253.

[4] Ibid., pp. 207–8.   [5] Ibid., p. 246.

impact of the native policy of the Government but also to other European influences. The most beneficent of these influences were the Christian missions.

For the missions the years after 1908 were years of continued advance, though in the case of the Protestants the opening-up of work in new areas continued to be prejudiced by the difficulty of obtaining new sites from the Government. Between 1906 and 1914, for instance, Protestant missions received only 978 hectares of land, whilst Roman Catholic missions were given 23,106 hectares.[1] The feeling against Protestant missions seems to have derived from the part which some of them had played —albeit sometimes belatedly—in the Congo Reform campaign; from the missions' continuing revelation of abuses in the early period of Belgian rule and the tendency of some of them to urge, with Morel, that British and American recognition of annexation should be conditional on effective reform.[2] It is also reasonable to impute to the governing Catholic party a reluctance to see a further extension of Protestantism, whilst there may also have been a continuing resentment towards Britain and America, stemming from what (from the Belgian viewpoint) was their bullying over Congo reform, a resentment which could now find expression against the predominantly Anglo-Saxon Protestant missions. Renkin and the Belgian Government may also have feared that Protestant missions could evidently not be instruments of a civilizing mission delegated to a Roman Catholic country, and might even spread dangerous ideas. Certainly there was a curious episode in 1909 in which a proposal, probably inspired by Renkin himself and in which the King was closely interested, was made that the Protestant missions should accept as their intermediary with the Belgian Government the Belgian Synod of Evangelical Churches and that their missionaries on the Congo should gradually be replaced by Belgian Protestants subsidized by the Belgian Government.[3]

Nor can relations between the Protestants and the Belgian Government have been improved by the continuing links—

[1] Rev. H. F. Drake, 'Some Contemporary Problems confronting the Protestant Church in the Belgian Congo' (unpublished S.T.M. thesis, Union Theological Seminary, New York, 1960), p. 52. See also Slade, *English-Speaking Missions*, pp. 337–58, 361–2.

[2] Slade, *English-Speaking Missions*, pp. 327–45.

[3] Ibid., pp. 347–56.

they had originated during the Congo Reform campaign—between the Belgian Socialists and the Protestant missions. Indeed there was a minor *cause célèbre* when in 1909 Vandervelde, who was by profession a lawyer, personally represented two American missionaries in a court case in Leopoldville in an action brought against them by the Kasai Company, following allegations of maladministration. One should perhaps add that, in general, it was a case rather of the Socialists hating the Catholics than of their loving the Protestants.[1]

Protestant converts sometimes experienced a certain persecution at the hands of Catholic administrators acting at the behest of priests, and a Protestant Missionary Conference in 1918 made a strong protest about this.[2] None the less the rate of Protestant and Roman Catholic advance was much the same and was certainly considerable, though in each case it was probably checked by the First World War. By the early twenties there can have been no *districts* and few *territoires* of the Congo in which a mission, Catholic or Protestant, had no footing.

Highly significant for the impact of Christianity was a change in missionary methods by the Roman Catholic Orders. From 1912 onwards, as a matter of principle, they abandoned the *ferme-chapelle* system (pp. 35-36). How far this was due to a fierce controversy over the alleged authoritarianism and harshness of the Fathers in charge—the Jesuits in particular—is not clear, but certainly many administrators and African chiefs opposed the system since it involved both the existence of communities close to, but not subject to the chief's jurisdiction and the too great isolation of the *ferme-chapelle* group from its traditional *milieu*. Some of the missionary Fathers shared this view.[3] Henceforth the emphasis was on the installation of the teacher-catechist in the heart of the village itself and the opening of a primary school, with the missionary priest continuing to visit as often as possible.[4] The Protestants, it has been seen, had already switched to the system of placing the teacher-evangelist in the village instead (p. 36). With steady

[1] Slade, *English-Speaking Missions*, pp. 364-75.
[2] Drake, 'Problems confronting the Protestant Church', p. 55.
[3] R.P. L. Denis, *Les Jésuites belges au Kwango, 1893–1943* (Brussels, L'Édition Universelle, 1943), pp. 78ff; R.P. de Meeus et R.P. R. Steenberghen, *Les Missions religieuses au Congo belge* (Antwerp, Van Dieren, 1947), pp. 82–83.
[4] Denis, *Jésuites belges*, p. 90.

European penetration of the country and the wider extension of administrative control, the new 'outgoing' approach brought rapid results. The mission came increasingly to be established in the village. Some lines of Dr. Slade concerning the Protestant teacher-evangelist bring home the nature of the missions' impact when the system worked at its best.

It was the missionaries, and perhaps to a greater extent the teacher-evangelists . . . who were to provide a link between the new pattern of life and the old. The personal knowledge of the evangelist was slight; he could read and write and manage simple arithmetic—sometimes not even that. His material equipment was meagre; there was the tumble-down grass hut which served as schoolroom and chapel, some Scripture paraphrases and reading books, and a few slates. His training period had been short in view of all he was expected to accomplish. But he was able to base his teaching on local customs and proverbs as the white man could never do. He possessed an inborn gift for story-telling, and could hold his listeners enthralled as he moved step by step to his climax. He could use emotional expression in a way which won their immediate response. He was himself an example to the children who sat at his feet of the heights to which they could rise. And where he was established conditions of life improved and Church membership increased by leaps and bounds.[1]

Other forms of the European impact on traditional African life and society were of a quite different nature. The itinerant European, Levantine or Indian trader, who was the expression 'on the ground' of the new Free Trade policy, was sometimes a rogue who took advantage of deficient supervision by the Administration, and of his own superior power, to perpetrate abuses to his own profit. Huts and provisions might be requisitioned without payment, his commercial dealings might be unfair. Van der Kerken noted these malpractices as particularly prevalent in Katanga, and in the Uele and Ituri regions.[2] Probably a more serious abuse, at least in regions reasonably close to the new industrial centres of Katanga and elsewhere, was the activity of labour-recruiters. Recruiters were licensed by the Governor-General, who also retained the power to close areas to recruitment, whilst the decrees governing recruitment also provided for sanctions against recruiters guilty of malpractices. But in practice recruitment seems to have been

---

[1] Slade, *English-Speaking Missions*, p. 193.
[2] Van der Kerken, *Sociétés bantoues*, pp. 291–3.

scarcely limited at all, whilst inadequate administrative control meant that there were occasionally veritable manhunts—or the taking hostage of women and girls until the men agreed to come forward. Outright violence was probably the exception, but the removal from villages of a high proportion of their able-bodied men had all sorts of harmful consequences.[1] Certainly the problem came to be regarded as serious enough for a Native Labour Commission to be appointed in 1924 with the consideration of the proper level of recruitment as its major task.[2]

The tasks so far attempted in this chapter have been to indicate the factors which conditioned Belgian policy in the Congo, to consider the nature of that policy and its working out from the viewpoint of the colonial power, and to point to other external forces operating on African society. It remains to attempt some assessment of the impact of European rule and culture on African society in this early period of Belgian authority.

A striking result of the coming of Europe to the Congo was that African society, already disrupted, was further weakened in its ability to respond adequately to its environment. In the long run that ability was still further reduced by the suggestion that certain, at least, of European goals were more worthy of attainment than some traditional ones. But the immediate impact of Europe was simply that it impaired the ability of traditional African society to respond adequately to life and its demands. Moreover, the coming of European rule, economic enterprise, values and religion imposed situations with which the weakened traditional institutions were, *ipso facto*, the less able to deal, whilst at the same time the positive tutelage necessary in such a delicate situation was lacking.

A vital function of the family and tribal hierarchy of African traditional life was, it has been seen, to confer at different levels the authority necessary for the performance of socially necessary tasks. At one level, for instance, the tribal chief and elders were entrusted with the overall welfare and security of the tribe and were by tradition accorded the powers necessary for the attainment of these aims. But this structure of authority was undermined by the practice of recognizing traditional authority

---

[1] Van der Kerken, *Sociétés bantoues*, pp. 169, 288–91.
[2] G. Hostelet, *L'Œuvre civilisatrice de la Belgique au Congo de 1885 à 1953* (Brussels, Académie Royale des Sciences Coloniales, 1954), I, pp. 257–8.

only at the level of the *chefferie* (or *sous-chefferie*), of frequently failing to discern or recognize the rightful authority, and of failing to recognize a hierarchy of powers or the real familio-political entities. At the same time the powers accorded to customary authority were, by traditional standards, very limited, whilst the failure to give specific recognition to elders may have further weakened the pattern of traditional authority. Finally the very fact of the imposition of European authority meant that there was henceforth a superior power—measured at least by the criterion of physical force. Traditional authority, where it was strongest, might continue to exercise power 'underground' but it no longer had an unquestioned finality, and in many respects it could not in the long run prevail against the will of the colonizing power. In short, traditional authority had begun to be undermined in the eyes of the African, and his whole sense of psychological security to be weakened, as a result of the declining ability of his customary institutions to play their age-old role. The problems, resulting from the coming of the European, with which the weakened and distorted customary authority had to deal were, to take notable examples, the land policy of the colonizer, whereby violence was done to traditional ideas of land tenure and whereby actual loss of land resulted; in certain areas the haemorrhage of able-bodied manpower as a result of recruitment; the imposition of unpopular tasks, such as the upkeep of the roads and, from 1917, the completion of the allotted stint under the policy of *culture obligatoire*, given full legal sanction in that year; the wide extension of a religion—Christianity—which unavoidably ran counter, or was presented as running counter, to deep-seated existing beliefs and institutions. Although the necessary positive tutelage was lacking in the enforcement of a rigidly European type of land policy, or in the failure of the colonial administration to protect traditional society from the depredations of the recruiter, that tutelage might sometimes be present in the enlightened and perceptive administrator or merchant. But it may well be that, despite the necessarily destructive effects of some of the teaching which he brought, and the unnecessarily destructive way in which he sometimes presented it, it was the missionary who most shielded the African from the difficulties of such a situation, and most effectively and sympathetically led him towards new ideas and new beliefs.

IV

AFRICAN ADMINISTRATION AND THE PRESSURES ON CUSTOMARY SOCIETY IN THE INTER-WAR YEARS (1)

THOSE who had so penetratingly criticized administrative practice during the first decade of Belgian rule in the Congo —Van der Kerken and Salkin in particular—had the rare satisfaction of seeing much of their diagnosis accepted when their books had scarcely left the presses. In a ministerial circular of the latter part of 1920, M. Louis Franck, who had succeeded Renkin as Colonial Minister in 1918, was forthright.

The great number of chiefs and sub-chiefs amongst whom authority is divided in many regions of the Colony is an evil and a danger. The *chefferies* are too small, many chiefs lack all authority. The means of obtaining obedience formerly possessed by the chief have disappeared. The time is not far distant when, if we are not careful, in many regions, the collapse of indigenous authority will be complete. Judicial anarchy will be the counterpart of administrative crumbling. . . . The chief who is no longer judge, and a respected judge, will lose what remains of his authority.

With considerable wisdom, the decree of the *chefferies* was concerned to base native authority on custom. This principle is essential and we must conserve it. An excellent work of revision and of organization has been carried out and ought to be proceeded with. Nothing which will be said modifies these governing principles.

But, Franck continued, it was also necessary to advance.

Today, on the same basis and in the same spirit, we can take a step further.

Not content with recognizing and maintaining chiefs of royal blood and traditional authority, we ought to strive to *develop* indigenous institutions.[1]

[1] L. Franck, 'La Politique indigène, le service territorial et les chefferies', *Congo*, II, 1, 2 February 1921, p. 194. (This article is a reproduction of portions of a

How was this to be done?

Franck's programme was threefold. First of all those *chefferies* and *sous-chefferies* which were too small to be viable were to be drastically reduced in number by amalgamation. To some extent this could be done by attaching the inhabitants of the small *chefferie* to an adjoining one on the death of their invested chief, but this was too slow a process to be sufficient in itself. The administrator had also to initiate a process of amalgamation by convening periodic meetings of those chiefs within a *territoire* who possessed some sort of common tribal affinity. These chiefs were to constitute the *conseil* of a new administrative unit called the *secteur*, and were not only to hold discussions with the *administrateur* or one of his assistants on matters of interest such as crops, taxes or markets, but were to be given judicial functions also. The seat of the council would be at the village of the chief considered by the administrator to be 'the most intelligent or the most influential and the most understanding, or who has preserved a traditional authority to a significant degree, or which is capable of revival'.[1] The chief thus selected would receive the particular attention and consideration of the administrator and would be quietly accustomed to taking the leading role amongst his fellow chiefs. Eventually, 'when the minds of his fellows had been sufficiently prepared . . . and as far as possible with the assent of the council',[2] the chosen chief would be formally invested as chief of the *secteur*. In that capacity he would enjoy specified administrative powers and would be the intermediary between the administrator and the other chiefs whilst, in the absence of the administrator, he would preside at meetings of the *conseil du secteur*. If there was an absolute lack of a suitable man occupying a traditional position, then recourse could be made to an *évolué*, to an African who had had some experience of administration as for example, a clerk, or as an N.C.O. in the *Force publique*. The ultimate aim in areas where the traditional groupings were too small was that each *territoire* would be divided into three, four or five *secteurs* whose centres, in

Preface which Franck wrote for the 1920 edition of the *Recueil à l'usage des fonctionnaires et des agents du service territorial*, and of a ministerial circular, n.d.) It may well be that Franck's concern for Flemish linguistic and racial integrity was a factor in his respect for African life, and custom (see R.P.E. Boelaert, 'Vers un état Mongo', *Bulletin de l'A.R.S.O.M.*, VII, 1961–3, p. 384).

[1] Franck, *Politique indigène*, p. 195.   [2] Ibid., p. 196.

addition to being the seat of the *conseil*, would be the location for a school, a dispensary and the all-important, in Franck's view, *tribunal indigène*.

Franck himself only sketched out a new structure of native courts, but he believed them to be the corner-stone of his system. Individual chiefs would continue to exercise a purely traditional jurisdiction over their own petty groupings, but the law must create *tribunaux de secteur* to deal with matters affecting more than the petty group, or in which the chief's decision had not been accepted. Beyond this would be a *tribunal de territoire* with correspondingly greater jurisdiction and powers.

If Franck's first policy sketch devoted most space to the proposed *secteurs*, it briefly but firmly endorsed the plea of Van der Kerken and others for the maintenance and strengthening, indeed for the revival of the large *chefferies*. The Administration should confirm the dependence of traditional sub-chiefs on their paramount chief.[1]

Franck was a strong-minded man and he retained the colonial ministry for almost six years. None the less it is surprising that his ideas left such a long shadow. Given wider and wider legal elaboration throughout the twenties and thirties, they remained the basis of native administration almost to the end of Belgian rule. Perhaps his influence begins to be explained when one sees his ideas and policies as the elaboration of an existing line of development rather than as anything really new; as essentially the tidying-up of a rapidly deteriorating situation.

The full flowering of the new policy was not until the decrees of 15 April 1926 on *Tribunaux indigènes*, and of 5 December 1933 on *Circonscriptions indigènes*, and in one respect—the proposal to revive and strengthen the large *chefferies*, to give them the status of *protectorats* (to cite the term used)—Franck's policies did not really get off the ground. The first application was to be to the old Ba-Luba empire. It was to be reconstituted under its paramount chief, Kasongo Niembo, and the boundaries of the Tanganyika-Moero district of Katanga were to be redrawn so as to make them coincide with those of the former Ba-Luba kingdom. There seem to have been two immediate reasons why re-constitution did not take place. The administration believed it to be impossible for the moment—it must be remembered that

[1] Franck, *Politique indigène*, pp. 191–201; Gille, 'Politique indigène', pp. 718–20.

Kasongo Niembo, after prolonged military operations, had only been arrested in 1917—whilst the sub-chiefs who had formerly owned allegiance to Kasongo Niembo refused to return to that allegiance.[1] Furthermore the Katanga sub-commission of the *Commission pour la Protection des Indigènes* came out against the encouragement of the large *chefferies* at its 1924 meeting, on the grounds that such a policy necessarily encouraged the perpetuation of undesirable and even barbarous customs.[2] This opposition may have played a minor role whilst there was also opposition from some of the Catholic missionary hierarchy to the whole Franck-inspired Belgian variant of indirect rule, on the grounds that it perpetuated two societies *en ordre parallele et incommunicable*, to use both the words and the italics of Monseigneur J. de Hemptinne.[3] Such opposition must have been particularly directed against the *protectorat* as the most extreme form of the policy. M. van der Kerken, with all the weight which his earlier criticism of administrative practice could command and all the influence which his pioneer role in applying the *secteur* policy to Equateur Province conferred, strove for a similar autonomy for the Mongo people as had been urged for the Ba-Luba. But it was not to be.[4] All that was ever attempted of the *protectorat* policy was a preliminary and possibly half-hearted strengthening of the authority of certain important chiefs, and even this limited measure did not survive the administrative economies of 1933.[5]

With the other two components of the Franck policy the case was different. The *secteur* policy was not generally applied until the decree on *Circonscriptions indigènes* of 1933 but important beginnings had been made, through administrative instructions, from 1921 onwards, when the first *secteur* was created.[6] At the same time, throughout the twenties, the task of organizing territory still virtually unpenetrated, or unadministered, into *territoires*, and into *chefferies* where there were thought to be viable units, continued. By the same token those *chefferies*

[1] Brausch, *Paternalisme*, p. 209.

[2] Report of C.P.I., Katanga sub-Commission, 1924, *Bulletin officiel*, 1925, pp. 195–7.

[3] Quoted in Brausch, *Paternalisme*, p. 212. Mgr. de Hemptinne was a member of the C.P.I. from 1923 onwards. See also Report of C.P.I., 1929, *Bulletin officiel*, 1929, II, pp. 118–19.

[4] Boelaert, 'Vers un état Mongo?', p. 384.

[5] Ibid.; Brausch, *Paternalisme*, p. 211.   [6] Ibid.

F

already recognized to be viable were left as they were. The application of the new policy in the twenties and early thirties was principally in Orientale province, which during much of the period was in the hands of governors wholeheartedly in favour of it.[1] At best a thorough labour of investigation was crowned with the creation of *secteurs* possessing a real homogeneity, but there are a number of indications that too often the investigation was too hurried and the result unsatisfactory, not least because administrators succumbed to the temptation to nominate an *évolué* as *chef de secteur* far more frequently than Franck envisaged or subsequent administrative instructions intended.[2] Certainly the Annual Reports of both 1929 and 1930 complain of the inadequacy of the majority of the chiefs,[3] whilst Van der Kerken believed that too often administrators resorted, in effect, to direct rule[4]—a likely enough result of a belief in the inadequacy of chiefs.

None the less, an important beginning had been made, a beginning which also made it possible to begin to apply to the *secteurs*, as they were established, the provisions of the decree on *Juridictions indigènes* of 1926 which Franck had from the first envisaged as the corner-stone of policy evolution. In close accord with his original circular the decree provided for, *inter alia*, the creation of *tribunaux de secteurs* and *tribunaux territoriaux*. Minor modifications were made in the system in subsequent years but the 1926 decree was the kernel of it. The system is succinctly described in the *African Survey*.

The *tribunaux indigènes* exercise jurisdiction over Africans in all civil matters which do not involve the application of the *droit écrit*; their criminal jurisdiction is normally confined to offences against customary law, but it may be extended by express authorization of law to specified statutory offences. The punishments which they may impose are limited to one month's imprisonment and a fine of 1,000 francs, or two months' imprisonment and a fine of 2,000 francs if the Court is sitting under the presidency of an Administrative Officer. Revision on question of fact lies with the *tribunal de territoire*; but the supervision of the proceedings of the Native Courts lies

---

[1] Gille, 'Politique indigène', p. 724. V. Vermeulen, *Déficiences et dangers de notre politique indigène* (privately published, 1952), pp. 43–44. It is relevant to note that, under Franck's impulsion, there was considerable administrative decentralization in the 1920's.

[2] Ibid., pp. 43–46. Gille, 'Politique indigène', pp. 726–7.

[3] *Rapports annuels*, 1929, p. 5, and 1930, p. 6.

[4] Opinion cited in A. Doucy, 'Politique indigène', *Livre blanc* (Brussels, A.R.S.O.M., 1962), I, p. 355.

with the *Parquet* (which may be loosely interpreted as the Attorney-General's department), which has certain administrative powers over them and sees their records. It can annul their decisions on grounds of law, or can order retrial.[1]

With the 1933 decree on *Circonscriptions indigènes* the legal expression of the modified system of native administration was complete. The terms of the decree closely followed the policy sketch which was Franck's original circular, but it is important to emphasize the administrative functions with which the chief, in his capacity as representative of the Administration before his people, was entrusted. They were numerous and their discharge had an important influence on the operation and impact of the whole system. The only strictly new power which the chief was given was the right to issue orders for the protection of public health and the maintenance of order. Otherwise his responsibilities were mainly those with which he had been entrusted since the decree of May 1910, but their enumeration in a decree intended to give general application to the new policy, and at a time when the colony had been opened up and economic development was being positively pursued, signified that henceforward the chief would be in a much more definite sense the agent of the Administration. He must help in the census, in tax-collection and conscription of labour, and must ensure the execution of the obligatory works imposed on his *secteur* or *chefferie*. These works might be either unpaid (such as the building of a school and the maintenance of local roads, the carrying out of anti-erosion measures) or remunerated, as in the notable case of the compulsory production of food or cash crops. All these works were the subject of an annual plan drawn up by the Administration. They were not to occupy the individual male African for more than sixty days a year.[2] The *chefferies* and *secteurs* were also to be provided with treasuries, fed from the proceeds of court fines, from a proportion of tax revenue, and from Government grants. They were to be used, in order of priority, first for the purposes of local native administration, and secondly for the provision of equipment necessary for the economic development of the local area. Thirdly they were to contribute in a small way to the provision of medical and social benefits. The treasuries would

[1] *African Survey*, p. 621.   [2] Gille, 'Politique indigène', pp. 729–30.

be supervised by the Administration and would help to strengthen the *chefferies* and *secteurs* as entities.

In the years after 1926, and still more after 1933, the application of this Belgian version of indirect rule naturally gained momentum. By the end of 1938 there were 340 *secteurs* and 1,212 *chefferies*, a far cry from the 6,095 *chefferies* of 1917 and a marked change from the 3,189 *chefferies* and 493 *sous-chefferies* of the beginning of 1933.[1] Following the same evolutionary pattern there were, by the end of 1938, 1,135 *tribunaux de chefferie*, 389 *tribunaux de secteur* and 105 *tribunaux de territoire*.[2] In both fields concentration was to go much farther.

These figures give a numerical indication of how the new administrative policy worked out and what its implications were, but these are questions which also need to be answered in terms, first, of how administrative officers applied the new policy and, secondly, of its implications for chiefs in particular and the traditional authorities in general.

M. Brausch, who had substantial experience of the operation of the revised system in Kasai, discerned an initial tendency to build up the *secteurs* as groups of related tribes which had in the past separated, or been separated, from each other. He also discerned a different, a geographical, basis for *secteurs* in the case of the ethnically mixed populations of the smaller centres, too small to receive full urban status. In such cases the principal determinant was the location of the existing European centre which gave the area its life. Brausch believed that it was not until after the outbreak of war that a full-blooded 'progressive' approach to *chefferies* and *secteurs* was adopted, not until then that administrative officers in general came to favour the creation of *secteurs* on a non-customary basis.[3] Grévisse, however, believes this attitude to have been present from the beginning. He described the notion of the *secteur* in its proper form as one which 'a considerable number of administrators have never succeeded in properly assimilating'.

Too many *secteurs* have been conceived in the most facile manner possible, either so as not to have to manage more than one native

[1] *Rapport annuel*, 1932, p. 9; 1938, p. 12.   [2] Ibid., 1938, p. 19.

[3] G.E.J-B. Brausch, 'Le Groupe social comme synthèse créatrice', *Bulletin du Centre d'Étude des Problèmes Sociaux Indigènes* (C.E.P.S.I.), 1948, No. 3, pp. 35–39; Brausch, 'Communes africaines', *Revue de l'Université de Bruxelles*, January–April 1957, pp. 241–6.

treasury instead of two or three, or to instal a creature of the white man who was expected to move mountains. As for the outcome . . .[1]

Grévisse's experience was in Katanga, but the *Commission pour la Protection des Indigènes* in its 1938 report, claimed that in general violence was being done to traditional rights and to custom by the absorption of small *chefferies* into larger units, as well as by the total suppression of the *sous-chefferies*.[2]

The most developed and authoritative assessment of the operation of the revised administrative policy came from an eminent colonial official in his retirement, Monsieur A. Maron. He believed that a strong anti-traditionalist tendency had been manifest right from the beginning, pointing out the significant fact that between the end of 1932 and the end of 1939 not only had the 493 *sous-chefferies* been abolished, in accordance with the decision to cease to acknowledge such units, but also that 2,149 *chefferies* had ceased to exist. The number of *secteurs*, of course, had risen—to 340 by the end of 1938. The main significance which he very persuasively claims for this development is that it made the chief much more the agent of the Administration and much, much less the representative of traditional society. Whereas a chief in a *chefferie* was, in principle at least, the man designated by custom, the chief of a *secteur* could not be because the *secteur* was by definition not a customary entity (though of course it might be a revival of one). Moreover, it was claimed, many viable *chefferies* had their status changed to that of *secteurs* in order to make it possible to get rid of a customary chief, whom the Administration regarded as unsuitable, and appoint at will a chief amenable to its purposes—and, in turn, get rid of him if he was no good.[3]

What were the implications of the predominance of this new type of chief in a situation where more was required of him? Consider first his administrative role. He was, it has been seen, entrusted with the supervision and enforcement of numerous tasks which mostly held the flavour of being the imposition of the white man—the maintenance of roads, the carrying out of hygiene regulations, compulsory crop production.

---

[1] F. Grévisse, *La Grande pitié des juridictions indigènes* (Brussels, I.R.C.B., 1949), p. 63.

[2] Report of C.P.I., 1938, *Bulletin officiel*, 1938, I, pp. 1020–6.

[3] A. Maron, 'Le Décret du 5 décembre 1933: son esprit et son application', *Bulletin de C.E.P.S.I*, 1947–8, VI, pp. 111–16.

In so far as the necessity of these tasks was not seen, or their performance was resented as a hardship, even the chief by customary right, in seeking to get them done, would begin to be regarded not as the 'Father and Mother' of his people, but as a mere servant of the white man. If he was a nominated chief, then here was simple confirmation that he was the creature of the Europeans. In short it seems clear that the position of even the most gifted of the customary chiefs, given the relatively high degree of Belgian intervention in customary life, was an almost impossible one, whilst the nominated chief, who was rarely accepted *other* than as a European nominee, had no more real authority than that of the armed force with which the Administration backed him. In the 1938 Annual Report for the Congo there is a note of reserve.

If the native chiefs render incontestable services in the administration of the peoples, it is self-evident that their value and their help remain very unequal. Many give proof of the greatest willingness but the majority is made up of men of average value whose co-operation only improves slowly.[1]

It may be that the chief's important role in the management of the new native treasuries sometimes enhanced his position, just as the introduction of the treasuries may have strengthened the integrity of the *chefferie* or *secteur*. The same Annual Report is quite glowing about the value of native treasuries,[2] but one senses that the Congolese rarely had a vital share in their management, whilst much of their revenue went to cover the chief's everyday administration. For these reasons they rarely seem to have become the crucible of an invigorated tribal life.

And what about the chief in his judicial capacity? What if, say, in his capacity as judge he was called upon by an administrator or other European authority to apply written law? He commonly was called upon to do so in a whole host of matters affecting the everyday life of his people.[3] He would then have to inflict punishment for non-production of the allotted stint of cotton, for failure to obey public health regulations and so on. In acting thus, whichever type of chief he was, his role as the enforcer of the white man's will is the more strongly underlined. In the performance of his judicial role the

---

[1] *Rapport annuel*, 1938, p. 12.   [2] Ibid., p. 16.
[3] Grévisse, *Juridictions indigènes*, p. 30.

customary chief, moreover, was in the grip of a yet deeper dilemma, a dilemma springing from the contrasting nature of European written and African customary law. It has been seen that the main objective of African customary law, since time out of mind, had been to maintain social equilibrium on the basis of custom (see p. 24). To quote a discerning passage by Grévisse, who had considerable experience of the operation of *tribunaux indigènes* in Katanga:

Native judges give the impression of wishing to superimpose two images: that which they have formed in listening to the arguments and another which lies at the roots of their memory. Their aim in doing this is to satisfy the most recent image with the intention of conserving it in its turn. This rectification eventually involves the punishment of a guilty person, but it tends above all to re-establish equilibrium, to make amends to the law which has been wronged, to suppress all injury and to integrate the new tendencies.[1]

As this last clause reminds us, there is in African customary law room for evolution. But such evolution took place only in the context of very gradual change in the life of the community. An only slowly evolving public opinion, which was the root support of customary law, was therefore unlikely to approve the sanctions which the European had prescribed for infractions of a written law which he had made, and which was designed to serve purposes which he had conceived. No less important was the frequent inability of an invested chief—especially when illiterate—to base his administration of written law on any coherent principle. A habit of mind attuned to custom often had no other points of reference.[2]

The problem for the nominated chief was different. More likely to be literate, an *évolué* even, he might have less difficulty with the administration of written law, but he completely lacked the necessary position, heredity and knowledge to administer customary law. Bearing in mind the partially spiritual position of the real chief—his intermediary position between tribe and ancestors, his responsibility to keep the life of the tribe in harmony and consonance with its earlier life and to pass it on inviolate to his successor—how could an imposed chief begin to function validly? The exception was perhaps in those situations where custom was already breaking

[1] Ibid.   [2] Ibid., pp. 32, 56.

down and where a fair-minded and discerning chief might even develop a reputation for good judgements given on the basis of equity.

An interesting official conclusion about the operation of the native court system was that even a partially corrupt court was much better than nothing. So argued Governor-General Ryckmans when addressing the Government Council in 1937.[1]

Looked at from the African side, the good traditional chief could be involved in a head-on clash with the Administration. An anthropologist, C. M. Turnbull, gained the confidence of one such chief in Orientale province and, in committing his experiences to paper, has provided a unique indication both of how European rule could bear hardly on the firmly traditional chief in particular, and of how that rule threatened traditional life in general. The words of Matungi, the chief, deserve quotation at length. His experience seems to span the period from the thirties to the fifties.

After some years the white men were so many that they were able to send parties of soldiers into the forest. Their soldiers were not white, they were black like us, but they came from tribes to the north who were our enemies, so they were not on our side. We were forced to move back to where the white men were building the big road that now runs from Kisanganyi [Stanleyville]. It took many years to build, and they demanded that we supply men—so many from each village—as well as food for all their soldiers, who stood with their guns in case we tried to escape. The white men did not always carry guns themselves, often they carried whips and they beat us like animals.

I remembered my father, and I said I would not let my people work for them. Because of the guns that had brought my people back to the roadside I said that we would supply whatever food we could spare, and for a time the white men accepted that. But they were not pleased. Then they came around and told us we had to plant cotton and other things we did not want to plant. They said they would pay us but I explained that if we planted cotton we would have to grow less food. They said we could buy food with the money we got for the cotton and I told them this was like the play of children, because we could easily grow our own food without money, and have enough left over to give them.

It was then that they told me that I was not a man, that I was evil, that I did not want to help my people, that I only wanted to

[1] Maron, *Le Décret du 5 décembre 1933*, pp. 123–4.

make trouble. Therefore, they said, I was no longer chief. Masoudi was to be chief in my place. Masoudi was a weak young man who had been to one of the first schools set up by the white men, near the village of Matadi. . . . He had come from a BaBira family, but had followed the BaNgwana and sold himself to the white man. He had no heart, had no spirit. He was as you see him now, an empty shell filled with the words and thoughts of foreigners. He was not one of us. I told the white men that Masoudi could never be chief, because of this reason. He was a Christian as well, and that meant he could not lead the people as the representative of their ancestors, and he could not initiate men into manhood. Nobody would follow him.

The white men simply said that the people might not follow him, but they would obey him because if they didn't the police would be sent in with their guns. In any case, they said, tribal initiation was thoroughly evil and a wasteful thing. Didn't we realize that all the time the boys were doing nothing in the initiation camp, for month after month, they could be working on the plantations or on the road gangs? I tried to explain that initiation was necessary for us, for only by initiation can we fit ourselves to join the ancestors when we die. The uninitiated have no right to respect in this life or after, and without initiation man would become an animal, living for himself alone, with no consideration for his family or his tribe. . . .

The chief of the white men came to our village himself and called all the people together. He told them that I was no longer chief, that Masoudi was. People were astounded, because to them this was a heresy, and they expected the white man to be struck dead. But I stepped forward and said that the white man's head was turned by the sun and he did not understand that Masoudi could never be chief. However, Masoudi was like white men, so let him call himself chief, and let him take on all the foolishness of trying to deal with them. I told my people that I wanted nothing to do with the white man, and I did not want to be responsible to the ancestors for polluting the soil of our fathers by following the white man's ways. I gladly gave up being a chief in the eyes of the white man, but to them, my people, I would remain as I had always been.

This pleased the village, and I think it even pleased Masoudi, who also knew that he could never really be chief. But the white men caught me and told one of their soldiers, an Azande, to beat me. For this I have never forgiven them. They could have beaten me themselves, for they had proved themselves stronger with their guns, and it would have been no disgrace. But to have me beaten by one of those savages from the north is a shame I shall never forget. Even our enemies we treat like men, not like children. For a long time this made me burn inside with a fire, eating at my stomach, eating my strength and my sense. But I became wiser, and now that I know the white man better I do not feel hot; because he will kill himself as surely as he kills others. In trying to destroy the pride of others he loses his own, and becomes a worm. Look at them now. They are truly a people who fight themselves. They pretend they fight us, but they eat out of their own hearts and their own souls, and they are empty flesh. When they are gone there will be nobody to weep, only rejoicing. They lie so much to others, they cheat and they steal from each other and they sleep with each other's wives. They may be more powerful than we, but we are greater, because we are men, not animals.

After Masoudi became chief I had nothing to do with the white men for some time. . . .

. . . Many disputes were brought to me because I was the senior member of our village; Masoudi was not. I come from the oldest branch of the family. Men who were having trouble with their wives would bring their cases to me; women whose husbands failed to give them children or who beat them too often also came. Complaints about the BaNgwana and their bad magic always came straight to me, because I knew how to deal with those savages, for I have magic of my own.

But Masoudi did not like this, and he complained to the white man. The white man came and told me I was to hear no more cases, for I was no longer chief. Masoudi was to hear them, and record them in a special book, or send the disputants to the tribunal at Matadi if the case was serious. The white man said that if he ever heard that I was trying cases again, he would have me locked up in one of his boxes. He had been building these boxes at Matadi and now he had a whole building full of them. Many men went in and never came out. There is a big graveyard right beside it, even today. and men are buried there without any consideration for the ancestors, and their souls are lost.

I paid little attention to the white man's warnings, because my people still would not go to Masoudi. I talked to Masoudi and told him that I would not interfere with his work, but that he was not to interfere with mine. If anyone brought a case to him he could enter it in his book and send it to the tribunal, but that he was not to let his eyes see what I was doing. He understood, and so I continued to be what I was, the real chief.

I had one other big fight with the white man though, and it was this fight that convinced me he was evil. Through Masoudi he managed to get all he wanted in the way of cotton, plantains and road workers. In time he came to collect taxes from all of us, out of the money he paid us for the cotton and plantains. The rest of the money he took back by fining us for various things, but none of this worried us very much. It was what we expected from a conquering people. But then the white man began to say that we were not to have more than one wife, and that we were to stop exchanging gifts of wealth at times of marriage. In this way he made many men and women lose their self-respect. What pride can a woman have if her husband does not think highly enough of her to give her parents a gift of many goats as a token of his esteem and trust? And what safety and happiness can the parents feel if they cannot say, 'Our son-in-law has given us so many goats; he must intend to treat our daughter well and to care for her, for no man could afford to lose so much wealth'?

But even worse than this, the white man began to try to prevent our holding our initiation ceremonies, celebrating the manhood of our youth. They said that if we wanted to educate the boys we should send them to a mission school where they would learn to recite from a book. They said that our initiation schools were savage, and a waste of time. For all those months the boys and their fathers were secluded they could not work in the fields, and so fell behind in their work demanded of them by law. And during all this time even the women fell off in their work because they were busy drinking and dancing. In addition the white man added their lie that these schools were for no other purpose than to stir up discontent. If it were not so, why did we not allow the white man in to watch and supervise?

I told the white man that we did not let him watch because he would defile our youth with his filth; that his eyes were evil, and he could only bring evil to our souls; that his body was unclean and he would desecrate the holy ground of the ancestors; that his mind was twisted and he would only see and tell untruths; that his heart was stone and he would not understand and respect, and so he could only bring unhappiness to us and to our ancestors. If it were otherwise, as it was with you, we would let him see—provided he purified his body and mind and heart in the way we do. But it would not be otherwise with him, for white men are what they are, animals. I told him that neither I nor my people would ever fail in our duties to the ancestors, and initiation is the highest duty, for only by initiation can we fit ourselves to join the ancestors when we die.

He did not like my words, but he listened. He was angry, but he saw that I and my people would never give way. He told me that people like myself should be locked away in a box for ever, that we were concerned only for ourselves, that we did not wish the good of our people. I walked away and left him talking to himself. . . .

I have tried hard to understand the white man and his ways, but I can only see harm. What happiness have they brought us? They have given us a road we did not need, a road that brings more and more foreigners and enemies into our midst, causing trouble, making our women unclean, forcing us to a way of life that is not ours, planting crops we do not want, doing slave's work. At least the BaNgwana left us our beliefs, but the white man even wants to steal these from us. He sends us missions to destroy our belief and to teach our children to recite fine-sounding words; but they are words we believe in anyway, most of them. And we live according to our beliefs, which is more than the white man does. . . .

The white man talks of law where we talk of the way of our ancestors; he talks of what is right or wrong where we talk of what is good or bad. I have looked at their way and do not like it, and I do not believe it is good for our people. It is better to do something because one believes in the ancestors than because one is afraid of being beaten or put in a box. And it is better to believe that something is good because goodness comes from it, than merely to say, 'It is so because we have written it so in our book.' Perhaps the white man believes in his own way; if so, let him keep it, and let us keep ours, and let us both be men, not animals. . . .

A man should behave the way he believes. To make someone else behave in a different way by pointing a gun at him, or by threatening him with a beating or with the box is evil, because it makes him less of a man, it makes him go against his beliefs; it makes him dishonest. Yet the white man says this is right. The white man has made it almost impossible for us to keep our beliefs, he makes us do bad things every day; he forces us to offend our ancestors. I do it myself, because I am afraid of the box. It is easier to plant the white man's cotton, to work for him on the roads, to treat him as though he were master of our souls as well as of our bodies. I hope the ancestors will understand and forgive.

I have tried to keep my dignity. I have tried to remain a man in the eyes of my father. Whatever I may have done with my body, I have never betrayed my beliefs with my mind. But for my children it is different. They do not know good and bad as I know it; the white man fills their heads with different ideas and they doubt. I circumcise my sons, but I cannot circumcise their minds and their hearts. I can make their bodies acceptable, but they have to make their souls fit for the afterlife.

I have seen too much uncleanliness to have escaped its touch myself. But I have tried. And until I die, which cannot be long, I shall keep trying, for myself and my people. After I am dead there will be no one left, unless somewhere I have planted a seed that has yet to grow and provide nourishment for those who live on. If I have done this, then maybe I too shall be thought fit to be given life at the side of my fathers.[1]

[1] C. M. Turnbull, *The Lonely African* (London, Chatto and Windus, 1963), pp. 60–70 *passim*.

In the working-out of African administration the work of the European administrator was at least as important as that of the chief. It was the *administrateur territorial* who was the lynch-pin of the system, though he was assisted by *agents territoriaux*, and under the supervision of the *commissaire de district*. A notable reform of Franck had been the foundation of the Colonial University at Antwerp with the result that both *administrateurs* and *agents*, at their respective levels, were better trained than their predecessors. The training given right up to the end of Belgian rule was authoritarian and made too few demands on the critical intelligence, but it did induce a professional sense of a high order, and for the moment advantage triumphed over limitation. It is reasonable to suppose that very many of the administrators were dedicated men and also that they shared the general Belgian inclination to hard work, and concern to do a job well.[1] They were specifically required to travel in their *territoires* during the greater part of each month. It may well be that, relatively, the 1920's were a golden age for the *service territorial*. At that period the size of the *territoires* was not excessive, and disturbing European pressures on customary life were at least not as great in most areas as they subsequently became. With the road network still rudimentary, much of the administrator's travel had to be on foot, which meant that he saw his 'parish' at close quarters. At night he would pitch camp and, if he were a man who inspired any sort of trust, low and high might come to talk to him, and perhaps seek his guidance. In his more official contact with chief and elders he would settle disputes, discuss problems and, no doubt, signify displeasure if something remained undone from his last visit, approval if it had been carried out. Moreover, the administrator had at his back the powers and the influence necessary for getting certain things done. Had there been food shortage in the village? Then each inhabitant could be compelled, under a decree of 1917, to grow a specified area of yams or other appropriate foodstuff. People had suffered from cold during the dry season— then pressure could be put on a proportion of the men to seek outside employment for a spell in order to earn the money for blankets. Moreover the dynamism and perspectives of Franck seem to have infused a wave of idealism into the *service territorial*,

[1] See G. Malengreau, 'Le Congo à la croisée des chemins', *La Revue nouvelle*, January 1947, pp. 7–8.

an idealism given scope by the administrative decentralization of the early twenties.[1]

The fact remains that the task of the administrator was a formidable one. As tax-collector, judge, census-taker, policeman, bridge-builder, and maid of all work, he had all too much to occupy him. On top of this he was administering a people about whose habits, beliefs, and customs there was widespread ignorance and yet whom he, with only the rudiments of anthropological knowledge, must learn to understand. A veteran administrator writes of those who introduced the Franck reforms in the twenties: 'Some administrators set themselves courageously to the task. They were pure idealists, seriously concerned with the fate of the ordinary African, resolved to devote their utmost efforts to the relief of the pitiable condition of the natives.' One may accept every syllable of this: but it is no less necessary to remark Monsieur Vermeulen's further words; 'But, in the Congo, as elsewhere, outstanding men do not abound'.[2] Time and again one comes back to the conviction that only men of exceptional qualities—especially insight—were really adequate for such a demanding position.

One may tentatively conclude that, in the twenties and thirties, Belgium deployed in the Congo an administrative service which by and large was conscientious and devoted, which included at least its share of outstanding men, which may have resorted to compulsion appreciably more than was common in, say, British Africa, but which was on the whole paternalistic in the best sense of the term. In addition, the officers of the *parquet*, which may be loosely described as the Attorney-General's Department, had as one role the investigation of alleged abuses,[3] and, since the department was quite separate from the Administration and not vulnerable to pressure from it, its activity as a protector of the African from abuses was significant.

In the early thirties, however, at much the same time as the second legislative instalment of the Franck ideas, harmful administrative reforms were also introduced. By an *arrêté royal* of 29 June 1933, supplemented by later legislation, the administrative divisions of the Congo were radically revised following

---

[1] This impressionistic picture owes something to a long discussion with a retired administrator.

[2] Vermeulen, *Déficiences et dangers*, p. 43.   [3] *African Survey*, p. 619.

the financial crisis which afflicted the colony as a result of the slump. Paradoxically, considering that economy was the aim, the number of provinces was increased from four to six, which may or may not have made much difference. But at the basic level of the *territoire* there had already been a momentous change between 1931 and 1933, the number being about halved, with a reduction from 183 to 104.[1] Since the Congo is about eighty times the size of Belgium, this meant that the average area of a *territoire* approached that of Belgium herself. The measure was defended on the grounds that a full acceptance of indirect rule made possible less close supervision, and that the road network and means of transport had so improved that fewer men could cover more ground. But many colonial pundits—and particularly administrators themselves—saw this measure as the *fons et origo mali*.[2] It may be that the administrator in the bush, the *broussard*, was rather too prone to make this measure the scapegoat for all later ills—and by the end of the 1939–45 war there was an anxious search for the reason why African administration was in such disarray. This is the more likely in that the redivision was also associated with some sort of centralization on Leopoldville.[3]

But even if this is so, and allowing for the fact that the new, enlarged *territoires* had an *administrateur-adjoint* as well as an administrator proper, there can only have been a serious loss of contact between the *administrateur* and his charges. 'They invested the traditional authorities with the task of co-operation with the European administration and they took away their tutors', said one administrator.[4] Grévisse was concerned to point out the inevitable loss of contact between the African and the now more distant *tribunal de territoire*,[5] whilst another administrator incisively portrays the implications for relations with the African population.

[1] *Rapport annuel*, 1932, p. 10, and 1933, p. 6.

[2] See, e.g., a collection of six articles on 'La Crise du service territorial' in *Dettes de guerre* (Elisabethville, Éditions de l'Essor du Congo, 1945), pp. 173–94. See also ibid., pp. 8–10. Also Vermeulen, *Déficiences et dangers*, pp. 51–53 and *Annales parlementaires, Chambre des Représentants*, 1933–4, cols. 1363–5.

[3] G. Van der Kerken, *La Politique coloniale belge* (Antwerp, Van Dieren and Co., 1943), p. 116.

[4] 'P.T.', 'L'Organisation administrative', *Dettes de guerre*, p. 182. See also *Rapport annuel*, 1935, p. 8 (in regard to Orientale).

[5] Grévisse, *Juridictions indigènes*, pp. 40–41.

To understand a region under all its aspects and in all its needs it is not sufficient to be stationed three or four hundred kilometres away, two days' road journey from it, and to visit it once or even twice a year. One does not properly understand what one sees. It is necessary to be involved in a problem at length and to be dealing with it almost every day to understand its essence and to be able to discover the rational and vital roots of a solution. This is especially true of human and social problems.[1]

Maron offers an interesting but very general statistical basis for this diminished contact, showing how the number of administrators in relation to population administered declined over the years. The ratio of population administered to one member of the *service territorial* was as follows:

1931	10,535	1935	14,363
1932	10,675	1936	14,700
1933	10,724	1937	14,900
1934	13,938	1938	13,800
	1939	13,292[2]	

These ratios make no allowance for the tendency for a higher proportion of administrative officers than formerly to be concentrated in Leopoldville as the necessary result of the policy of centralization.

Maron also makes the important claim that the main reason for the draconian way in which *chefferies* were abolished was the imperative need for the fewer administrators in larger territories to have fewer local authorities to deal with.[3] This development Maron went on, was pushed much farther during the war, as we shall subsequently see.

In the years after 1933 the original rigour of this measure was modified to the extent that a few additional *territoires* were established. A form of organization also grew up—ex-Governor Moeller de Laddersous in 1952 termed it an adaptation of function stemming from the 1933 measures[4]—whereby a *territoire* was subdivided into a number of separate parts, each

[1] 'Le Dernier des Mohicans', 'Un abîme . . .', *Dettes de guerre*, p. 190. See also Vermeulen, *Déficiences et Dangers*, p. 53 'The size of the new *territoires* . . . did not allow the better *chefs de territoires* any longer to make more than one short appearance a year at the headquarters of *chefferies* and in the principal villages'.

[2] Maron, *Le Décret du 5 décembre 1933*, p. 115. These figures are evidently taken from the *Rapport annuel*, 1939–44, p. 7.

[3] Maron, *Le Décret du 5 décembre 1933*, p. 116.

[4] A. Moeller de Laddersous, 'Quelques aspects du Congo, 1952', *Bulletin de l'I.R.C.B.*, XXIII, 1952, 2, pp. 1048–50.

in the immediate charge of the *administrateur-adjoint* or of an *agent territorial*.[1] It might be argued—and doubtless was— that contact with the African population was therefore not essentially reduced. There seem to be at least three reasons why that contact, even on the assumption that it was not quantitatively lessened, would often have been less beneficial, or even harmful. In the first place the deputy to the administrator would, in view of the fact that *administrateur-adjoint* was the initial grade in what may be termed the professional administrative service, be more or less inexperienced and thus be able to make only a limited contribution. While he was likely to be inexperienced, the *agents* were men of a different grade which might be compared to that of Warrant Officer. It has been seen what strictures Van der Kerken and Rolin reserved for the majority of those who made up this category in the early years of Belgian rule (pp. 53–54). It is reasonable to suppose that their quality was much better in the twenties and thirties as a result of such factors as improved training. But even supposing that most of these men were competent within the limits of their rank, dedicated and humane, it can still be argued that they did not as a class possess the necessary education and insight to be entrusted with the supremely difficult task of handling at the grass-roots level (in some ways the most vital of all) the relations of the European Administration with the village African. The third of the reasons is that there was no sufficient substitute for day-to-day contact between the African traditional authorities, and Africans generally, and the man who was in a measure equipped to make the relationship positive and fruitful, who possessed reasonable discretionary powers, and who felt a particular sense of responsibility for the people of his territory.

It was not only that contact suffered. It is a reasonable inference that a cause of the arbitrary composition of *secteurs* which sometimes took place was the sheer inability of an *agent territorial* to analyse the society with which he was confronted, and the insufficient time available to the *administrateur* to make his own investigation. Recognition of a *secteur* and investiture of its chief might theoretically rest with the *commissaire de*

[1] The *Rapport annuel*, 1935, p. 8, expressed concern at this development in Orientale precisely because the direct, personal influence of the *administrateur* was thereby lessened.

G

district, but he would inevitably draw heavily on the representations of his subordinates.

A further factor which affected the work and impact of the *service territorial* during the thirties was that an additional burden was placed upon them—the implementation in a much more rigorous way and on a much more general scale of the policy of compulsory cultivation. The original legislation of 1917 had been inspired by E. Leplae, the Director-General of Agriculture at the Ministry of the Colonies, from a conviction that compulsory cultivation was justified on educational and humanitarian grounds.[1] Dietary deficiences could be alleviated by the growing of certain food crops, real hardships avoided with the income obtainable from the sale of cash crops. The extension of the policy, under the terms of the decree of 5 December 1933, reflected the same—and additional—motives. A commission of the Senate, doubtless influenced by the particularly serious effect of the slump on a Congo economy dominated by large-scale industry, drew up proposals for a positive agricultural programme. Agriculture should enjoy the same prestige as commerce and industry, and peasant production should be encouraged by the provision of specialist assistance, by customs changes, by improvements in communications, by persuasion—and by compulsion.[2] A further impulse to the extension of compulsory cultivation came from a striking speech in the Senate by Prince Leopold on his return from a visit to the Congo,[3] in which he pleaded for the encouragement of the peasant producer, and stressed the social desirability of diversifying the economy. He urged

the establishment of the peasantry in the most integrated form, permitting the native to acquire property and to enjoy the economic liberty which is guaranteed him by our *Charte coloniale*.[4]

But however elevated the motives, the implementation of the policy meant that the *service territorial* came to spend an important part of its time backing up the representatives of the Agricultural Department as they allocated stints, and seeing that the *tribunaux indigènes* took appropriate action against

---

[1] E. Leplae, obituary notice, *Bulletin de l'I.R.C.B.*, XVIII, 1, 1946, pp. 127–8.
[2] Hostelet, *L'Œuvre civilisatrice*, I, pp. 267–8.   [3] Ibid., p. 269.
[4] *Annales parlementaires, Sénat*, 25 July 1933, 1932–3 Session, cols. 586–8.

those who did not fulfil their norms. The new policy therefore both seriously distracted the administrator from his proper job, and cast him, in the African view, too much in the role of an oppressor. In Grévisse's words

The alteration in the territorial ideal began in about 1935 with the introduction or extension of compulsory cultivation. When this happened some of the representatives of the Agricultural Service assumed a very great ascendancy over certain authorities to the extent that numerous *administrateurs territoriaux* saw or believed themselves obliged to neglect their proper mission and to take their share in propaganda just like any *agent territorial* or *agricole* of their *territoire*. The submission of some of them has been to the extent of 'closing' the courts during the agricultural season.[1]

Both the Katanga sub-Commission of the *Commission pour la Protection des Indigènes* in its 1936-7 meeting, and the main Commission in 1938, expressed concern, albeit mild, at the operation of the compulsory cultivation policy.[2]

It has also been alleged that the impulse behind the policy of compulsory cultivation in the mid-thirties was in part provided by the pressure of European produce-buyers, purchasing for export, who presumably saw in the existence of compulsory powers a means whereby they could buy cheap and still sell at a profit on the depressed world markets of the period.[3]

The Governor-General himself can only have had the policy of compulsory cultivation in mind when he wrote in 1938:

It is appropriate to underline that the excellent situation [the morale of the African population] is maintained with a *personnel territorial* which is numerically insufficient, overburdened with work and whose task becomes heavier every day. It would be sufficient for the task if it was permitted to devote itself more completely to its essential mission, that is to say to the administration of the native populations, which requires constant contact with the latter and prolonged stays amongst them. But the tasks which have devolved upon the members of the *personnel territorial* are multiple and diverse and distract them from their primary task as the Colony continues to develop, when

[1] Grévisse, *Juridictions indigènes*, p. 42.
[2] Report of C.P.I., Katanga sub-Commission, 1936–7, *Bulletin officiel*, 1938, I, p. 1174; Report of C.P.I., 1938, *Bulletin officiel*, 1938, I, pp. 1044–6, 1056. *See also* ibid., p. 1006.
[3] Hostelet, *L'Œuvre civilisatrice*, I, pp. 359–61.

the non-indigenous population is increasing and when new activities of every kind are more and more appearing.[1]

Behind what is officially a concern primarily for the future, it may be legitimate to detect a private disturbance about the present.

[1] *Rapport annuel*, 1938, p. 7.

V

AFRICAN ADMINISTRATION AND THE PRESSURES ON CUSTOMARY SOCIETY IN THE INTER-WAR YEARS (2)

IMPORTANT as was the administrative impact on customary society, other European influences were of course also at work. Of major significance was European medicine, its most obvious manifestations being the hospital or dispensary of the Government or of a Catholic or Protestant mission. But the big companies also maintained their own extensive medical services and commonly made them available to other Congolese as well as their own employees. In addition, the Congo had a number of private or para-statal organizations, the most important of which was the *Fondation Reine Élisabeth pour l'assistance médicale indigène* (FORÉAMI), founded in 1930, whose capital was provided mostly by the colony and by the Belgian Government, but which included gifts from Queen Elizabeth of Belgium and other private donors. FORÉAMI, in its early years at least, was distinguished by a concentration of effort in a defined area aimed at eradicating endemic diseases before work was begun in another area. Thus it had marked results in the Bas Congo *district* of the Lower Congo in the mid-thirties. But this thoroughness was, to only a lesser degree, a characteristic of the whole Belgian approach to endemic diseases. In regard to sleeping sickness, for example, whereas the population in affected areas was some five million—about half of the Congo population in the mid-thirties—the average number examined annually over the period 1935-9 was 4,984,906. This was an increase from the 2,038,275 average over the period 1927-9. The rate of new infection had declined in the same period from 1·108 per cent. to 0·302 per cent.

While sleeping-sickness and malaria were the two most common endemic diseases, a whole series of others also claimed attention, just as a certain amount of research and laboratory work was also a feature of the Belgian medical effort.[1] A characteristic feature of medical organization was the extensive use made of European public health inspectors (*agents sanitaires*) in the public health campaign. Thus the distinction between *fonctionnaire* and *agent*, between the professional man and the 'warrant officer', was reproduced in the medical service—as it also was in the agricultural service.

The mission hospitals were not on the whole as well equipped —the Protestant ones enjoyed no significant subsidy—but many people, both in this period and later, believed that the standard of care was often higher in them. And even a poorly equipped hospital came to be seen as providing a ray of light by a population which was often quick to appreciate the advantages of European medicine.

But even in the twenties administrators and doctors did not have a vacuum in which to operate. Traditional society, viewed as an organism, was being subjected to assault from two quite different directions—the labour-recruiter and the missionary.

A constant lament of post-1945 Congo was over the voluntary flight of Africans from their villages to the towns and industrial centres. This voluntary exodus seems to have begun on the eve of, or during, the Second World War; during the twenties, on the other hand, and certainly well into the thirties, Congo Africans, when left to themselves, were prone to stay in their villages. To some extent the need to earn money to pay head-tax drove men to leave the village for a spell in search of wage employment, or even to leave it permanently. A young un-married man, at least, might prefer to earn a living in the city or mine rather than undertake, without the help of a wife, the sometimes considerable cultivation—as much as twelve acres— necessary if he was to earn his tax money and still remain at home.[2] To an extent, therefore, the rural African lent, if not a

[1] Hostelet, *L' Œuvre civilisatrice*, I, pp. 247–54.
A. Dubois et A. Duren, 'Soixante ans d'organisation médicale au Congo belge', *Liber Jubilaris A. Rodhain*, (Brussels, Ad. Goemare, 1947), pp. 1–36.
C. C. Chesterman, 'The Contribution of Protestant Missions to the Health Services of the Congo', ibid., pp. 37–46.
[2] Hostelet, *L' Œuvre civilisatrice*, I, p. 356.

ready, at least a resigned ear to the recruiter, and it was certainly an aim of Belgian policy—realized in frequent encouragement of recruitment by the administrators on the spot—that a certain number of Africans should leave their villages and take a job in some European enterprise for periods of a few months. In the unreflecting and convenient view that was then orthodox in colonial circles, the needs of industry would be met, whilst the worker would both acquire some acquaintance with (superior) European habits and customs and, on his return, spread the knowledge of them in his village. But by the early twenties it was apparent in some areas that the level of recruitment was such that the whole demographic balance of the community was upset and its way of life threatened. A commission was therefore appointed in 1924 to consider the proper level of migrant labour. It laid down that a maximum of 5 per cent. of the able-bodied men in a community should be allowed to take work at a distance, that this level might be raised to 10 per cent. if it was a question of work within two days' travelling radius, and that a further 15 per cent. should be permitted to take employment close to their homes. The commission also recommended that certain districts should be completely closed to recruiters for a number of years.[1]

The commission's recommendation were accepted as a norm and administrators were repeatedly advised to see that the percentages laid down were respected. But though attempts were made to keep within them, it is difficult to believe that there were sufficient resources and techniques to operate what was in any case a somewhat ambiguous policy. Even though the overall level might be according to rule, there were, whilst prosperity lasted, always some *districts* which were admitted to have been denuded of men above the proper levels. One does wonder how determined to adhere to the policy some administrators were—and even how accurate were some of the figures given. Perhaps from a conviction of the need to raise the usual standard of living through wage-earning, perhaps through inability, possibly from a sense of the importance of industry to the colony, perhaps out of compliance with the pressure of employers, the Administration in the bush did not always withstand the pressure of employers for ever more labour for

[1] Ibid., I, pp. 257–8, 347–53; *African Survey*, pp. 1402–3.

expanding industry.[1] It is likely that the most effective of the Commission's recommendations was the complete closure of certain areas, because this was not a question admitting of more or less misinterpretation. Certainly areas were thus closed. The slump brought a respite—indeed the return of many discharged labourers to their villages—but with the revival of the economy in the middle thirties the old process began again with the percentage limits, at one or another level, being widely exceeded, with administrative officers again succumbing to the pressures of industry and plantation-owners.[2] Because of the frequently occurring practice whereby administrative and other officers took appointments with private enterprise after an official career which commonly ended between forty and fifty, it is often implied that they were sometimes vulnerable to pressure.[3] (It is certainly commonly said that the reason why Governor-General Ryckmans, in his retirement, quite exceptionally held no directorships in colonial companies until a long time after his retirement had begun, was that some of his policies had not met with the approval of the big Congo companies.) Already by 1939 there was a serious lack of able-bodied men in many areas.

Although it had an impact of a quite different kind, the work of the Christian missionary also contributed to the undermining of traditional society. Missionary methods continued along the course that had been charted during the second decade of the century. Protestants and Roman Catholics alike continued to base their work on the central mission station, where was concentrated the higher primary school and frequently a technical, professional, or a 'normal' (i.e. lower secondary) school, and where the missionary staff was based. Here there might also be a mission hospital. From this centre the work of the catechists or teacher-evangelists in the villages would be supervised by missionaries 'on itineration', to use a Protestant missionary term. If methods did not change, the reach, the coverage of the missions became ever more extensive in this period. A History of the Jesuit Order in the Congo, whose work covered a substantial part of Leopoldville province,

---

[1] Hostelet, *L'Œuvre civilisatrice*, pp. 259–62, 354–9; *African Survey*, p. 1403; *Rapport annuel*, 1925–30 *passim*, and esp. 1928, pp. 11–13.

[2] Hostelet, *L'Œuvre civilisatrice*, pp. 359–69.

[3] See, e.g., Vermeulen, *Déficiences et dangers*, pp. 52–53.

asserts quite unequivocally that the major impetus for advance
was rivalry with Protestantism. 'The motive of action which
dominated all others, which most often led to the precipitate
establishment of a station, was the presence or the threat of
concurrence hérétique.'[1] In the Roman Catholic view it was
acceptable that the first impact of an operation thus conceived should be superficial. Experience had shown that
Roman Catholic work was extremely difficult in areas where
Protestantism had taken firm root: consolidation could come
later.[2] It is reasonable to suppose that such considerations also
influenced the rate and direction of expansion of other Catholic
missions, as they may also have affected the strategy of the
Protestants.

A factor which must also have contributed to the rate of
Catholic advance was the favour shown to Roman Catholic
missions by the Government. There was no secret about this.
In the words of the authors of a history of Belgian missions in
the Congo, published in 1947: 'The State on humanitarian
grounds protects religious missions in general, and, on patriotic
grounds, it favours the missions represented by its nationals.'[3]
There are, in fact, very few Belgian Protestants and it is
difficult not to believe that a country where believers are almost
entirely Catholics did not have religious reasons for favouring
Catholic missions. This favoured position of the national
missions was given legal endorsement in the so-called Convention
de Jonghe of 1925–6, the collective term for a series of agreements concluded by the State with the individual national
missions, by which specified annual subsidies were made to these
missions in return, particularly, for their agreement to apply a
specified educational programme. This important reform was yet
another measure which owed its inspiration to Franck. The
national missions were defined as those missions which had
their headquarters in Belgium, which were directed by Belgians
and which included a certain number of Belgians amongst
their missionaries.[4] The discrimination was explicit against
foreigners, implicit against Protestants; the terms of the agreement did not, however, prevent the recognition of the Mill Hill
Fathers, with headquarters in London and a missionary staff

[1] Denis, *Jésuites belges*, p. 102.   [2] Ibid.
[3] De Meeus and Steenberghen, *Missions religieuses*, p. 41.
[4] Ibid., pp. 39–40, 136–40.

composed of Dutch and Irish priests, as a national mission. It is
not inappropriate that the Irish should have been associated
with this arrangement![1]

The results of this major reliance on the National Missions
for the Colony's educational programme were, quantitatively
at any rate, most impressive. In 1938 the 4,268 subsidized
schools of the National Missions contained nearly 222,500
pupils, whilst the non-subsidized schools of the Catholic
missions, mostly village schools which did not meet the
conditions necessary to qualify for a subsidy, contained a further
half-million pupils. In addition the completely unsubsidized
Protestant schools could number a further 300,000 pupils. In
sum there was a school population of over one million in an
estimated population of some 10,300,000, a ratio which was
much better than that in any other African territory.[2] The
experience of the post-Independence years may possibly have
given rise to doubts of the wisdom of the Catholic Church in
accepting a position in which it was seen not least in the role of
agent of the State.[3]

What is no less noteworthy is that privately some ecclesiastics
seem to have enjoyed an improper influence over the Administration,[4] whilst it appears to be an accepted fact that the
Catholic missions were an important influence in policy-
making.[5] Certainly, in 1933, the Congo Protestant Council
accused the Government of being 'completely dominated by
the Catholic Church'.[6] These are strong words and one does
not have to take them literally. Nevertheless it is significant that
a body whose public pronouncements were likely to be informed by a sense of the delicacy of its position should feel
moved to such a strong protest.

In the inter-war years, then, traditional society was subjected
to important external pressures. The crudest and perhaps most
harmful of them was excessive recruitment. Immediately, by
upsetting the demographic balance of whole communities, this
simply destroyed the bases of the traditional apportionment of
work between the sexes and between old and young. In measure,

[1] Drake, 'Problems confronting the Protestant Church', pp. 56–57.
[2] De Meeus and Steenberghen, *Missions religieuses*, pp. 142–3.
[3] Varied personal information.
[4] I have personal information of two such cases.
[5] Malengreau, *Politique coloniale*, pp. 37–38.
[6] Drake, 'Problems confronting the Protestant Church', pp. 57–58.

too, as the village communities were put under pressure to work and to produce, so the burden on those who remained increased. More intangibly, demographic imbalance led to a lassitude, an *ennui*, even a despair. So many of the able-bodied men were away—rarely returning except for visits—that the whole spirit of the community was upset. It was believed by some authorities that the plunging birth-rate in some rural areas was a result as much of the psychological disturbance to village life as of direct physical causes, not least the absence of so many of the young and virile. To quote an observer:

It is not difficult to imagine the sombre *ennui*, the profound demoralization into which a village is plunged where 54 per cent. of the able-bodied men are normally absent. . . . Everything weighs on the women: the cultivation of food crops, the care of children and of cattle, the upkeep of dwellings. The wage of the husband scarcely permits him to maintain himself and to buy certain indispensable household articles and items of clothing for himself and his family.[1]

While such conditions were not universal, they were sufficiently widespread to be a major social problem. External pressure was also felt in the realm of authority. Where traditional authority had been harsh, the intervention of a superior European authority was doubtless welcomed: where European authority was discreetly and intelligently applied it did the minimum violence to traditional notions of law and government. But in both cases the accepted institution, the omnicompetent customary authority, was undermined by the fact that it was seen to be subordinate, not to another tribe as the result of a perhaps marginal—and often reversible—victory in battle, but to a European authority possessed of an overwhelmingly superior strength, skill and mastery. Strive, therefore, as some administrators did to shore up customary authorities, the slow leaven of the realization that power really lay with the European administration was already at work, and seriously detracted from respect for customary authority. The case was more or less serious depending on how much pressure was placed upon traditional authority, on the degree of African acceptance of the invested chief and, of course, on his capacity.

The most definite impact on customary beliefs and practices was that of the Christian missions. It can be persuasively argued

[1] Quoted in Hostelet, *L'Œuvre civilisatrice*, I, p. 366

that Christianity can be presented as the consummation of Bantu religion rather than as a contradiction of it; that the appropriation of Christianity by the African need not involve a wholesale rejection of traditional religious beliefs. In very recent years Katanga has witnessed an important missionary work of this positive kind, stemming from the approach to Bantu religion worked out by Father Tempels (see above, pp. 26–29) and others associated with him.[1] but the impression gained from conversation with older missionaries is that in the inter-war years, though necessity might exact grudging compromises with deep-rooted African practices, the most common evangelistic approach was the clean sweep. Sometimes the missionary might be fiercely iconoclastic. For various reasons—the degraded manifestations of Bantu religion, a sense of the uniqueness of Christianity, the legacy of the pre-1914 intellectual climate of Europe in which its civilization was seen as superior in every possible respect—he insisted on breaking down before building completely afresh. In other cases the sheer inability of a busy man to achieve the supremely difficult task of understanding the beliefs of those to whom he preached led to a result not so very different. To the essentially communal ideas of Bantu religion was opposed the doctrine of individual conversion and salvation; to the extended family was opposed the 'Christian', the nuclear family; to a belief in magic as a use of power, sometimes beneficent, was opposed the doctrine quite foreign to Africa, that all magic was evil, a pact with the Devil; to the common African belief in the necessity of maintaining community with the ancestors, and in their vital influence—when this belief was not branded as utterly wrong—was opposed a flabby, Western concept of the Communion of the Saints which abstracted from that doctrine much of its true content and much of what could have made it meaningful in Africa. Malinowski makes a noteworthy comment on this. 'Ancestor worship seems to me in many ways the crucial problem and the touchstone of missionary work.'[2] The result of such preaching was division—division within the tribe, division within the clan, division within the mind of the individual convert. Christian converts inevitably ceased unquestioningly to accept all forms

[1] See Anstey, 'Christianity and Bantu Philosophy', pp. 320–2.
[2] B. Malinowski, *The Dynamics of Culture Change: An Inquiry into Race Relations in Africa* (New Haven, Yale University Press, paperbound edition, 1961), p. 69.

of customary authority and often expressed their new loyalty
and new affinities in removal to a separate corner of the village.
At the level of the individual the cleavage could be acute.
Turnbull quotes the tragic *cris de cœur* of two Congolese, whom
he got to know during the 1950's, who had superficially
accepted Christianity and as a result found themselves sus-
pended between two worlds.

I am alone in this world. You made it impossible for me to be true
to the ways of my ancestors, yet I can not understand the ways of
your Bwana Yesu, I can not believe his beliefs. When I die, very
soon, shall I still be alone? Will you talk to me then? Will my people
talk to me? Will anyone speed my spirit on its way to some resting
place, or shall I be as I am now, alone?[1]

Secondly, there was the case where the subject, as a boy, had
been the focus of a dispute between his Christian father and a
missionary on the one hand, and a traditional claim for submission to the initiation ceremony on the other; the missionary
had had the boy circumcised in a mission hospital. This had
been a traumatic experience. The father subsequently re-
nounced Christianity. Matungi, the man entrusted with the
performance of initiation rights, says to him

'You have been made one of Bwana Yesu's children by the water
ceremony . . . and if you still believe in Bwana Yesu, you may still
go to his afterworld. You cannot come to ours. . . .' All this Matungi
told me, and my father said that Matungi had spoken well. We would
have to accept that in the afterlife we would be separated forever,
for my father had decided to go back to the ways of his ancestors.
. . . I met some Ba-Ngwana the other day, and they told me that they
have a god who will accept me and take me into his afterworld if I do
certain things. But they are unclean things, and we all know the
Ba-Ngwana to be an unclean people. Perhaps I shall have no after-
life, and in that case I can only do what I can with this life. . . . In
my heart there is only the knowledge that the white man has taken
me away from my fathers and brothers for all time . . .[2]

A more generalized comment is found in some words
quoted approvingly by a Ghanaian minister of religion and
university teacher:

Most Christians [i.e. African Christians], it is suggested, live on two
unreconciled levels. They are members of a Church, associated all

[1] Turnbull, *The Lonely African*, p. 43.   [2] Ibid., pp. 135–7.

too often in their minds with benefits and discipline rather than with loyalties and fellowship. As such they subscribe to a statement of faith. But below the system of conscious beliefs are deeply embedded traditions and customs implying quite a different interpretation of the universe and the world of spirit far from the Christian interpretation. In the crises of life—birth, marriage, death—the 'Customary' matters more than the Christian; the Church is at these moments an alien thing.[1]

To summarize the impact of Christianity solely in these terms is perhaps to give an unfair impression. Missionaries may well object, for instance, that scant heed is paid to all the problems presented by polygamy, or matrilineal society. It should be remembered, however, that we have been concerned with the impact of the Christian missions on traditional ideas and on traditional society conceived as an organic whole, and the destructive nature of that impact has necessarily been emphasized.

The assessment must certainly be completed by a consideration of the more positive impact of the Christian missions. At the lowest level of all, the missions introduced children, and to a lesser extent adults, to various elementary European skills, particularly reading and writing. More generally, the missions were the primary agency for introducing the Congolese to the ideas and values of Europe. Moreover it was in the missions that Congolese advance was first encouraged. The first Congolese priest was ordained in 1917 and, to look ahead, by 1959 there were six hundred Congolese priests, including one bishop. Their training had been every bit as rigorous as their European brethren's and the same level of attainment had been demanded of them. The pattern was similar amongst the Protestant missions.[2] Again, a very great deal was achieved at the humanitarian level. In the early days this achievement might take the form of emancipation from oppression, as in the case of the

[1] L. B. Greaves quoted by E. A. Asamoa, 'The Christian Church and African Heritage', *International Review of Missions*, XLIV, 1955, p. 293. Note also J. V. Taylor, *The Growth of the Church in Buganda* (London, S.C.M. Press, 1958), p. 191: 'It is only after the advent of Christianity, and especially the conception of dualism which it implies, only after the undifferentiated unity of existence has been broken, that magic takes on, as it did in Europe, the fascination of darkness'. I am indebted for all these references to Drake, 'Problems confronting the Protestant Church', pp. 162–3.

[2] Ruth Slade, *The Belgian Congo*, 2nd edition, with an additional chapter by Marjory Taylor (London, O.U.P. for the Institute of Race Relations, 1961), pp. 33-37.

Baptist Missionary Society in the Bolobo area (see p. 35); in later days it was perhaps the hospital and dispensary which particularly exemplified this aspect of the missions' work.

At the level which was the essential *raison d'être* of the missions there was a real element of success. For many converts the faith which they had adopted was a meaningful thing. This remains true even if acceptance of Christianity had involved wholesale rejection of earlier beliefs. And it is very much to the point to weigh in the scales the undoubted fact that Christianity was a faith which could and often did liberate from haunting and ever-present fear, and which could refine a traditional life which rarely had that cosy and satisfactory quality which it often seems to bear in the anthropologist's monograph. In all corners of the Congo converts can be found—albeit a minority of professing Christians—for whom Christianity is a release from darkness, and a totally new life. And despite the tragic cases which Turnbull has recorded, he can also say of Christians: 'But even though their difficulties are often the greatest, at least they retain some sense of values and standards, however confused. Together with the would-be traditionalists they alone have any firm basis of inner morality in their lives.'[1]

A further aspect of the process by which African culture is weakened is depicted by the French West Indian intellectual, Aimé Césaire, in these rather different terms, in which the role of 'linguistic imperialism' is brought out:

The colonial régime destroys the framework which gave structure to the cultural life of the colonized people. It is a question, right at the beginning, of the political organization which the people had freely developed. Then comes the language: from being no longer the official language, the language of the school, the language of ideas, the native language experiences a loss of prestige which thwarts its development and sometimes even threatens its very existence. In thus limiting the civilization of the colonized, in suppressing or bastardizing its structure, they end by suppressing what is one of the characteristics of all living civilization: the faculty of renewal.[2]

Analysing the process of culture contact in a yet different way there is much support for the view that traditional African culture began to wither particularly as the result of the association

---

[1] Turnbull, *Lonely African*, p. 179.
[2] Quoted in G. Mosmans, *L'Église à l'heure de l'Afrique* (Brussels, Casterman, 1961), pp. 93-94.

of two factors. The first of these is what seems to be a basic African concern—a concern with power. In the words of J. C. Carothers,

> The indigenous African's approach to life was mainly governed by the question of 'power'. He saw the world around him as a battlefield populated by conflicting forces. Quite apart from supernatural aspects, but always reinforced by these, he saw in the real world dangerous beasts imbued with power to harm, alien and inevitably hostile tribes, successful men within his group who had achieved their ends (usually at the expense of others) by reason of the power within them. He saw his own survival and possible success as an outcome of some power in him or of some other source of power that might be tapped through, say, a witch-doctor.[1]

E. W. Smith calls Westermann to his aid in putting the matter like this:

> [The African] wants to feel safe in this uncertain and hostile world ... To meet all [his] clamant needs, physical and psychical, he seeks power.
> 'This craving for power' as Dr. Westermann says, 'is the driving force in the life of African religion. It has its origin, not in logical reflection, but in a feeling of incapacity and in an obstinate desire to overcome it; it is a search for help and comfort, a means of maintaining and strengthening life in the midst of a thousand dangers, and a way of conquering the fear which shoots its arrows from every hidden ambush. Man is weak and what he needs is increased strength. ... The absorbing question for him is how to acquire some of this power so that it may serve for his own salvation or that of the group for which he is responsible.'[2]

The second factor was the palpable possession by the European of a greatly superior material and technical power. It was in measure as the European was perceived to be the possessor of such immeasurably superior power that the culture which had hitherto been a sufficient source of physical and psychical power began to be abandoned and the new culture of the

---

[1] J. C. Carothers, *The Psychology of Mau Mau* (Nairobi, Government Printer, 8th Impression, 1955), pp. 6-7. The section of the Report from which this extract is taken is a summary of Carothers' monograph, *The African Mind in Health and Disease* (Geneva, World Health Organization, 1953).

[2] E. W. Smith, 'The Whole Subject in Perspective', *African Ideas of God* (London and Edinburgh House, 1950), pp. 28-29, quoting D. Westermann, *Africa and Christianity* (London, O.U.P., 1937), p. 84.

European anxiously sought. If some Europeans were characterized by idealism and benevolence, all were characterized by the
possession of superior power, and every contact with a European drove this impression home. The result was the quest by
the African for this power for himself, frequently ignorant of
the inability of European 'power' to meet all the needs of the
European mind and spirit, still less the African with its infinitely richer communal life. Those scholars who see the
process in these terms describe it in various ways. Westermann
puts it thus:

[The African] may heartily disagree with much of what the European does and plans, yet the great majority of the leading natives in
Africa have no greater ambition than to resemble the white man. . . .
Even those Negroes who, as educated men and conscious representatives of their race, regard European domination critically or with
hostility, claim for themselves the right to possess fully the white
man's culture, for they are convinced that they are able to compete
with him and hold their own only when they possess his weapons.[1]

In this context 'power' is synonymous with 'weapons'. In
Carothers' view,

. . . wherever the arrival of the alien was crowned with success and
that alien (be he a soldier, an administrator, a missionary, a trader,
or some other) was able to maintain himself in a superior fashion, the
local culture was doomed precisely in the degree of his success and
the extension of his influence. It is the material success of the
immigrant which is first recognized and which sounds the death
knell of the earlier culture.[2]

'The new ruler', Carothers also says, 'is seen as possessed of a
power of a different order; one's own old gods are impotent
and this new power must be tapped.'[3]

The great reality, then, in the Congo as in any other colonial
situation, was the overshadowing might of European 'power'.
Whatever aspects of European culture might subsequently be
rejected by the Congolese as he developed more discrimination,
whoever much he might also come to a reasoned conviction of
the value of elements of his own culture, it appears that he

---

[1] D. Westermann, *The African Today and Tomorrow* (London, 3rd edition, 1949),
p. 138.

[2] Carothers, *Psychology of Mau Mau*, p. 7.

[3] Ibid. See also M. Richelle, *Aspects psychologiques de l'acculturation* (Elisabethville, C.E.P.S.I., 1960), pp. 35-36, 82, 176.

always recognized the superiority of this European 'power' in the sense in which Westermann and Carothers are using the term. And, to look ahead, he was recognizing it no less when he sought to use it as the vital weapon against European colonial rule.

Most authorities would agree that a more or less destructive assault on traditional ideas, institutions and practices was an unavoidable outcome of the coming of Europe to the Congo. The question may nevertheless still be put as to whether the process could have been less brusque, and one is all the more moved to pose this question in view of the claim sometimes made that a paternal relationship between European and African, between colonizer and colonized, was both natural and possible. If such a relationship did generally exist, then it would surely have been a shock-absorber in the process of culture contact.

The 'old colonial hand' would probably require little persuasion that, in the conditions of the twenties and thirties, a paternalistic relationship was both natural and necessary. Natural because of the disparity between the cultures of colonizer and colonized: necessary on account of the African's need of guidance in a situation where the props and pillars of his customary world were being shaken. The instinct of the 'old colonial' can certainly command some support of a more considered kind. Brausch, for instance, in an article on Belgian paternalism, claims that

. . . often traditional entities easily lend themselves to this paternalism. Numerous ethnographers have in effect shown that, before the arrival of the Europeans, the Africans already lived under a paternalistic régime; they conceived the relations between superior and inferior as similar to the relations between forefathers and descendants; the suzerain is for his vassal a father to whom he owes the respect and services due to an ancestor, but of whom he can also claim the help and protection which every man owes to his child.[1]

Some would accept the interpretation of the paternal relationship which Tempels sets out.

The African considers the European as possessing a life higher than his own. He considers him as possessing a life which he communicates to him, which 'he brings to birth' in him. He is not only loyal

[1] Brausch, *Paternalisme*, p. 204.

towards the European who has proved his strength and power, a mysterious and external power, but he esteems in us the inmost capacity of being [*la capacité intime de l'être*], a dominant existence [*le degré d'existence majeur*], the ontological quality itself. He expresses himself by saying artlessly, according to the logic of his traditional thought, that the European is his father and his mother.[1]

// 790/

Assuming, then, that there was a sound psychological basis for paternalism, to what extent were the necessary conditions present? Half an answer is that these conditions were present when there was some sort of personal relationship between a European and an African. The term 'personal' must here be given an extended meaning so as to include the relationship between, say, an administrator and a clan as a whole. The administrator might never speak to most members of the clan: none the less, if he concerned himself in a generally sympathetic way with the affairs of the clan, through dealings with the clan head, he may be considered as having entered into a personal relationship with that clan.

The possibility of a personal relationship clearly does not arise only from the existence of a state of psychological dependence, or from a felt need of external support in the African: it requires even more a readiness on the part of the European to concern himself with the African. That such concern was often forthcoming is quite evident. Though my own personal evidence that the ensuing relationship was often a reality comes mostly from the post-1945 period, it is reasonable to infer that it was more rather than less widespread in the twenties and thirties. In all corners of the Congo there were doctors, missionaries, administrators, settlers and others who, in the natural way of things, exhibited a concern for the Africans with whom they dealt which earned them respect and sometimes reverence.

The qualities which were manifested by the Europeans might vary a good deal but appear to have had as a necessary common base concern and authority.[2] A most interesting commentary on the nature of paternalism, which emphasizes the latter element, is the claim made by an observer of events

---

[1] P. Tempels, 'La Philosophie de la rebellion', *Dettes de guerre*, p. 17. For a closer examination of psychological dependence in a colonial situation see O. Mannoni's fascinating *Prospero and Caliban* (London, Methuen, 1956). This book was first published as *Psychologie de la colonisation* (Paris, Éditions du Seuil, 1950).

[2] I have here drawn partially on personal information.

in Katanga before and after Independence, that the European who continued to command respect and obedience, when there were no physical sanctions to enforce it, was the man whose authority had always been clear-cut. He might even have had a reputation for harshness; his employees, or subordinates, none the less remained loyal to him, and actively protected him and his interests. What mattered, it is claimed, is that the European had personified authority and had in some sense entered into a personal relationship with his employee or subordinate.[1]

A necessarily impressionistic assessment as regards the Congo during the twenties and thirties is that there were not enough good paternalists and that, as far as the important category of administrators in the post-1933 years (especially) is concerned, they were often too busy to establish paternal relationships. The implication of this was that the African disposition towards a satisfying dependence—a relationship which contained the richest possibilities for African development *beyond* dependence and tutelage—was frequently thwarted. It may be that the pace of change, stemming primarily from economic development, was too rapid, even in the twenties and thirties, to permit of the general diffusion of paternalism as here defined. It may also be that the human material was inadequate for the widespread creation of such a relationship— as it might be inadequate anywhere, given the degree of intervention in customary life which was implicit in Belgian policy. But when one reads, for example, of such exciting achievements as Father Van Wing's success at Kisantu in bringing about, through discussion, a significant agreed modification of custom in regard to succession and inheritance in a partly Christianized and matriarchal society; when one sees this rich result of an enlightened paternalism,[2] one must have some regrets for a lost opportunity. The shock-absorber was simply not found under all parts of the European juggernaut. It might be in place here and there but this meant that it could only play a very partial role in limiting impact.

[1] P. Rousseau, 'Relations entre chefs d'entreprises blancs et employés autochtones avant et après l'indépendance du Katanga', *Bulletin des Séances de l'A.R.S.O.M.* VII, 4, 1961, pp. 622-42.

[2] J. Van Wing, 'Une évolution de la coutume Bakongo (Congo belge)', *Les Élites en pays de mission* (Louvain, Semaine de Missiologie, n.d. (1927)), pp. 3-15. This valuable paper is printed as an Appendix.

This chapter has been concerned with the varied impact of Belgian rule on customary life. In fact paternalism had its most striking results in the new *milieu* of the mining or other industrial centres, and it is to the development of industry and the towns, and to the consequences of this development for the contact of European and African culture, that we must now turn.

VI

ECONOMIC DEVELOPMENT AND THE GROWTH OF TOWNS IN THE INTER-WAR YEARS

What are we doing in the Congo?

We are pursuing a double aim: the extension of civilization and the development of outlets for Belgium and of Belgium's economic activity. These two aims are inseparable.[1]

MEDICAL and missionary work, even native administration, all could claim to be civilizing influences. But what about the working-out of Belgium's complementary, economic purpose? Franck's statement of Belgian aims went on to state the broad lines of economic strategy:

The merchant, the industrialist, the planter are the motive power of a colony. Without them, without their initiative and their labours, without the return from their exertions, no country in the world would be able to bear the considerable expense of colonization. The State cannot itself attempt the economic development of our extensive territories. Also, the policy of the Government is to industrialize the Colony by giving an autonomous commercial organization to its own economic services and by everywhere encouraging private enterprises.[2]

It has been seen that a fair beginning in economic development had already been made by the beginning of the twenties. Important trunk railways were in operation, plantation agriculture was well established and mineral exploitation had reached a point where, for example, the Kilo-Moto mines in Orientale province were already amongst the world's major gold mines, and where, by 1923, Katanga was the third largest supplier of copper. It is significant, however, that the

[1] Franck, 'Politique indigène' p. 189.   [2] Ibid., p. 191.

Union Minière, whose virtual monopoly of production of a major mineral in growing demand, copper, as well as of other valuable minerals, might have been expected to make its operations quickly profitable, began to show a profit only in the early twenties. The fact that Congo economic development was not always sufficiently profitable to tempt Belgian or other outside investors led to the promise of a minimum interest on capital invested. The payment of this interest was made possible by the grant of advances by the Belgian Government, and £3,000,000 were in fact paid over between 1921 and 1925. Though this was only a small sum in relation to the metropolitan budgets of those years, it was a considerable augmentation of Congo receipts—by 20 per cent. in regard to the 1921 Budget. The grant of these advances aroused little interest in the Belgian Parliament or amongst the public. To look ahead, Belgium, for various reasons, never asked for repayment.[1] This technique of the guarantee on interest—wholly delightful to the investor—was principally used to finance railway construction.[2] At the same time the State continued the practice, dating from the days of the Independent State, of claiming a financial share in, and directorial representation on the boards of, Congo companies, by virtue of land, mineral or other concessions which those companies had received from the State.[3]

The results of this policy were impressive. By 1928 the Bukama–Port Francqui rail link had been completed and large areas of the Lomami, Sankuru and Kasai country opened up; the creation, in this way, of a rail and river route between the Lower Congo, Leopoldville and Katanga was the first major step in integrating Katanga with the rest of the Congo. Hitherto its link with the outside world had been via the Rhodesia Railways and Beira. In the years after 1923 construction of the Vicicongo network, in the country between the Itimbiri and Uele rivers in Orientale province, was begun and, though the system was built to a narrow gauge, it was capable of carrying considerable traffic and joined a large tract of country to the farthest point of river navigation on the Itimbiri tributary of the Congo. More important was the realignment and reconstruction to the 3 ft. 6 in. gauge of the Leopoldville–Matadi

---

[1] J. Stengers, *Combien le Congo a-t-il coûté à la Belgique?* (Brussels, A.R.S.C., 1957), pp. 87-97, 320-1, 344-5.
[2] Van der Kerken, *Politique coloniale belge,* p. 157.　　　[3] Ibid., p. 156.

railway. In all, 2,450 kilometres of new railway were built in the twelve-year period 1920–32, whilst the other facets of the development programme have been summed up in these terms:

Boma, Matadi, Ango-Ango, Leopoldville, Coquilhatville, Aketi, Stanleyville, Kabalo, Albertville, Uvira, Bukama, Port Francqui were endowed with ports possessing most sophisticated equipment. The large towns came to have mains water and electricity. Aviation and wireless telegraphy were greatly developed. The telephonic link between Brussels and Leopoldville was realized. Project succeeded project. Capital sums were expended one after the other. . . .

If one adds to this equipment in the public sector the formidable equipment in the private sector, one is not surprised that the Congo has become the finest colony, the best equipped, in many respects at the very least, in Africa.[1]

In the twenties and thirties the new railways were the great harbingers of change in the Congo, though in the thirties, especially, the building of roads came to have an important ancillary role. In a work which represents a unique and very desirable type of railway history two geographers, MM. Nicolai and Jacques, have shown in some detail the immense social and economic changes brought about by the B.C.K. railway. This railway, linking Bukama with the Kasai river at Port Francqui, and constructed between 1924 and 1928, had demographic results which are partly measurable. Not only did many of the labourers, mostly Kasai Ba-Luba, brought in to build the line, settle permanently in villages close to it, but when the line was completed numerous Congolese, again mainly Kasai Ba-Luba, were attracted to the belt of land flanking the railway. This accentuated the already existing problem of Ba-Luba expansion, resulting from their greater amenability to European influence, into areas hitherto dominated by the conservative Bena-Lulua. The existence of the railway, and this movement to it, brought the Kasai railway zone into the realm of production for the market and facilitated emigration to the mines of Katanga. The new production, however, was by traditional techniques, of which the new opportunities for profit demanded too much, so that soils were rapidly exhausted. The railway also made possible European enterprise in timber exploitation and

[1] Comment by O. Louwers, quoted in Stengers, *Combien le Congo a-t-il coûté à la Belgique?*, p. 357.

ranching, provoked the growth of new centres and the decline of old ones, the main example being the decline of Lusambo, the original provincial capital, and the rise of Luluabourg. As a result, firstly, of settlements of railwaymen along the lines, especially at the main centres, much new wealth was brought into the region. The opening of the railway zone to European-inspired development followed.[1]

There was also human investment in the Congo—settlers. Originally consisting only of farmers and planters, this category came to include men in business of their own account in other fields—for instance, proprietors of building firms, transport-contractors, merchants of various description. They can best be defined as men running their own enterprises who had made the Congo their permanent home. In later days lawyers and other professional men who had come to live permanently in the Congo swelled their ranks, but the typical settler remained the agriculturist. Principally for climatic reasons, they were most densely concentrated in Kivu and Katanga.

In the early days of Belgian rule quite considerable financial aid to Belgium colonization was given by the Colonial Ministry —a credit of £150,000 in 1912, for example—with the aim of both strengthening the European presence in the Congo and providing Belgians with economic opportunities lacking in their home country. The establishment of a number of agricultural settlers in Katanga was financed but the scheme came to a halt in 1913; according to one theory, because the local administration was at best indifferent to it. But official encouragement revived a little in the inter-war years, and, provided that the intending Belgian settler had some capital (the dangers of breeding a 'poor white' class were seen), he received such benefits as exemption from the caution money otherwise demanded; an advance of passage money; a period of training; advances of livestock and equipment; and the cession of land at a low rate. In 1936, for example, the settlement of rather over 250, including members of their families, were subsidized at a cost of £17,143 to the Colonial Budget.

In economic terms the settlers certainly did their share in adding to the colony's economic wealth, and at the same time some of them developed a good paternal relationship with their

[1] M. Nicolai et J. Jacques, *La Transformation des paysages congolais par le chemin de fer: l'exemple du B.C.K.* (Brussels, I.R.C.B., 1954), *passim.*

African labourers. But their presence also had economic and social implications harmful to the Congolese living in the bush. In a colony which, as we have seen, was short of manpower, here was a further demand upon the reservoir. A continuous call of the settlers was for more help from the Administration in recruiting labour; a continuing lament its failure to do enough. Here undoubtedly was a factor which was responsible in some areas for the fact that Administration permitted recruitment quotas to be exceeded. Again, the simple fact that there was a growing class of settlers meant that the pattern of the colony's economic life was woven so as to include them. Specifically, this meant that it was assumed that such fields of enterprise as haulage contracting, and trading beyond a petty level were for the settlers and not for the Congolese. Here was a notable difference compared with, say, Nigeria or the Gold Coast where the African entrepreneur was already in the inter-war years an established figure. The Tshombe family, which built up a trading and transport business in Katanga, was very much an exception.

In the twenties, production in almost all fields increased markedly, attaining a crescendo in 1929–30. Measured by exports, the level had risen from £6,237,400 in 1923 to £8,620,200 in 1930.[1] The expansion of copper production was particularly marked, jumping from 56,221 metric tons in 1923 to 138,949 tons in 1930, during which period the Congo retained its place as the world's third-largest copper producer.[2] Even more considerable was the growth in diamond output—from 318,979 carats in 1920 to 2,518,258 carats in 1930.[3] In this period there was also a notable export of agricultural produce—mainly cotton, palm oil, palm kernels and coffee.[4]

As regards the balance of agricultural and forestry production on the one hand, and mineral extraction and processing on the other, the preponderance, as measured by exports, lay with minerals.

Mineral development certainly had its head in the boom days of the twenties, whilst in production for the market as a whole it was European enterprise which predominated. This is almost self-evident in the case of minerals, but was only a little less marked in the case of agricultural produce. Certainly cotton

---

[1] *The Belgian Congo* (Naval Geographical Handbook), p. 414. (In this source all amounts are given in sterling.)
[2] Ibid., pp. 402-3.   [3] Ibid., p. 408.   [4] Ibid., p. 417.

was actually grown by Africans but the processing was exclusively in European hands. Palm produce was mainly, and coffee almost entirely, the preserve of European plantation enterprise.[1] The reasons for this emphasis seem to have been the conviction, in Van der Kerken's words, that 'cheap, large-scale agricultural production cannot be the fruit solely of native agriculture'[2] and, possibly, the belief that European techniques and control were necessary to maintain quality. It is certainly true, for instance, that oil palms generally give a declining yield after twenty years or so. A rigorous policy of replanting is therefore necessary if quality is to be kept up. As further reasons it is legitimate to suggest that there were, in the twenties, no influential advocates of really effective encouragement of peasant production, whilst the Belgian concern to 'do a good job', the entrenched position of plantation interests and the whole tradition of granting out blocks of land to companies, and to some extent individual planters, combined to produce this same outcome. European plantation interests undoubtedly received favours and inducements. There was, of course, the grant of the land itself, but in addition the State would undertake not to give other concessions within a certain radius for a period of years. Though partly designed to protect local labour from too severe demands, this provision also conferred on the grantee the advantage that he did not have to compete for labour, whilst in some cases it was intended to protect him from competition generally.[3] Again, the proprietor of a cotton gin, from 1921 onwards, was accorded a *zone de protection* in which he enjoyed the exclusive right to buy the appropriate product from peasant producers at a price fixed by the State.[4]

It has already been seen that exports increased markedly in the twenties. If one considers imports, then a much more striking increase is apparent. Whereas in 1923 imports amounted to £4,408,110, six years later they had attained the figure of £11,135,770.[5] In the fact that imports had, from 1925 onwards, come greatly to exceed exports lies the reason for the particular severity with which the slump hit the Congo, for hit it it did in 1929–30. The disparity was due to the heavy capital expenditure of what one might term the Franck

<hr />

[1] Ibid., p. 386.   [2] Van der Kerken, *Politique coloniale belge,*p. 200.
[3] Ibid., p. 175.   [4] Ibid., pp. 160, 175.
[5] *The Belgian Congo* (Naval Geographical Handbook) p. 414.

period, but it seems clear that the rate of investment was such as would bring only a good return in the very long run and if the terms of trade remained steady.[1] The investment boom has also been criticized on at least three other grounds—that, latterly, it was accompanied by intense speculation, that too much was devoted to luxuries, and that there was overcapitalization in railways and harbour installations as a consequence of a piecemeal rather than an overall approach. The speculation of the period—sometimes, it is said, of a frantic kind in the cafés and hotels of Leopoldville—was perhaps a consequence simply of the atmosphere generated at that time and of the fact that the Congo had the most sophisticated economy and financial structure of any territory in tropical Africa. Luxury building there also was. Some of the boom's progeny survived the slump. In 1934, for example, two English travellers were much impressed by the 'Metropole' hotel at Matadi and the 'A.B.C.' at Leopoldville in point of size and sumptuousness. The former had five stories, lifts and a cinema, a European manager, reception clerk and head waiter.[2] Certainly economic development had been intense and a concern to carry it yet farther spilled over into apparently non-economic fields. It is significant that the decisive factor in a marked increase in the strength of the *service territorial* during 1930, the height of the boom, was that 'the Colony was, at that moment, enjoying full prosperity and commerce demanded the more and more effective occupation of the posts in the interior'.[3]

But come, of course, the slump did, leaving in the centres of European penetration a legacy of new, but derelict, plant and equipment. Once the slump had happened there were many who could define the causes and apportion the responsibility.

The report of the Congo Budget Commission of that year was quite definite that the development programme had exceeded necessities and that the colony's *train de vie* had been geared to an artificially high level of short-term activity in capital construction.[4] The following month, M. Leyniers, one of the few

[1] *The Belgian Congo* (Naval Geographical Handbook), p. 415; Van der Kerken *Politique coloniale belge*, pp. 156-7.

[2] R. L. Hill and C. Cooper, 'Notes on a Journey through the Belgian Congo' (unpublished), pp. 70-1. Kindly lent by Mr. Hill.

[3] *Rapport annuel*, 1930, p. 5.

[4] *Documents parlementaires*, Sénat, 13 February, 1934, Rapport de la Commission du Budget du Congo belge et Ruanda-Urundi, 1934, Document 85.

acute and persistent critics of Congo policy, implied that much unnecessary capital expenditure had been incurred through a failure to co-ordinate Congo transport policy as a whole.[1]

The effects of the slump were certainly severe in the Congo. The value of exports dropped sharply but not catastrophically —a notable defensive success when it is realized that the price of copper fell from £100 to £30 a ton.[2] The real shock is seen in devaluation of the Congo franc and in a more than two-thirds drop in imports between the peak year, 1929, and 1933.[3] With the cessation of capital projects coming on top of the world depression, there was widespread dismissal of both Europeans, who mostly returned to Belgium, and African wage-earners. During 1932 no fewer than 72,000 African workmen were discharged, whilst in industrialized Upper Katanga the number of wage-earners had, by 1933, fallen by 70 per cent. in relation to 1929.[4] In so far as urban and industrial unemployment meant the return of the unemployed to their villages, and, of course, the cessation of recruitment, the results were not without benefit to rural society. Even in the towns and industrial centres, those unemployed who contrived to stay put may not have suffered too greatly, given the system of mutual support built into the African clan and tribe.

The slump and its effects upon the Congo gave rise to one of the few debates on Congo policy that Belgium has witnessed either before or since. The usual attitude of both the Belgian public and political leaders generally in the inter-war period was one of indifference to the Congo, mixed with distrust. 'I have no need to tell you, gentlemen, with what distrust public opinion welcomes colonial projects', said the Colonial Minister in the Chamber of Representatives in 1934,[5] whilst it was rare for the annual debates on the Congo Budget to be very lively.[6] But a system whose defects had been masked by prosperity became vulnerable to criticism when the protective padding of profit was torn away. In July 1932, for instance, the close connexion between the Administration and the cotton companies

[1] *Annales parlementaires*, Sénat, 1933-4, 27 March 1934, M. Leynier, cols. 801-6.
[2] *The Belgian Congo* (Naval Geographical Handbook), p. 414.
[3] Ibid. [4] *African Survey* (1938 ed.), p. 647.
[5] *Annales parlementaires*, Chambre des Représentants, 1933-4, 3 May 1934. M. H. Tschoffen, col. 1390.
[6] See also, for example, Stengers, *Combien le Congo a-t-il coûté à la Belgique?*, pp. 91-92, 345-6.

in the matter of cotton processing and purchasing aroused criticism in the Chamber of Representatives.[1] Again, in 1931, a Colonial Commission of the Senate (moved, one surmises, by a realization of the unfortunate consequences that had resulted from excessive concentration on, and investment in, the European sector of the economy) made specific proposals for a programme of peasant agriculture. Agricultural policy should be accorded the same prestige as commercial and industrial policy; great efforts, backed by compulsion if necessary, should be used to persuade chiefs and people to augment their production of food and cash crops; specialist assistance should be provided and co-operatives encouraged; peasant agriculture should not be prejudiced by excessive grants of land to European concerns; communications should be improved and customs policy modified to permit peasant cash crops to compete effectively in the world market.[2] These recommendations were accepted by the Colonial Minister, whilst the heir to the throne, on returning from his Congo visit, as well as giving his own impulsion to the new policy of encouraging the emergence of a Congolese peasantry, frankly criticized the assumptions which in the past had governed Belgium's 'comportment'[3]—policy is not an appropriate word—towards the Congo. His speech in the Senate was a pointed one.

This economic development of the Congo we have carried out, like most colonizing powers, through the exclusive intervention of capitalist enterprises, regarding the native as a simple tool of production. . . .

But whilst elsewhere this method has progressively been abandoned, in the Congo we have persevered in the same course. . . .

If one also considers that an ever increasing number of industrial enterprises has been created, that even more extensive public works have been undertaken, calling for an even greater labour force, one will grasp the elements of a system where the native continued to be regarded as a simple tool of production. People scarcely concerned themselves, in the beginning at least, with the social and health consequences which such a policy inevitably involved. . . .

But whilst a certain prosperity has become visible, it is not less apparent that, on the one hand, the moral and material conditions of the native has not improved sufficiently and that, on the other

[1] *African Survey* (1938 edition), p. 635.
[2] Hostelet, *L'Œuvre civilisatrice*, I, pp. 267-9.
[3] 'Comportment' is here and elsewhere used in this semi-technical sense.

hand, the administration of the colony, the cost of which has progressively increased, has seen itself get deeply into a budgetary deficit of really alarming proportions.

The responsibility of this state of affairs falls, in my opinion, on all of those who have taken part in the colonial task, for all, some more, some less, have believed that the future of the Congo rested solely on the prosperity of private enterprises.

With respect for existing enterprises, the Duke continued, the Congo economy must be diversified, and agriculture, basically the peasant agriculture of the Congolese themselves, developed.[1]

A further attack on traditional attitudes to the Congo was made in the Senate the following year. Indirectly the attack was occasioned by the Depression, but directly by the clamant need for the subvention of the Congo Budget by the mother country for the second year in succession. In 1933, curiously, the provision for help to the tune of £942,857—necessitated by a budget, in which receipts only half covered expenses— had been passed with no more than formal opposition.[2] The following year, however, probably under the inspiration of M. Leyniers, the *rapporteur* of the Senate Commission on the Congo budget, and a non-parliamentary group concerned about the colony, a hard-headed and pointed analysis of Congo economic policy was made in a forty-six-page report. The first allegation has already been cited—the colony's standard of living had been geared to an artificially high level of short-term activity in capital development. This ill-conceived policy, the report continued, had already cost Belgium more than 'a demi-milliard francs'[3]—it is not at all clear how this figure was arrived at. Moreover, the development programme had exceeded necessities and had been coupled with the 'troublesome' (*fâcheux*) system of guaranteed interest. A major cause of the colony's difficulties was its poor productivity and this was due to four main factors. Premature regulation of labour recruitment had arrested free competition and had conferred a *de facto* monopoly on existing enterprises; there had been harmful variations in mining policy and restrictions on prospecting;

---

[1] Sénat, 1932-3, cols. 586-8, 25 July 1933.   [2] Ibid., cols. 103-8, 345-4.
[3] Converted into sterling at the 1934 Par of Exchange, 500 million francs is £2,857,142. But it is not clear whether the figure of a *demi-milliard* francs meant francs exclusively at their 1934 relationship to gold.

ill-founded industrial hygiene regulations had involved tremendous expenditure; finally there was the fatal influence of the formula 'Africa for the Africans'. The Congo was Belgium's and control should not be in the hands of those who spent the money, but should rest principally with those who found it. However, Belgium ought not to withhold help from the Congo, though the provision for control should be improved.[1]

Precisely what was meant by the formula, so strongly criticized, of 'Africa for the Africans' is not clear. Its meaning would seem to be such as to rejoice the heart of an anti-colonialist propagandist, and certainly M. Wauters, a leading Socialist and member of the Budget Commission, later somewhat disociated himself from it.[2] In a later intervention Leyniers made further criticisms of financial arrangements with Congo companies. Transport contracts made by the Congo Administration were too favourable to the companies concerned whilst, at the same time, Leyniers alleged, a variation of 'dividend stripping' was practised. Mining companies owing an agreed share of their profits to the State would declare artificially low dividends and would place the "undistributed dividend" in a bank which was a shareholder in the company. As a result the State did not receive its due and the company and the shareholding bank benefited improperly.[3] In the same debate criticisms were also made by Wauters.[4]

One reason for the Commission's emphasis on free competition and objections to Government intervention, whether by way of guaranteeing interest or in social and industrial legislation, and one source of its vision of the Congo as a place to make money, doubtless lie in the general attitudes of the Belgian business world at this time. But it may also be true that the exceptionally strong expression of these attitudes owed something to a particular feature of the Congo economy, the fact that it was dominated by trusts. References to the predominance of the big companies in the Congo's economy certainly suggest that the invocation of the virtues of *laissez-faire* was an appeal against monopoly—resorted to because the book prescribed no other remedy for its evils. The evils of the

---

[1] *Documents parlementaires*, Sénat, 13 February 1934, Report of Congo Budget Commission, Doc. 85.
[2] *Annales parlementaires*, Sénat, 1933-4, 22 March 1934, cols. 752-60.
[3] Ibid., 27 March, cols. 801-6.
[4] Ibid., 22 March, cols. 752-60.

highest stage of capitalism were to be met by an un-Marxian, enforced return to the lesser peak below the summit.

Preoccupation with the dominant position of the big companies is demonstrated in an analysis included in the 1934 report of the Senate Budget Commission, already referred to. There were four principal financial groups active in the Congo. The *Groupe Empain* controlled five companies with a capital of £2,560,000; the *Groupe Cominière* controlled nine companies with a capital of £2,497,143; the *Banque de Bruxelles* sixteen companies with £2,240,000 capital. By far the most substantial was the *Société Générale*, controlling forty-one companies with a total capital of £27,725,714. If the minority holdings of these groups are also taken into account, the four groups controlled about three-quarters of the capital of all colonial companies.[1] The most important group, the *Société Générale*, is a phenomenon without English parallel, so varied and extensive are its holdings in Belgian industry, commerce and finance. But it has been suggested that an American equivalent might be a combine consisting of the Bank of America, United States Steel, General Motors, Trans-World Airlines, the Baltimore and Ohio Railway, and the Mutual Life Insurance Corporation of New York.[2] Nor was the influence of the *Société Générale* to be assessed by the size of its holdings alone. Back in 1928 M. Sap, who, apart from Leyniers, was the only notable parliamentary watchdog on Congo policy, had written as follows (it should be observed that he was a member of the conservative Catholic party):

The *Société Générale*, if it wishes, has several methods at its disposal for concealing all the participation which it wishes to conceal. But, I repeat, the percentage of shares held by companies does not interest me and is not interesting; what is interesting are the representatives of the *Groupe Générale-Outremer* on the Boards of Directors.

When on the Boards of Directors of Congo concerns one finds MM. Francqui, Van Bree, Lippens or Cattier, then it is they who order, who direct, who control and no one would think of disputing it.[3]

---

[1] *Documents parlementaires*, Sénat, 13 February 1934, Report of Congo Budget Commission. For a detailed analysis of Congo companies see Joye and Lewin, *Les Trusts au Congo*.

[2] Smith Hempstone, *Katanga Report* (London, Faber, 1962), p. 47.

[3] Sap, quoted by Wauters, *Annales parlementaires*, Sénat, 1933-4, 22 March 1934, cols. 752-60.

I

Between 1931 and 1934, therefore, Congo economic policy did come under fire, at least within the restricted area of parliamentary discussion. The most notable outcome of the debate was clearly the new encouragement given to peasant agriculture, an encouragement backed by compulsion; the operation of this policy has already received some consideration (pp. 82–83). The established position and role of the big Congo companies did not suffer as a result of the criticisms made of them; it would be interesting to make a Namier-type analysis of the influence of the *Société Générale* and other kindred interests on voting in the Belgian Parliament—though henceforward peasant agriculture became more important in the economy.

As in the rest of the world, the mid-thirties saw recovery, and by 1937 exports, at £16,976,075, were in value more than three times the plummet level of 1932.[1] While the expansion of the diamond industry was considerable—from a production of 2,518,258 carats in 1930 to 8,344,765 carats in 1939[2]—copper did not surpass its 1930 level until 1937.[3]

It has been seen that one of the results of the Depression was some movement of discharged wage-earners back to their villages. This was sometimes quite marked. In the case of Leopoldville, the African population declined by some 15,000 —that is, over one-third of the total population and about one-half of the men—between 1929 and 1933.[4] But over the inter-war period as a whole the movement was clearly upward. In the case of Leopoldville there was an increase from some 17,000 in 1923[5] to 40,000 in 1938, by which year a number of other centres had also, by African standards, attained a substantial size. These were: Elisabethville, 18,000; Matadi and Stanleyville, 12,500 each; Coquilhatville, 8,500; Albertville, 5,500; Jadotville, 3,500; Costermansville (later re-christened Bukavu), 2,000.[6] Nor do these figures indicate the full extent of detribalization. Allowing for the populations of lesser centres, of mining camps, for soldiers and others, the African population living out of its traditional environment may have

---

[1] *The Belgian Congo* (Naval Geographical Handbook), p. 414. Note that the Belgian Congolese currency had been devalued on 2 April 1935.

[2] Ibid., p. 408.   [3] Ibid., p. 403.

[4] J. Denis, *Le Phénomène urbain en Afrique Centrale* (Brussels, A.R.S.C., 1958), pp. 91–95.

[5] Ibid., p. 91.   [6] Gille, 'Politique indigène', p. 736, n.

been as high as 8·33 per cent. of the 10,300,000 total population of that year.[1]

Here, evidently, was a growing problem which presented itself at various levels. Ethnically heterogeneous, even the *secteur* was scarcely an appropriate unit of administration for the new *centres*; from the twenties onwards measures were taken to bring under control by administrative means a problem which had attracted attention at least as early as 1913 by the vagabondage which was its most obvious symptom,[2] and which was clearly a matter of continuing concern.[3] A first measure was taken in 1926 in the same decree as laid the foundation of a system of native jurisdiction for the rural areas. The decree's urban application was the creation of *tribunaux de centre*, having similar characteristics to the *tribunaux de territoire* and *tribunaux de secteur* which the decree authorized for the rural areas. Just as they had been intended as the juridical precursor of changes in native administration in the bush, so the new native courts in the towns—of which there were forty-one by 1931[4]—were intended 'to give substance and prestige to the political institution which was to follow'.[5] Follow it did, in an important decree of 23 November 1931: up to that time urban administration was authoritarian, consisting in police measures and in public health and building legislation.[6]

The central provision of the decree—modified by a number of later decrees[7]—was the creation of a completely new unit of administration, the *centre extra-coutumier*, a status to be conferred upon the African quarters of the larger towns. The governing authority of the C.E-C. was a chief, aided by a council of between five and twelve members, some of whom (the judges of the *tribunal de centre*) were members as of right. The remainder, like the chief himself, were nominated by the authorities, whilst the chief, or any councillor, was subject to penalties and even dismissal if he abused his powers or neglected his duties. Not the least of those duties was the maintenance of law and order in the C.E-C., and to this end each C.E-C. was entitled

---

[1] *African Survey*, p. 557.
[2] Report of C.P.I., 1913, *Bulletin officiel*, 1913, pp. 283-7.
[3] Reports of C.P.I., 1919, *Bulletin officiel*, 1920, pp. 671-3 ; 1928, *Bulletin officiel*, 1929, II, pp. 91-94.
[4] Gille, 'Politique indigène', p. 724.   [5] Ibid., p. 721.   [6] Ibid., p. 732.
[7] In the period up to the war by decrees of 6 and 22 June 1934 and 20 January 1939.

to raise its own police force by an ordinance of 2 February 1934. The chief himself had limited powers of detention in the case of breach of the peace, whilst the council could impose up to seven days' imprisonment for offences against such rules as it had itself drawn up. (It must be remembered that the *tribunal de centre* also had authority in the C.E-C.; its competence was wider and its penal powers more extensive.)

The rules which the council was empowered to draw up were upon matters of local interest not regulated by general legislation. The council could also levy taxation for local purposes. In the Stanleyville C.E-C., for instance, taxes were levied on musical instruments, on plots of land allotted by the council, on shops, on palm-wine and on huts occupied by unmarried women. The *centres extra-coutumier* were closely supervised. Supervision of a general kind was the prerogative of a *comité protecteur*, which had competence over all the C.E-C. in a province, which was nominated by the provincial governor and whose chairman was either the provincial commissioner or the *commissaire de district*. At the local level, an administrator attended all meetings of the council and had a veto as well as advisory power. This potentially authoritative position of the administrator was underlined in the provision made for the direct administration of a C.E-C. by him, on the authority of the *commissaire de district*, if the chief and council proved unequal to their task.[1]

Here, then, was an attempt both to create practical administrative units and at the same time to create living communities out of the atomized, detribalized populations of the towns. These communities were to be encouraged to develop morally and materially by a paternalistically supervised policy of self-help. By 1939 there were thirty-two such *centres extra-coutumiers*.[2]

The other major way in which the Colonial Government sought to meet the problems of urbanization was through its considerable activity in matters of public health. The remarkable Belgian achievement in the rural areas between the wars has already been noticed: in the towns the achievement was no less impressive and, indeed, work here began earlier for the simple reason that the new towns, by their very nature, represented an immediate and considerable risk to health.

[1] *African Survey* (1938 edition), pp. 525-6; Gille, 'Politique indigène', pp. 732-7.
[2] Ibid., p. 736.

The urban Congolese did not only benefit from various health and hygiene measures: there was also a body of detailed welfare regulations contained, principally, in a decree of March 1922. This first decree may have been inspired, at least in part, by the revelation of abuses in the Kilo-Moto gold mines in the period 1917–20. There, according to Godding (later to be Colonial Minister), speaking in 1934, were 'tasks which were too severe, with the sanction of corporal punishment; insufficient food, a non-existent medical service'.[1] The decree empowered local authorities to prescribe a statutory scale of diet for workers, a provision which has been generally implemented by a series of local regulations laying down balanced scales of diet, and requiring employers to supply manual workers with prescribed rations in addition to their cash wages. Provincial advisory councils on labour questions were also created and a labour inspectorate was set up by an ordinance of February 1934.[2]

The 1922 decree also regulated conditions of employment by its provisions on labour contracts. This legislation extended to all such contracts between '*indigènes et maîtres civilisés*', even though they might be merely verbal, and conferred upon the employee a number of important rights and safeguards: dismissal was allowed, for example, only in the case of serious failings. The welfare legislation, generally, pinched employers sufficiently to produce attacks upon it in the 1934 Senate debate, as we have seen. The 1922 decree, however, also provided for both civil and penal sanctions for breaches of the contract of employment and it has been alleged that an important role of the decree was to provide employers with the means to discipline their employees by recourse to the courts.[3]

Such, then, was the provision made by the Colonial Administration for the Congo African detached from his traditional *milieu*. The effect of these provisions upon him, and the impact of the town generally, will be considered when the more rapid urbanization of the forties and fifties has been studied. But a consideration of the implications of the widening diffusion of a European economy in the Congo, which is an important part of the burden of this chapter, would be incomplete without

[1] *Annales parlementaires*, Sénat, 1933-4, 27 March 1934, col. 800.
[2] *African Survey* (1938 edition), pp. 680-1, 695.
[3] Ibid., pp. 661-2; *African Survey*, pp. 1416-17; H. Léonard, *Le Contrat de travail au Congo belge et Ruanda-Urundi* (Brussels, Ferdinand Larcier, 1935), *passim*.

reference to the initiation by private companies of what was to prove much the most radical and constructive attempt to meet the problems of detribalization in the Congo.

The pioneer was the *Union Minière*, and its apologists would not deny that it initiated a policy which was to have positive and beneficial social results principally in the interests of the efficient production of minerals. This was reasonable enough; as a later president of the company was to put it: 'The policy of *Union Minière* is to produce copper.'[1] In the boom conditions of the mid-twenties, labour shortage and low productivity were serious hindrances to efficient production. A crucial factor was the low population density of Katanga—appreciably lower than the low density of the Congo as a whole. From the beginning this meant that labour had to be sought from outside Katanga, though much disadvantage and expense was involved. Recruits from Rhodesia, by British colonial legislation, were allowed to take up industrial employment for maximum periods of six months only and though the recruiters' net might be flung ever wider to take in Kasai, Lomami, Maniema and Ruanda-Urundi, what might be saved through the greater efficiency of men on longer contracts was counter-balanced by the enhanced expenses of recruitment and transport. In any case few accepted contracts as long as three years—though some, presumably, undertook two or more short-term engagements—and this in an occupation in which the ordinary miner or labourer attained maximum efficiency only after two or three years. Moreover, desertions were frequent, and the basically unsatisfactory nature of the workers' living conditions (with, for instance, a very low proportion of women and children in the camps) may well have been seen as a cause of low productivity. Finally, the *Union Minière* was susceptible to the steps taken by the Colonial Government to limit recruitment on the one hand, and to enforce quite high standards of welfare on the other.

The *Union Minière's* answer was, in 1925, to take the first steps in a policy of labour stabilization; within a very few years the policy was fully established and by 1939 had abundantly proved itself. The essential components were the renewable three-year contract, the encouragement of workers to bring their wives with them, and an assiduous concern for the welfare of the worker and his family. To this end the worker was

---

[1] Quoted in Hempstone, *Katanga Report*, p. 47.

provided with rations well above the (generous) minimum officially prescribed by the Colony for wage labour, he was given good housing and regular medical attention, and was allowed to work no more than nine, but more commonly eight hours a day, with four free days a month. The company paid for a man's wife to accompany him to the *cité des travailleurs*, or to join him there, and gave to bachelors all encouragement, short of actual provision of the bride-price, to acquire a wife. Welfare services were extended to the worker's family no less than to himself, with, amongst other things, the provision of rations for wife and children, of maternity and infant welfare clinics and of primary schools. Priests and nuns were closely associated with the welfare work and were given facilities for carrying on their purely religious work. Overall supervision of a *cité des travailleurs* was entrusted to a *chef de camp* who had to keep a dossier for each worker and who was issued with comprehensive instructions. He would spend time in listening to complaints and a good deal of time in settling 'palavers'. He was urged to give sympathetic consideration to reasonable requests for time off to return to the village of origin. No pressure was to be put on a man to re-engage on the expiry of a three-year contract in the belief that a voluntary decision so to do was a pre-condition of good performance in the job.[1]

The results of the policy were striking. Whereas between 1921 and 1929 the *Union Minière* had had to recruit an average of 10,000 men a year, in the period 1935–42 the annual average had fallen to 1,800—and this in a period which included the rapid wartime expansion of copper mining. This decrease in recruitment was, of course, made possible by the fact that, despite some initial aversion to the three-year contract, men were increasingly prepared to accept it *and* to re-engage on the expiry of a three-year term. By 1940 between 77 and 78 per cent. were ready to re-engage. By that time, of those who had completed one three-year term, about 50 per cent. had had between three and six years' service, a further 25 per cent. had had from six to nine years', whilst another quarter had been employed by the company for more than ten years.

[1] L. Mottoulle, *Politique sociale de l'Union Minière du Haut-Katanga pour sa main-d'œuvre indigène* (Brussels, I.R.C.B., 1946), pp. 6-52. See also the same author's 'Historique, organisation et résultats obtenus d'une œuvre de protection de l'enfance noire dans la population indigène industrielle de l'Union Minière du Haut-Katanga', *Bulletin de l'I.R.C.B.*, II, 1, 1931, pp. 531-44.

Statistics of life in the camps are no less impressive. Between 1925 and 1929 the annual average percentage of days spent by workers in hospital was, in man-days, 3·3 per cent.: by the period 1935–9 this had dropped to 2 per cent. Mortality rates were also much improved. In 1914 the rate was no less than 117·7 per thousand. In the period 1925–9 it had dropped to 39·1 per thousand, and by 1935–9 to 7·1, whilst between these same two quinquenniums infant mortality had decreased from 161 per thousand to 43·1. The demographic balance of the camps was also improving a good deal. In the 1925–9 quinquennium the total number of women was only 26 per cent. of the number of men: by 1935–9 this percentage had more than doubled to 54. Finally, whereas in 1929 deaths in the camps still exceeded live-births, by the period 1935–9 births exceeded deaths by an average of 22·6 per thousand.[1] All these figures, it will be seen, were to improve yet more in later years.

Such a policy clearly cost money and the *Union Minière* estimates that the policy of stabilization cost £166,667 in 1926, rising to £291,429 in 1929.[2] Without doubt, however, by reason of increased productivity per man and more efficient production generally, the policy more than paid for itself and the company was soon in the position where it could genuinely believe that 'everything which can harm the physical, moral or social well-being of its workers is contrary to the interests, properly understood, of the *Union Minière*'.[3] The example of the *Union Minière* was followed by FORMINIÈRE (*Société Internationale Forestière et Minière du Congo*), by the Kilo-Moto mines, by the *Huileries du Congo Belge* (the Lever organization in the Congo) and by many other large companies. Between 1934 and 1938, for instance, the H.C.B. spent about 22 million francs on medical and educational work.[4] It is understandable that in the thirties the Belgian Congo had come to enjoy a high reputation for the welfare services provided for wage-earners and their families.

In these ways did Belgium seek to meet the problems arising from the increasing tempo of economic activity. The reaction of the detribalized African population to these measures has

---

[1] Mottoulle, *Politique sociale de l'Union Minière*, pp. 53-67; *African Survey* (1938 edition), p. 681.

[2] Mottoulle, *Politique sociale de l'Union Minière*, p. 64.

[3] Ibid., p. 6.   [4] *African Survey* (1938 edition), pp. 681-2.

yet to be considered, but there is much in a socio-religious phenomenon of the twenties and thirties—Kimbanguism and other messianic prophet movements—to suggest that in some areas the impact of European rule had been too great for traditional society to sustain. It is now time to consider these movements.

VII

PROTEST AND SYNTHESIS—
THE BLACK MESSIAH

Catechism

1.   Who is *Mfumu* S.K. [i.e. Simon Kimbangu] in the first person?

Answer: *Mfumu* S.K. is the executor, he who realizes the revelation through the words of grace, through the words of power and through the words of miracles, he is the one who realizes the blessing. He is the one in whom lives the Lord God, the gracious father of the Blacks.

2.   Who is *Mfumu* S.K. in the second person?

Answer: *Mfumu* S.K. is the priest that the Lord God has exalted to be an eternal priest, like the priesthood of Melchizedek. He is the priest of the black race.

3.   Who is *Mfumu* S.K. in the third person?

Answer: *Mfumu* S.K. is the . . . calabash with the oil of blessing that the Lord God has given to the black race that it may be blessed in Him. He is the cup with the oil of blessing for the black race.

4.   Who is *Mfumu* S.K. in the fourth person?

Answer: *Mfumu* S.K. is the sacred sceptre of dominion, which the Lord God has given to the black race that it may have dominion through it. He is the ruler's rod of the blacks.

5.   Who is *Mfumu* S.K. in the fifth person?

Answer: *Mfumu* S.K. is the mighty sword of government that the Lord God has given to the black race. He is the sabre with the keen edge or the three-edged bayonet, in him is the message of salvation for the wicked that the Lord God has given to the black race.

6.   Who is *Mfumu* S.K. in the sixth person?

Answer: *Mfumu* S.K. is the banner of dominion that the Lord God has given to the black race that it may rule through it. He is the banner of dominion for the black race.

7.   Who is *Mfumu* S.K. in the seventh person?

Answer: *Mfumu* S.K. is the shining lamp over the way that the Lord God has given to the black race so that the blacks, when they come to the valley of the shadow of death, may be able to take this lamp in their hand, and thus the night shall be no more for their eyes. And they shall see clearly the way to the city above; all stumbling blocks, all pits, the whole North and the wicked lions, all who are enemies of the Saviour. All people, when they journey on the way, shall see many evil things on the way and they shall fight with them. They shall fight and gain the victory and enter in God's heaven. This is why he is called the lamp on the way to heaven.

8.   Who is *Mfumu* S.K. in the eighth person?

Answer: *Mfumu* S.K. is the open and prepared way that the Lord God has opened on the earth in the heart of the black race so that they may journey thereon to God's heaven. He is the prepared way upon which the black race may enter heaven.

9.   Who is *Mfumu* S.K. in the ninth person?

Answer: *Mfumu* S.K. is the shield of battle on the way to heaven that the Lord God has given to the black race so that when they have stood up to travel the road to heaven they may arm themselves and fight the fight against Satan who is our enemy on the way to heaven.

10.   Who is *Mfumu* S.K. in the tenth person?

Answer: *Mfumu* S.K. is the river with the living water that the Lord God has given to the black race. The blacks wish to drink from this river and they shall receive eternal life and enter the gate of heaven. He is the river with the living water for the black race.

11.   Who is *Mfumu* S.K. in the eleventh person?

Answer: *Mfumu* S.K. is the canoe that the Lord God has put in the river of death, so that the blacks shall go on board that boat and cross death's river courageously. He is the ferry of the black race.

12.   Who is *Mfumu* S.K. in the twelfth person?

Answer: *Mfumu* S.K. is the sacrifice of atonement that the Lord God has allowed to descend among the black race so that they may enter in at the gate of heaven as a group. He has become the ladder on which the human race reaches up to God's heaven. He has become the stair on which they reach the heaven of their God.

13.   Who is *Mfumu* S.K. in the thirteenth person?

Answer: *Mfumu* S.K. is the open door that the Lord God has

opened among the black race that they may enter by it.
It is the city of the new Jerusalem, the Jerusalem of the
blacks and God's very holiest city. He is the door
through which they enter the heaven of their God.

Amen, Amen.

So runs the catechism used by a congregation of followers of
Simon Kimbangu a quarter of a century after the movement
stemming from him had been born.[1]

Simon Kimbangu was born, sometime in the 1880's, at
Nkamba in the Lower Congo, in an area which was already a
centre of Protestant missionary work. The son of a renowned
nganga ('native doctor',—a term which will be more adequately
explained later), Simon was put to school, presumably one
belonging to the Baptist Missionary Society since that particular society was the expression of Protestantism in that
region, and subsequently seems to have become a B.M.S.
catechist. He came to be regarded in Protestant missionary circles as a conscientious worker and a good and quiet man who
regularly read his Bible. Towards 1921 he began to have
dreams and visions which enjoined him to go home to his
village, for God wished to enrol him as one of his labourers.
After at first resisting this call, Kimbangu eventually yielded to
it. The dreams and visions continued until one day, in Andersson's words,

when Kimbangu, according to the custom of his people, was going to
a near-by village with a gift of a piece of cloth as his contribution to a
friend's funeral, he fell into a fit and lay unconscious on the road.
On the way home from this visit (accompanied by his parents) and
later in his own village, he had new visions in which a stranger,
neither white nor black, nor mulatto, appeared to him.

One night, when this being came with a Bible in its hand and
said, 'This is a good book. You must study it, and preach', Kimbangu
replied: 'Nay . . . I am no preacher or teacher, I cannot do it',
whereupon the stranger urged him to give the Book to his mother,
so that she might preach, and then told him that there was a sick
child in a village near by, and ordered him to go and pray for it.
Still he would not obey. His mother now had a dream in which the

[1] Quoted in translation in E. Andersson, *Messianic Popular Movements in the
Lower Congo* (Uppsala, Studia Ethnographica Uppsaliensia, XIV, 1958),
pp. 195-6. Andersson adds in immediate explanation that the questions constitute an application of the doctrine of the Trinity to Kimbangu, here multiplied
to thirteen persons, reflecting the twelve apostles together with Kimbangu himself.

stranger repeated his command that her son should go out and preach and heal the sick, but this summons too he ignored. It was repeated again in a tone of great authority: 'There is a sick child in a certain village. You must go there, pray, lay your hands on the child and heal it. If you do not go, I shall require your soul of you.' Now, as in Kinshasha [when told to return to his village], Kimbangu was forced to yield. He went next day to the village in question and found the child. He laid hands on it and prayed, whereupon he was subjected to violent convulsions. The child, however, was cured of its sickness and put to its mother's breast.[1]

According to Balandier, this crucial revelation took place on 18 March 1921.[2]

News of the healing of the child spread through much of the Lower Congo like wild-fire. Labourers in Thysville and workers on the railway left their work to come to see the new prophet at Nkamba—soon renamed 'Jerusalem'; extra carriages had to be provided for pilgrims on the railway; hospitals were emptied of their patients. Soon the small village of Nkamba was host to a shifting population running into thousands. Undoubtedly it was Kimbangu's repute as a healer which brought the people, but an eye-witness is quite definite that the attempts at healing took place only in the course of services of worship. There would be prayers, hymns, a Bible-reading and a sermon. Only after more prayers were the sick treated, usually after admittance one by one into the prophet's inner sanctum where it seems that, staff in hand and trembling violently, Kimbangu bade them 'Be healed, in the name of Jesus Christ'.

'Were the cures effective?' is the question that naturally arises. Andersson has sifted a good deal of evidence, and made clear its character, to arrive at the conclusion that the great majority of attempts were a failure but that here and there cures probably took place. The cases which he cites of cures of yaws, sleeping-sickness, blindness and sterility, and the authority on which the cures were reported, give grounds for supposing that this overall verdict is somewhat too conservative.

It is clear that these gatherings were emotionally very highly charged. But while the people came primarily to obtain healing for themselves or their relations, Kimbangu seems to have had a

[1] Andersson, *Messianic Popular Movements*, pp. 50-51.

[2] Ibid., pp. 48-52; G. Balandier, *Sociologie actuelle de l'Afrique noire* (Paris, Presses Universitaires de France, 1955), pp. 427-8; J. Van Wing, 'Le Kibangisme vu par un témoin', *Zaire*, XII, 6, 1958, pp. 566-7 ('Kibangisme' is an optional spelling).

real concern to preach and to have imparted positive doctrine based upon Scripture. There was, indeed, an unprecedented run on Bibles and hymn-books at all the Protestant mission stations round about, and even Kimbangu's detractors commonly admit his devotion to Scripture. Unhappily there is no available knowledge of the precise content of Kimbangu's sermons: we have only the word of a local Protestant missionary, quoted by Andersson, that 'one should abolish and abjure all *nkisi*, practise monogamy, and worship the one true God'.

The reference to *nkisi* is understandable only in its Ba-Kongo context. Van Wing, in describing the conception of *nkisi* held by the eastern Ba-Kongo, writes: 'It is an artificial object supposedly inhabited or influenced by a spirit, in any case endowed by it with a superhuman power; and this spirit is under the domination of a man.'[1] The whole *raison d'être* of *nkisi* is to combat witchcraft or sorcery, called *kindoki* by the Ba-Kongo, belief in which is universal and deep-rooted. *Kindoki*, writes Van Wing again, is 'the cause of almost all illness, of almost all deaths, and of most adversity'.[2] In turn, the man who controls the *nkisi* is the *nganga*. This term may be interpreted as 'fetish priest', provided that it is understood that the Ba-Kongo owned no priestly caste (the French term *féticheur* is more accurate), and provided that it is realized that basically the *nganga* fulfilled an accepted and proper function in Ba-Kongo society—though certainly constantly tempted 'to exploit the taste for the miraculous, for the strange, for the invisible and, let it be said, the vilest passions of [his] clients'.[3]

But the efficacy of the *nganga*, working through the *nkisi* which he controlled, was by no means universal, for he was still all too often countered by the sorcerer, the *ndoki*, the practitioner of black magic. Periodically in Ba-Kongo history a desperate sense of the inadequacy of their *nkisi* seems to have overwhelmed the people, and these *nkisi* were destroyed in outbursts of mass passion. The last such occasion seems to have been amongst some of the Angola Ba-Kongo in about 1872.[4]

---

[1] Van Wing, *Études Bakongo*, p. 383.   [2] Ibid., pp. 421-2.
[3] Ibid., p. 421.
[4] Ibid., p. 423. Van Wing, 'Kibangisme vu par un témoin', pp. 574-5. Andersson has a valuable discussion of Ba-Kongo beliefs, especially on pp. 1-28, and 259-62, but Van Wing's *Études Bakongo* remains the most authoritative and comprehensive source.

Kimbangu was therefore to some extent echoing a not unfamiliar refrain from the past when he ordered the destruction
of *nkisi*. The complement of this destruction, general throughout
the Lower Congo, was, according to Van Wing, the conferring
of baptism upon the followers of the new prophet. Here then
was the new armour for the Ba-Kongo which, together with the
insistence upon monogamy, was clearly of Christian inspiration.
So, if less obviously, was the third element in Kimbangu's
teaching, the injunction to *'worship* the one true God' (my
italics). Such a conclusion is justified positively by Kimbangu's
upbringing on, and undoubted and continuing familiarity with
the Christian Bible, and negatively by the fact that the one true
God of the Ba-Kongo, *Nzambi*, was, while revered, remote from
day-to-day religious practice.[1] The overall Christian content of
Kimbangu's teaching is attested, not just by the already
mentioned boom in Bibles and hymn-books, but also by the fact
that preachers in all the Protestant missions round about
preached to capacity congregations.

Andersson's judgement of Kimbangu himself is that, at least
in the early days of his ministry, the prophet 'was motivated by
a genuine zeal to preach the Word of God' and that 'doctrin-
ally he upheld the tenets of pure Christianity'.[2] But the movement soon aroused the fears of the authorities, and in a measure
the foolishness of Kimbangu justified these fears. Following
complaints from employers that their workmen were leaving
them in order to visit Nkamba, and information that the hazards of the pilgrimage were leading to deaths, the local
administrator went to investigate. According to one account,
when he arrived he found Kimbangu surrounded by four
lesser prophets, by about fifty catechists and by a crowd of some
seven or eight hundred. The sick were lying in the centre of the
crowd and songs were being sung. The atmosphere was emotional. Then, whilst the administrator's tent was being erected,
Kimbangu positioned himself opposite him and, in a loud
voice, read the story of David and Goliath, while a girl held up
a picture of the unhappy Philistine to ensure that the point
should not be lost! The administrator then tried to begin a
conversation with Kimbangu but was soon interrupted by the

---

[1] This whole section on the birth of Kimbanguism is based, save as otherwise
indicated, on Andersson, *Messianic Popular Movements*, pp. 52-61.
[2] Andersson, *Messianic Popular Movements*, pp. 57, 60.

prophet's turning away and, somewhat disconcertingly, addressing the Holy Ghost.[1]

Even though the prophet's deportment on this occasion may have been the result of spirit possession, or hysteria, it has an anti-European appearance. The further question arises, and has been strongly debated, whether Kimbangu's teaching was specifically anti-European in any way. The Congo newspaper, *L'Avenir colonial belge*, probably reflecting the common opinion of local Europeans, believed that he was anti-European; that 'he preaches Africa for the Blacks, preparation for war against the Whites'.[2] More weighty is the official charge brought against him at his trial in October 1921 that Kimbangu, amongst other things, 'has declared himself to be the redeemer and saviour of the black race, pointing to the white man as the enemy, calling him the abominable enemy'.[3] Andersson, on the other hand, cites a good deal of African evidence that there was no such teaching—this, for instance: 'give the rulers of the country all that they ask of you, but give your heart to God. I am the first to pay my taxes.'[4]

The constant fear which a colonial government must have of a breakdown of law and order may suggest that, in its anxiety, it read more into the movement than was there. The fact remains that, if Kimbangu's aims were not overtly and intentionally subversive, his teaching inevitably had revolutionary implications. Here was a man who not merely spoke with the authentic voice of Scripture but who seemed by his knowledge of Scripture, by the authority with which he preached, to be the embodiment of it. Moreover, it was an African who was doing this, who could command an insight into the Christian faith greater than that of the European missionaries who brought it, and who could make its—by European standards—more exotic characteristics take on a fire not known in the more reserved practice of the missions. From this it was but a step to the feeling summed up by a contemporary Protestant missionary witness in these words: 'They rejoiced to think that one of their number had become a prophet. Not only white people could become great and powerful, for a mighty one, a man worthy of note could arise

---

[1] Andersson, *Messianic Popular Movements*, pp. 61-63.
[2] Quoted in ibid., p. 61 n.   [3] Quoted in ibid., p. 67 n.
[4] Quoted in ibid., p. 61.

Plate I

VOTEZ PSA

A. GIZENGA
Président Général

Cl. KAMITATU
Président Provincial

Un Gouvernement PSA
promet dans l'immédiat

1. - Réduction totale du chômage et de travail à tous.
2. - Multiplication des écoles surtout dans les milieux ruraux - Gratuité de de l'enseignement primaire et secondaire.
3. - Augmentation des salaires à tous.
4. - Amélioration de l'habitat dans les milieux ruraux.
5. - Gratuité des soins médicaux à tous les non salariés.

Kana PSA kusala gouvernement
beno atakubaka mambote yai :

1. - Kubasisa bisalu mingi sambu na bantu yonso.
2. - Kusala ba inzo ya nkanda mingi. Kulonga bana malongi ya mpanmba na primaire ti secondaire.
3. - Kupesa meya ya malunga na bantu ya kisalu yonso.
4. - Kusadisa ti kuyidika banzo ya mbote na babwala yonso.
5. - Bantu yonso ya kele na kisalu ve, na ba dispensaire ti na ba hôpital, kupesa nkisi ya mpamba, kufuta ve.

P.S.A. poster used in the 1960 election campaign

Plate II

Batabwa figures: 'If African ancestor figures in their innumerable styles have a quality in common, it is surely that of *gravitas*, expressing the deep reverence (tempered with familiarity) in which the deceased elders of the tribe are held. They have been promoted by death to a higher status, in which they perform an indispensable function as intermediary channels of life force for the tribe; at the same time they are in a reciprocal relationship with their living descendants, on whose survival as a line and unbroken service they are dependent for their own well-being in the after-life. This example (Royal Scottish Museum, 31 *in*) is from the Batabwa, a Baluba or Baluba-ized tribe at the south end of Lake Tanganyika.'

William Fagg and Margaret Plass, *African Sculpture*
(London, Studio Vista, 1964), p. 140.

Plate III

Cité des Travailleurs of the B.C.K. Railway

Plate IV

Leopold II of Belgium

from the ranks of the Africans whom they had scorned.'[1]

The racial element thus admitted, political implications began to be drawn from Kimbanguism by some of the movement's members and by interested parties. A number of auxiliaries had had to be ordained by Kimbangu, and it may well be that shaking and the other ambiguous criteria of spirit possession had led to the admittance of a proportion of rogues and charlatans, as well as men who erred simply in attributing to Kimbangu more than he claimed for himself. In some places Africans were urged not to pay their taxes, whilst in Leopoldville, it is alleged, a pre-existing group of revolutionary-minded Africans gave to Kimbanguism an anti-European slant for their own purposes.

With excitement mounting throughout the Lower Congo, the Government acted. On 6 June Kimbangu was arrested, but escaped, only to come again into the Government's hands after he had intentionally courted arrest by returning openly to his own village on 10 September. The area being by this time under martial law, Kimbangu was tried by a military court at Thysville the following month. In Van Wing's view, the case was tried according to the proper judicial procedure; but Andersson cites evidence that inaccurately translated documents were used against Kimbangu. The upshot was that Kimbangu was condemned to death on a number of counts. He had spread false rumours of healing and resurrection from the dead; he had posed as the emissary of God; he had called the white man '*l'ennemi abominable*'; despite being forbidden to do so, he had preached the coming of a new God who would be more powerful than the State and claimed that he, Kimbangu, was the representative of God, and so on. Considering that Kimbangu himself seems never to have initiated even a breach of the peace, the sentence was excessively severe and the fact that the *parquet* joined in appeals by Protestant missionaries against the sentence is significant. The result was the commutation of the sentence by King Albert to life imprisonment in face of a violent press campaign by the *L'Avenir colonial belge* and of a petition from Europeans in Thysville for Kimbangu's speedy execution.[2]

[1] Quoted in ibid., p. 57.
[2] Ibid., pp. 57-67; Van Wing, 'Kibangisme vu par un témoin', p. 580. Comments by Roman Catholic missionaries are prone to take the line that the movement was an

K

During the remainder of the twenties and up until the mid-thirties, the Lower Congo, and parts of adjoining French Congo, witnessed the appearance of several prophetic sects, all according a greater or lesser place to Kimbangu himself. In the French Congo, in the mid-twenties, the authorities took very harsh action against Ngunzuism, the 'prophet movement', whilst in the Belgian colony there was periodic repression and coercion both before and after the prohibition of Kimbanguism by the Governor of Congo-Kasai province in February 1925. To begin with, the Swedish Protestant mission made a real and partially successful attempt to keep Ngunzuism within the fold of the mission but the somewhat pliant attitude which it displayed, in face of Government demands that it act against the Ngunzu movement within its ranks, generated in French Congo some feeling that the Protestant missions were definitely on the side of the Administration. In the Belgian Congo, the circular which accompanied the prohibition of Kimbanguism, by its request that all missions should help the Administration in the struggle against the sect, further enhanced the ambiguous position and difficulties of the Protestant missions.

Broadly speaking, the policy of repression, together, possibly with a sense of being abandoned by the Protestant missions, gave to the prophet movements a more anti-white character, whilst in doctrine there was also a turning in on itself, some decline from the generally high level of preaching and conduct of Kimbangu himself, and some positive reversion to traditional practices and beliefs. Thus one finds the First Person of the Trinity losing prominence and becoming remote somewhat in the sense that Nzambi had always been remote. Certainly great importance continued to be attached to the Person and example of Christ, but it was the Third Person of the Trinity who was the most 'popular'. Supreme importance was attached to revelations, or 'revelations' of the Holy Spirit which had to be attested by outward signs, and especially body-shaking. In Andersson's words, 'the doctrine of the Spirit is the wide gate

---

inevitable product of Evangelical Christianity (see e.g. L. Philippart, *Le Bas Congo: état religieux et social* (Louvain, Saint-Alphonse, 1929, pp. 100-1). In Protestant accounts there is a greater sympathy with Kimbangu and informing them, one senses, a feeling that Kimbangu's work *might* have had wholly positive results if Protestant missionaries had consistently and sympathetically sought to guide it. Andersson spent many years in Ba-Kongo country as a Protestant missionary.

through which a number of pre-Christian conceptions have entered'. An example of such was the commandment of one prophet that 'To fornicate is no sin; God's Spirit declares that the prophets must have female servants'. On the other hand there were many cases of continued acceptance of the rigorous Puritanism of Kimbangu himself.

Another major characteristic of Ngunzuism, which recalls the element of taboo in traditional religion, was the considerable number of prohibitions. For instance, it was forbidden to kill the *mbemba* bird, since a particular prophet was alleged to find this bird a convenient vehicle in his journeyings from place to place. To kill the bird might therefore be to kill the prophet. As to anti-white feeling, one missionary even went so far as to assert that 'the whole movement has at bottom the single aim: we shall ourselves govern and rule our own country. All whites must get out.' (This opinion of mid-1935, it should be pointed out, apparently related to French Congo, which was at that time more disturbed. It is none the less significant of the growth of the racial element in the movement, which took little account of colonial frontiers.) Finally, there was frequently a messianic element in the *ngunzu* movement. To quote Andersson again, 'Simon Kimbangu quite evidently plays the role of his people's Messiah. The aims of the movement are more political than religious. There is more talk of "Ntotila's" [signifying Kimbangu] coming and of the establishment of the national Kingdom than of Christ as Saviour. . . .'[1]

It was, indeed, in French Congo that, in the thirties, two further interesting developments took place in the Ngunzu movement. The first centred on the Mukongo, André Matswa, who first came into prominence over his attempts, in 1929–30, to raise money for the support of indigent French Africans in Paris, where Matswa himself had lived for a time. There seems to have been an element of the charlatan in Matswa but, by means which are not clear, he acquired a great ascendancy over the Ba-Kongo in French Congo and founded a still-thriving Ngunzuist cult, *Nzambi ya Minda* which is significant for the extent to which it has reverted to traditional Ba-Kongo religious

[1] This section is based on Andersson, *Messianic Popular Movements*, pp. 68–116. The quotations are from pp. 109, 112 (twice), 100. The *Courrier africain* (Leopoldville, Centre de Recherche et d' Information Socio-Politiques), I, 8 January 1960, is also useful here, and as a useful summary of Kimbanguism as a whole. See also Balandier, *Sociologie actuelle*, pp. 442-7.

practices and for its surpassing of anything acceptable by even the most relaxed Christian standards. After his death in 1942, for instance, 'Father Matswa' was directly invoked in the prayers of his followers.[1]

Of much greater positive interest is the extraordinary phenomenon whereby the coming of the Salvation Army to the Congo in 1935 was widely interpreted amongst the Ba-Kongo as the return of Kimbangu himself and the consummation of his work. That such could be the case is clearly indicative of the importance of the messianic strand in the Ngunzuist movement. Throughout the twenties and early thirties Kimbangu was actually imprisoned in distant Elisabethville (it really was life imprisonment, for he was to remain there until his death in 1951). But there was considerable uncertainty about what had actually happened to him, some Ba-Kongo apparently believing that the original death sentence had actually been carried out. Given a proclivity to think in supernatural terms, however, it mattered little whether he had been executed or simply committed to prison. Distance and uncertainty gave rumour and legend every possible opportunity and the belief that Kimbangu would in due time return as saviour was an important element in the prophet movement. A Ba-Kongo belief—widely shared throughout Africa—is that the spirits of the departed are white. With this belief, with the expectation of the return of Kimbangu as Messiah, with the martial aspect and accoutrements of the Salvation Army and, of great importance, the letter 'S' (for 'Simon'!) on the collars of the Army's officers, we have all the elements of the explanation of why the first Salvationists were widely regarded as the reincarnated Kimbangu with some of his prophets. (Many Kimbanguist prophets had been exiled to other parts of the Congo and the uncertainty amongst the Ba-Kongo of their fate gave the same opportunity for legend and rumour as had been given by the uncertainty regarding Kimbangu.) In the words of the report of Palmborg, a Swedish missionary,

Their Simon Kimbangu had been for many years an exile in Upper Congo [*sic*]. His followers believed implicitly that he would return to them, by supernatural means. Their time of waiting was long-drawn-out. But when the Army came, their hopes were fulfilled. *L'Armée du salut* did not come from *Mputu* (Europe), like other

1 Andersson, *Messianic Popular Movements*, pp. 117-26.

missions, it did not come to Congo by sea or by air, no, it was a miracle. . . . The Salvation Army is Simon Kimbangu himself, who has returned to his country and his people. By an act of God he left the place or the prison in which he was confined, he transformed himself into a European, was granted the power of a white man, and now the Whites cannot imprison him again or prevent him from doing his work. The imagination of the Africans was fired by this illusion. Simon Kimbangu has come back![1]

When the Salvation Army was seen in this light, it is not altogether surprising that the most remarkable powers were attributed to it and the most remarkable expectations of it entertained. In short, the Army was seen as the Deliverer from the sorcery which the destruction of *nkisi* had still not always rooted out, and against which the still more radical test by poison could no longer be applied for fear of the authorities. The detail of this development is admittedly not clear, but it was evidently helped by the music, the drums and the flags, whilst the custom grew up of clasping the Salvation Army officer's hand as the necessary preliminary to a sign from Heaven proclaiming guilt or innocence of sorcery. The usual indication of guilt was subsequent illness and death, and since it was generally believed that a person could practise sorcery without knowing it, and since people often made long and difficult journeys to attend Army meetings, the death of a proportion of the pilgrims as a result of the hazards of travel was taken as proof of the Army's efficacy in unmasking witch-craft.

Eventually the Army's leaders became partially aware of what was being read into their mission and their ceremonies, and curbed their more extravagant practices. But in measure as this was done, the Army's mass appeal waned—though it continued to enjoy evangelistic success of a more conservative order—and a 'popular' Salvation Army grew up beside it in which, by the standards of Western Christianity, the bizarre and the extravagant had full play. This development was aided by the somewhat uncritical acceptance into the ranks of the Army, by the original Salvationists, of men who had too often been dismissed by one or other of the Protestant missions for misconduct, or who were 'under discipline' for some sin or offence. It was one such, Simon Mpadi, who after being

[1] Quoted in ibid., p. 128.

appointed lieutenant in the 'official' Army, in 1939 founded yet another variant of Ngunzuism, *La Mission des noirs* or the 'khaki movement'.[1]

Another and more purely millenarian movement of quite different origin was to be found in the Congo between the wars —the Watchtower or *kitawala* movement. As the name indicates, this movement was of North American origin, the term *kitawala* in various spellings having the meaning of 'tower'. During the twenties the movement was established in Rhodesia which, of course, had a common frontier with the Katanga province of the Belgian Congo. Before that the Watchtower movement had been active in Nyasaland. Its teachings—and the movement is better known under its present European name of Jehovah's Witnesses—are frankly and vigorously millenarian. Its importance in our context is that both the existing Churches and the State are creatures of Satan's kingdom and will eventually be destroyed at Armageddon, along with all unbelievers. Moreover, though Jehovah's Witnesses reject the divinity of Christ, they have a very distinct place for messianism since they believe that the second coming of Christ has already taken place, invisibly, in 1914. Little seems to be known of the movement's Congo expression—it moved into Katanga in the twenties—but Balandier has pointed out, in general terms, that there is a similarity between the *kitawala* movement and Bantu messianic sects. The similarities include the declaration of war against sorcery and the belief in a further golden age for the black race. A distinct xenophobic element is therefore implied here. Certainly the *kitawala* movement led to rioting in the Mweru-Luapula district of Katanga in 1936.[2] Its principal importance in the Congo, however, was after 1939.

Both Kimbanguism and its variants, and the *kitawala* movement, are of considerable interest to the student of comparative religion: but in the context of this book they are principally of interest as protest on the one hand, and synthesis and fulfilment on the other. They were protest, first of all, against the missions, and especially the Protestant missions. It was not the rigorous attitude of the missions towards monogamy that offended—Kimbangu's own crusade against polygamy is sufficient testimony to that. It was, rather, that the missions

---

[1] This section is based on Andersson, op. cit., pp. 126-38.
[2] Andersson, op. cit., pp. 247-8. Balandier, *Sociologie actuelle*, p. 420.

ignored faith-healing and failed to persuade all of their converts that Christianity could be the answer to sorcery, that
endemic fear in traditional life; it was that they failed to
provide sufficient emotional satisfaction in worship, and paid
too little heed to the central position of the ancestors in traditional life and thought. At the root of each failure was the
cultural arrogance of the West which, it is not surprising, all
but exceptional missionaries shared. Such an attitude not only
dictated the 'clean sweep' approach, whereby everything
African, being crude and pagan, was to be attacked, or at best,
ignored, but also reflected the deficiencies to which contemporary Western Christianity was itself subject. These included
acceptance of what might be described as the mechanical
conception of medicine which then prevailed and a consequential failure to bring to Africa any lively sense either of the
mental element in 'physical' illness or that faith-healing could
in any sense be part of the Christian mission.[1]

Given such attitudes, evangelical piety, preaching and witness might still gain its triumphs, but disbarred itself from
making fundamental conversions on a wide scale by not
realizing the need thoroughly to analyse African religion,
magic, custom, and African need generally as the pre-condition
of presenting Christianity to the African in a way meaningful
to him in terms of his own culture. Again, evangelical Christianity, it can be argued, has consistently neglected the doctrine of
the Communion of the Saints—many evangelical Christians,
it may be conjectured, would be at a loss if asked when All
Saints' Day fell. In consequence the absolutely basic African
cult of the ancestors was not often seen as a supreme opportunity for the missionary, for he rarely saw the Communion of
the Saints in terms of the consummation of the ancestor cult.
Partly determined by cultural arrogance was the content of the
teaching offered in mission schools. Because the mission school
was not equipped to teach Christianity in positive relationship
to traditional African religion, nor European culture in
positive and demonstrable relationship to African, the school
came to be valued primarily as the golden and almost exclusive way to the understanding of the technical superiority of

---

[1] That this was but a passing fashion in Western theology and Western medicine
is possibly debatable. But one can point to the much greater awareness that now
obtains of the interrelation of medicine, psychology and religion, and to a theological concern with demonology.

the white man. The acquiring of a limited understanding of the white man's skill and ways was, in any case, the principal reason for which mission schools were valued by the Government and commercial firms, though it would be fair to add that they were, in a general way, valued for their moral function.

The great emphasis in Kimbanguism on spirit-possession, ecstatic states and especially shaking, suggests, by its very disproportion, a reaction against the lack of emotional outlets in evangelic Christianity. It is a truism to say that people, generally, need a physical outlet for their emotion and some sort of periodic escape from omnipresent care. The English Baptist of the early twentieth century, say, would, in his chapel, know the emotion aroused by the sinners' bench, the appeal for converts to come forward, the whole, perhaps, against a background of fervent but controlled 'Hallelujahs'. Anything more emotional than this he would regard as the extravagances of extremist Christian sects. The Baptist minister, transplanted to Africa as a missionary could not, commonly, recognize the positive element of emotional health and satisfaction in traditional dances, because it was frequently characterized by obscenity, nor comprehend that dancing could become an outlet for religious emotion. Nor, by the very fact of belonging to a different civilization, could he appreciate what seems to be a greater African receptivity to supersensory phenomena. For example, it is apparently the case that immigrant workers from the Upper Volta who are not fully adjusted to life in urban Accra go out at week-ends to a place where they enter into possession states and are seemingly better adjusted the rest of the time.[1] At a rather different level Dr. Bengt Sundkler has pointed out how very frequently the call of an African to the Christian ministry or priesthood is experienced in a dream.[2] Of such dispositions and of the needs which they imply, the Protestant missions in the Ba-Kongo country took little account. There is then, overall, a real sense in which Kimbanguism and the prophet movement were a protest against the Protestant missions.[3]

[1] M. Banton, 'African Prophets', *Race*, V, 2, October 1963, p. 53.

[2] B. Sundkler, *The Christian Ministry in Africa* (London, S.C.M. Press, paperback edition, 1962), pp. 22-30.

[3] This section owes something, but only something, to Andersson, *Messianic Popular Movements*, pp. 264-8. It may be felt that this comment takes too little account both of the difficulties and of the achievements of the missions, that it

The movement was also a protest against traditional religion, and especially against the inadequacy of *nkisi* as protection against sorcery. This protest was expressed in the wholesale destruction of *nkisi* and was coupled with implicit protest against the remoteness of *Nzambi*, for it was on a God conceived of as able to be worshipped and entreated that reliance was placed to fulfil the function formerly carried out by recourse to *nkisi*.

Moving beyond the sphere of religious belief and practice there is some direct and more circumstantial evidence that the original Kimbanguist movement, and, still more, the varied prophet movements which followed it, were protest against European domination in both the religious and the political fields. It has been seen that, from the time of Kimbangu's trial, a messianic element entered into the prophet movement and it seems clear that this messianism was, in its looking to Kimbangu's return as a religious and political saviour, a protest against European domination in both of these sectors. It is also significant how much emphasis came to be attached by followers of Kimbangu to the fact that, because of him, they were members of a world religion on a level with Protestantism and Catholicism; it is no less significant that Kimbangu himself was sometimes given the stature of other great religious leaders and prophets, including Christ himself. 'He has given us Simon Kimbangu who is for us the Moses of the Jews, the Christ of foreigners, the Mahomet of the Arabs.'[1]

We must also ask if in both its origin and continuation the prophet movement was not a protest at the way in which the European presence bore so heavily on traditional society. The starting-point here must be that, whatever rubbish may be

ignores the dangers of emotionalism in religion and of distorting the Christian message; that it undervalues, for instance, the important medical work of the missions and the undoubted genuineness of the faith of some of their converts. But my remarks are not intended as a pontifical judgement on Protestant missionary work at a particular time and place, but are speculation on why the Ba-Kongo found Protestant Christianity dissatisfying, in so far as they did, particularly as indicated by the popularity of some, especially, of the elements of Kimbanguism. It is, after all, not surprising that in any circumstances a Christianity, embedded in Western culture, should have difficulty in establishing a real *rapport* with African traditional religion. And to arrive at such a *rapport* would have been, and is, a supremely difficult task. It is relevant to suggest that certain of the religious, cultural and intellectual assumptions of the late nineteenth- and early twentieth-century Protestant missionary were such as to make this task particularly difficult.

[1] Balandier, *Sociologie actuelle*, pp. 431, 476-7; Andersson, *Messianic Popular Movements*, p. 57.

talked about colonialism, the specific fact of there being a 'colonial situation' is the principal fact of life in a colony. By this is meant the concentration of authority in politics and administration, over land, in the economic life of the territory, in technology, in religion and in education, in the hands of the colonizer. The fact that, in the colonization of tropical Africa, the colonizer was white and the colonized black made the mastery of the one group, and the subordination of the other, crystal-clear. Malinowski, concerned to point out the 'selective giving' of the colonizer, illustrates the fact of his domination. He was writing in the early forties.

1. We do not give them the instruments of physical power: fire-arms, bombing planes, poison gas, and all that makes effective defence or aggression possible.

2. We do not give our instruments of political mastery. Sovereignty remains vested in the British or Belgian Crown, French Republic, or Italian or Portuguese dictatorship. The natives, except for an insignificant minority, have no votes.

3. We do not, in most territories, share with them the substance of economic wealth and advantages. The metal which comes from the gold or copper mines does not flow into African channels, except the inadequate wage. Even . . . under indirect economic exploitation [when] . . . we allow the Natives a share of profits, the full control of economic organization remains in the hands of Western enterprise.

4. We do not usually admit them as equals to church assembly, schools, or drawing room. Full political, social, and even religious equality is nowhere granted.[1]

It of course remains true, and Malinowski himself recognized the point, that, on the other side of the ledger, there have been displayed by the colonizer qualities such as generosity, devotion and self-sacrifice. But the immediately relevant point is that authority and the instruments of power are in the colonizer's hands. When one turns specifically to the Ba-Kongo, it does seem that ever since the coming of European rule in the 1880's, and through the 1920's and 1930's, European authority pressed heavily upon them. There had first of all been incessant demands for porters to carry loads from the Congo estuary round the cataracts to Stanley Pool; then had come a sustained, heavy demand for workers to build the Matadi–Leopoldville

[1] Malinowski, *Dynamics of Culture Change*, pp. 56-57. For the notion of a colonial situation see also Balandier, *Sociologie actuelle*, pp. 3-36, and O. Mannoni, *Prospero and Caliban, passim.*

railway, to be followed by a devastating epidemic of sleeping-sickness of which the ill effects were made worse instead of better by the policy of re-grouping villages, adopted by the Independent State. Further upset resulted from the seemingly frequent investiture of the wrong men as chiefs when the 1910 decree on native administration was being applied.[1] Scarcely was the scourge of sleeping-sickness mastered in the second decade of the century than European rule again began to bear heavily on the Ba-Kongo. Van Wing sees this in terms of the compulsion levied upon the people to carry out the road building programme which was one of the most important features of the Franck plan for economic development, whilst Balandier attaches weight to the crises of 1921 and 1930–1 in the world commodity market for palm produce[2] (one of the Ba-Kongo staples), crises which were after all, to the Mukongo, European-made. To these various experiences of the weight of *Bula Matari's* domination must be added, in the French Congo, the protracted construction of the Brazzaville–Ocean railway which made as devastating demands on African labour as had its Belgian counterpart thirty years earlier.

All in all, however good its intentions might sometimes have been, European domination had been seriously felt by the Ba-Kongo. This being so, there is, we have seen, some direct evidence that the prophet movement was a religious protest, though with evident and growing political implications, against a European domination concerning which no other form of protest was possible.

There is also circumstantial evidence. It consists in the fact that the Ba-Kongo experience seems to fit into a pattern. The anthropologist R. Linton has said that the development of messianism is 'a common enough consequence of relations of domination and submission'.[3] Coming specifically to Africa, the writer of a study on the so-called Ethiopian Christian sects of South Africa stated, as long ago as 1902, the hypothesis that

Ethiopianism is a social movement of a people claiming its rights at the precise moment when it becomes conscious of itself, and of the

---

[1] Van Wing, *Études Bakongo*, pp. 81-82, 128-9 ; Van Wing, 'Le Kibangisme vu par un témoin', p. 565.
[2] Van Wing, *op. cit.*, pp. 583-4 ; Balandier, *Sociologie actuelle*, p. 427 ; Andersson, *Messianic Popular Movements*, pp. 231-2.
[3] Quoted in Balandier, *Sociologie actuelle*, p. 495.

oppression of which it is the object on the part of a foreign government. [It] is caused: by the restrictive laws of English native legislation; by the ill-will of some Whites; by the mistakes and the lack of
flexibility and of preaching skill on the part of several missionaries.[1]

Examining this same South African theme fifty years later, Dr.
Sundkler concludes that race discrimination in Church and
State and especially in the Government's land and labour
policy, the whole of which constitutes an oppressive European
domination, has caused the rise of the African Separatist sects.[2]
Balandier, taking cognisance of the spread of sects into Central
and East Africa, makes a larger claim.

Such a distribution shows that the Negro Churches coincide in
large measure with the domain of the Bantu; which could be linked,
according to a widely held pre-conception, to a lesser resistance of
the socio-cultural systems of the Bantu. But it is, rather, proper to
insist on the fact that this distribution corresponds to the regions
where Christianization was the most intensive, where racial
discrimination was the most marked—between the Cape and the
River Congo—or the modern economy the most sensitive in virtue
of the position soon occupied by mineral extraction. It is therefore a
question of a zone where the factors of social transformation are
most numerous and most active, of a zone where the situation of the
dominated is most acutely felt.[3]

Exciting though this hypothesis is, it should be said that it
has yet to be translated from the realm of persuasive hypothesis
to proven explanation. But with the case of the Ba-Kongo
more narrowly in mind, it may be concluded that the prophet
movements, in the twenties and thirties, were, amongst other
things, certainly a protest against European domination. But
lest this conclusion may seem too exclusively to rationalize a
religious phenomenon, it will be well to quote the penetrating
comment of Banton. To that comment it is worth adding that
the Ba-Kongo in the twenties and thirties were basically still
living in the bush and their experience even of lay Europeans
would have been of people who usually professed, or for form's
sake appeared to profess, Christianity.

[1] Quoted in Balandier, *Sociologie actuelle,*, p. 417.
[2] Bengt Sundkler, *Bantu Prophets in South Africa* (London, Oxford University
Press, second edition 1961), pp. 32-37 especially.
[3] Balandier, *Sociologie actuelle*, p. 419.

There seem to be more fundamental factors on the cultural and intellectual planes which explain the priority of changes in the religious sphere. Religious beliefs provide an answer to the question all people ask: 'How did we get this way?' For colonial peoples this can be an acute problem; why should the Europeans be so powerful? What had they done to deserve the machines and other goods that outclassed anything the Africans had ever conceived of? Because, in traditional African belief, the spirit world is usually regarded as controlling human fortune, it was logical for the Africans to suspect that the secret of the white man's power lay in his religion. They had received *their* messiah. If only the Africans were to have theirs too, they would soon be on an equal footing with the Whites.[1]

If protest is the predominant characteristic of the Congo prophet movement, it is also to be seen as a notable synthesis. At one level there was no conflict between the traditional notion of *Nzambi* and the Christian idea of God—both are monotheistic. But the 'prophetic' (one can only speak in the most general terms) conception inherits the Christian rather than the traditional notion, for God is conceived of as accessible, concerned with the world of men, and to be worshipped. There is, again, an interesting synthesis in the idea of a Messiah or Saviour. Traditional religion had a strong belief in the continued and benevolent potency of the original tribal ancestors who were held to inhabit some of the *nkisi* and in that way to be supernatural agents of good for the tribe. In the prophetic belief, in so far as it was in Christ as the Messiah, the origin is clearly in orthodox Christianity: in so far as Kimbangu, or any other prophet, is looked to as the coming Messiah, there is something of a synthesis between the old and the new. In regard to the supremely important role accorded to the Holy Spirit in the prophet movement, there is an obvious derivation in Christian doctrine, but behind that is the traditional belief in a world ruled by spirits—'force-beings' in Tempels' terminology. Prohibitions played a central role in traditional religion, in Christianity and, as a blend of the two, in prophetic religion, whilst Balandier cites the case of one congregation—there could well be many others—in which the pagan annual festival commemorating the ancestors became in prophetic religion associated with All Saints' Day.[2] Again—though this analysis is in no way exhaustive—there is the obvious parallel between

[1] Banton, 'African Prophets', p. 51.   [2] Balandier, *Sociologie actuelle*, pp. 474-5.

initiation rites and the baptism both into the Christian faith and into a prophetic sect. As a generalization, it is evident that, both in the teaching of Kimbangu himself, and still more in the later forms of the movement, the Old Testament was a particular source of inspiration, as portraying a world not too dissimilar to that of traditional Ba-Kongo society.[1]

Finally, the Congo prophet movements were, for their followers, commonly some sort of synthesis at the personal level. What they had entered into was a lively personal involvement in a religion which offered a reassuring familiarity in its reliance on traditional religion, and a convincing answer, in its appropriations from Christianity, to the problems of living in a changing world. Moreover, common membership of a prophetic sect would give a comforting sense of membership of a group. As J. V. Taylor and Dorothea Lehmann have put it, writing of the *kitawala* member on the Rhodesian copper belt :

He is already one of a brotherhood which is linked closer together than a clan, and which lives in firmer expectation of a glorious future than any political party or trade union can anticipate.[2]

Finally, the satisfactions which membership of a prophetic sect conferred were such that they could in part be enjoyed in the present. In so far as they could not, their attainment did not, in the view of most Kimbanguists, at least, depend on direct action, but on an apocalyptic event. In relation to law and order, this meant that the prophet movement was much more a safety-valve for tension, than a combustion chamber for explosion.

[1] Balandier, *Sociologie actuelle*, pp. 456-7.
[2] J. V. Taylor and D. Lehmann, *Christians on the Copperbelt* (London, S.C.M. Press, 1961), p. 235.

VIII

WAR

On 10 May 1940 the German Army invaded Belgium; on 27 May the Belgian Army was forced to surrender. Until this fateful early summer of 1940 the effect of the Second World War on the Congo had been little more than somewhat to disturb its pattern of overseas trade, but with the resolve of the Belgian Government-in-exile to carry on the fight, and with Governor-General Ryckmans' alignment of the Congo on the Allied side, the Congo was at war.

Militarily, the Congo's contribution was to expand the *Force publique* by calling up reserves and by new recruitment, and to make contingents of the *Force* available to the Allies. One such contingent had a fighting role in the Abyssinian campaign against Italy, but the units sent outside the Congo seem otherwise to have been mainly deployed in garrison and support duties in West Africa and the Middle East. That their direct part in the war was no greater was hardly their fault, but the Belgian concern to keep an army in the field against the Axis powers and thus to be visibly a part of the Allied war effort did exact a price in the Congo itself. After all, an immediate implication of the German occupation of Belgium was the ending of all recruitment for the Congo in the mother-country and the loss of most of those who chanced to be on home leave in May 1940. The *Force publique* could therefore be expanded only from the Congo's own resources, and this was especially serious in its effects on the static pool of administrators, doctors, and so on, from amongst whom some of the best were taken.

This shortage of manpower was to have its own repercussions, but even more serious was all that followed from the tremendous economic expansion of the war years, far and away the Congo's most significant contribution to the war effort. 'Our work must pay for our defence', said Ryckmans and, through a series of commercial and financial agreements with the Allies, Ryckmans' slogan was given reality.[1] Economic mobilization appears to have begun in the autumn of 1940, when the first Anglo-Belgian agreement was concluded, but the really strong pressure on the Congo to produce, produce and produce seems to have resulted from the entry of Japan into the war, the fall of Malaya, and the ensuing shortage of such necessities as tin and rubber. Certainly there was a steep rise in the production of both these commodities, tin production rising from 2,750 *tonnes* in 1939 to as much as 17,300 *tonnes* in 1945, and rubber from 1,142 *tonnes* in 1939 to 11,337 in 1944, the peak year. But there was a major increase in almost all mineral production over the 1939–45 period—a virtual doubling in the case of zinc, cassiterite and coal, and a one-third increase in copper. Katanga also had reserves of uranium, and the Congo in fact enjoys the ambiguous distinction of having provided this essential ingredient of the first atomic bomb. In the field of natural products the growth in the production of major commodities was nowhere as marked as with rubber, but there were substantial increases in palm oil and timber production—from 89,947 to 144,271 *tonnes* in the former case and from 75,000 to 175,000 in the latter.[2] Related to this growth in a production principally geared to export was a necessary increase in farming for the internal Congo market. The workers of the expanding towns and mineral centres all had to be fed.

Enough has been said to demonstrate that the economic achievement of the Belgian Congo during the war was a considerable one and her role in providing significant quantities of strategic materials for the Allies was important in the broader context of the fortunes of Europe and the world as a whole. But the concern of this study is primarily with the Congo itself, where the effects of these wartime exertions were felt at all levels of society. It has already been argued (pp. 78–82 above)

[1] *Rapport de la mission sénatoriale au Congo, 1947* (Brussels, 1947), E. de Bruyne, 'L'Économie congolaise', pp. 189-90.

[2] Ibid., pp. 191-2. M. de Bruyne's figures are taken in part from the *annexes* to the Vice-Governor-General's address to the *Conseil de gouvernement*, 1947, and in part from the *Bulletin de la banque du Congo belge*, July–August 1947. The author points to discrepancies between the two sources, mostly relatively small, but there is a remarkable difference between the two as regards tin production in 1945, the Government figure being much less at 8,667 *tonnes*. Such a discrepancy must presumably be due to differing classifications of tin in the later stages of processing.

Plate V

Patrice Lumumba

Plate VI

(*a*) Leopoldville: the business quarter and Boulevard Albert

(*b*) On the Congo River

Plate VII

School

Plate VIII

Church of the Disciples of Christ Congo Mission at Coquilhatville

that the administrative reforms of 1933 reduced both the quality
and the quantity of the contacts between the *service territorial*
and the African. Certainly the extreme rigour of the amalgamation of *territoires* had been relaxed to the extent that
the number of *territoires* had risen slightly to 117. It can also be
argued that the administrative burden was reduced, and
contact with traditional authorities rendered more manageable
and effective by the further progress, between 1939 and 1950, .
of the *secteur* policy; in that period the number of administrative
units was reduced from 1,453 to 993, the 383 *secteurs* and 1,070
chefferies of 1939 having given place to 517 *secteurs* and 476
chefferies (the process was particularly marked in Leopoldville
and Kasai provinces).[1] But against this must be reckoned the
decline in the numerical strength of the administrative *cadre*
from 1940 onwards, and the substitution of temporary officers
who, for the most part, in the opinion of one authority, 'shone
neither by their moral qualities nor, especially, by their
intellectual qualities'.[2] Furthermore the inevitable decline
in efficiency of men too long resident in the tropics must also be
reckoned with.

With this deficiency in numbers must be coupled the overburdening of those who remained. As the war progressed,
administrators necessarily became a part of the machinery for
the rationing of scarce commodities like petrol and tyres,
but the greatest single cause of their overwork was the necessity
of a policy of production. Its pervasive dominance, everywhere attested, is made clear in the report covering the war
years in the Colony. 'Since 1940 the Administration has had
above all the economic aim of production: it has adopted
economic programmes to the circumstances of war and has
provoked the growth of native resources to the maximum.'[3]
'All the black population,' says Van Wing, 'has been
mobilized to produce the maximum possible as fast as
possible.'[4]

It has been seen (in Chapter IV) that as long before as
1917 the principle that Congo Africans should be obliged

---

[1] Gille, 'Politique indigène', p. 730.
[2] G. Malengreau, 'Le Congo à la croisée des chemins', p. 8. See also A. Rubbens,
'La Relève', *Dettes de guerre*, p. 193.
[3] *Rapport annuel*, 1939-44, p. 11.
[4] J. Van Wing, 'La Situation actuelle des populations congolaises', *Bulletin des
séances de l'I.R.C.B.*, XVI, 3, 1945, p. 584.

to work in their own immediate interests had been given legislative sanction, and that this principle had received a more developed expression in the important decree of 5 December 1933. The essence of the relevant part of that decree was that a male African living in customary society could be obliged to devote a total of sixty days a year to paid and unpaid work of importance to his local community.

In the category of unpaid work the maintenance of roads of local importance and the production of food or cash crops were the major obligations. Any income accruing from the sale of crops, it should be noted, was exclusively the producer's. In the category of compulsory paid labour was labour devoted to the construction and maintenance of roads of general importance and of rest-houses. Constraint was justified on the grounds that the activities concerned were either socially desirable or had an educative value. It has also been seen that the policy of compulsory cultivation—along with the 1933 administrative reforms generally—began to be implemented on a significant scale in the mid-thirties (see Chapter IV), that is to say, appreciably before the war, and that the operation of *culture obligatoire* was already causing some disquiet.

What had been writ small in the later thirties was to be writ large in the war years—especially, it would seem, from 1942 onwards. The production of native agriculture was augmented by more intensive application of the 1933 decree—clearly production is production even if imposed *à titre éducatif*— and by a number of further legislative enactments geared specifically to wartime requirements, so that by 1944 the maximum of obligatory labour appears to have been increased to 120 days. To the administration of this policy of production the remaining administrators had evidently to devote an increasing proportion of their time. Working in collaboration with officers of the agriculture service and, at the grass roots level, through African *moniteurs agricoles* and the chiefs, lands to be cultivated had to be marked out, the harvesting of such natural products as wild rubber arranged for, and any necessary preparation of a raw product for the market likewise seen to. On the face of things production was but one among several of the administrator's preoccupations, not therefore to be singled out as of excessive importance to him. But there are indications that during the war years administrators tended to be judged by

the productivity of their *territoires*,[1] whilst doubts that the policy
of production might be bearing too heavily on the peasant in the
bush would often be stilled by the conviction that it was
supremely necessary to defeat Nazi Germany.[2] This being so,
the tendency was inevitably to countenance the higher rather
than the lower estimate of what could be achieved in the
mandatory 120 days, and the same considerations caused the
tribunaux de police to become principally significant for their role
in enforcing the policy of production.[3]

Whilst the judicial system became to that extent a positive
part of the apparatus of production, preoccupation of the
understaffed administration with production resulted in serious
harm to the system of native courts simply through inadequate
supervision. Enough has been said about the fragility of many
of these courts, especially if they pertained to other than the
natural unit of the *chefferie*, and of their need of close nurturing.
Whilst Grévisse could write of a particular *administrateur
territorial*, who rarely presided at the *tribunal de territoire*, but
whose patient presence at numerous sittings successfully led
to the true nature of custom being brought out and the guilty
substantially judging themselves in the light of it,[4] he was
basically concerned to point out that this sort of situation was
exceptional, and that the necessary supervision was usually
lacking. Too common, indeed, must have been the situations
harshly described in these terms:

At the lower level, the *tribunaux de chefferie*, a corrupt *greffier* (clerk to
the court) composes in honour of his always overburdened administrator a beautifully written account, concise and convincing, without the least relationship to the depositions of suborned witnesses nor
to the iniquitous sentence pronounced by a venal judge. . . .

At the *tribunal de territoire*, the *administrateur territorial*, on the point
of transfer, not knowing the language of the proceedings, deals with
his correspondence whilst one of the assessors reports on the case in
an elliptical and familiar *lingua franca*. Provided that the case has
been correctly presented to him, the president judges in equity. He
has no time to found his sentence on a vanishing custom in which no

---

[1] See, e.g. 'P.G.', 'L'Administration des indigènes', *Dettes de guerre*, p. 29,
and L. Mottoulle, 'Pour la protection et l'amélioration des conditions d'existence
des populations rurales du Congo belge', ibid., p. 64.

[2] A. Rubbens, 'La Grande pitié du paysan indigène', op. cit., p. 49.

[3] Idem, 'Évolution', op. cit., p. 25.   [4] Grévisse, *Juridictions indigènes*, p. 44.

doctrine nor jurisprudence can guide him. . . . Moreover, District and Province are awaiting Table A and Report B.[1]

In a word, the consequence of wartime conditions in general, and of the policy of production in particular, was that administrators were in even less of a position to give adequate attention to all facets of their work than they had been immediately before the war—when the larger *territoires* were in existence, and the policy of *culture obligatoire* in process of extension from the mid-thirties onwards. What usually suffered were the varied expressions of paternal (in the best sense of the word) care for 'their' Africans.[2] Nor did the Congo Administration wish to deny that contact suffered, as official laments testify.[3]

Whilst one effect of the war was to overburden the *service territorial* and distract it from its true task, the effect on the structure of indirect rule was no less serious. M. A. Rubbens, the editor of *Dettes de guerre*, describes it in this way:

The *circonscription indigène* has lost all stability. The mistaken decree of 1933 is the root cause, but the vagaries of regrouping [into *secteurs*], the break-up of custom, the decrepitude of the chiefs, and especially the employment of these frail institutions in tasks exceeding their strength, has completed the dislocation of these pseudo-traditional creations.[4]

Maron, whose criticisms of the implementation of the 1933 decree in the pre-war years have already been seen, sees wartime conditions as carrying the undesirable a stage farther.

The fact that the decree of 1933 has transformed the native chief into an official executor of the orders of the Administration, that a later legislative ordinance, that of 3 June 1942, has given native courts competence in regard to compulsory tasks and particularly in regard to export crops and harvesting, has allowed the territorial authorities

---

[1] 'P.G.' 'L'État de nos juridictions', *Dettes de guerre*, p. 32.

[2] See, e.g., G. L. Ballegeer, cited in *Dettes de guerre*, pp. 12-13. This, essentially, is the 'debt' which the colonial power had contracted as a result of the wartime, and to a lesser extent pre-war distortions of native policy. The colonials who thought along these lines felt so strongly about the question that they discussed it in the columns of the Elisabethville newspaper, *L'Essor du Congo*, during 1944-5. *Dettes de guerre* is therefore an appropriate title for the book in which the correspondence appears in an edited form. I have attached a good deal of importance to the policy criticisms contained in it as coming from men with considerable knowledge—which though it related especially, did not relate exclusively to Katanga—and who evidently felt so strongly that they went to the lengths of publicizing their views in open forum.

[3] *Rapport annuel*, 1939-44, p. 11.

[4] A. Rubbens, 'Évolution', *Dettes de guerre*, p. 25.

to free themselves from a part of their task by placing it on the shoulders of the chiefs. It was necessary to decrease the number of subordinate authorities and that is what has been done. It was also necessary, in order to have more control over them, after having replaced *chefferies* by *secteurs*, to get rid of insufficiently amenable customary chiefs and replace them with auxiliaries removable at will.[1]

Grévisse, for his part, had referred to the wartime period, as well as to the year before 1939, in his observations (pp. 68-69) about the facile way in which *secteurs* had too often been constituted for administrative convenience.

Altogether these are persuasive analyses. Clearly a *secteur* created for such reasons of expediency, and almost certainly including a varying customary law, would present the new chief and his council with a difficult enough task, even assuming his own competence and good intentions, and effective administrative supervision. An additional factor was that, in practice, *secteurs* seem sometimes to have been created because the population of existing *circonscriptions* had declined to the point of patent unviability, since most of the adult males had emigrated to the towns and centres; this imbalance in age and sex constituted a serious threat to the successful administration of the new *secteur*.[2] It certainly seems that many chiefs simply were not up to their prescribed task as the administrative link between the European administration and the tribal African.

This could be seen in the most important field of all, that of the *tribunaux indigènes*. One harsh verdict on their operation has been noted. Rubbens goes on to talk of the native courts as having 'lost all prestige, as much by the uncertainty of the law applied in them as by the dawdling procedure and competitive venality of judges and *greffiers*'[3] whilst Grévisse's whole lament in *La Grande pitié des juridictions indigènes* is of the maloperation of too many native courts.

The official view, however, was that though their operation was by no means perfect, it was mainly owing to them that the African population as a whole remained in good heart.[4] To the extent, however, that traditional authorities were inadequate for their administrative task—and a number doubtless were

[1] Maron, 'Le Décret du 5 décembre 1933', p. 116.
[2] Gille, 'Politique indigène', pp. 730-1.
[3] Rubbens, 'L'Ébranlement de la société indigène', *Dettes de guerre*, p. 25.
[4] *Rapport annuel*, 1939-44, p. 24.

adequate—the whole system of indirect rule was weakened. But when to the performance of purely administrative tasks was added compulsory cultivation, compulsory harvesting of rubber or copal, or compulsory work on road-maintenance, then the situation in the case of a bad or inadequate chief would become yet more disturbing. Rubbens claims to be voicing widely held experience when he writes:

Those who work in the native *milieu* know that too often the chiefs have neither the courage to represent to their administrators the growing burdens on their subjects which result from the accumulation of tasks, nor the strength to apportion them equitably and enforce their acceptance. Incompetent figureheads, whose true place would be in a museum of native life, they become a target for the hostility of their better subjects in making known, without understanding them, commands always more overwhelming without having the strength to enforce them.[1]

The effect of the policy of production in particular, and the whole wartime comportment of the Administration and of the colonial power in general, on the African living in the Bush can be sampled at various levels. At the level of a diminished contact between the administrator and the ordinary African, which has already been seen to have been one of the great concerns of the contributors to *Dettes de guerre*, there might and often did arise in the case of the African a feeling of abandonment. 'P.G.' attests how the Africans in the bush

feel themselves at the mercy of chiefs, of the *tribunaux indigènes*, subjected to the exactions of judges, to the swindling of *greffiers*, of policemen, of messengers, of *moniteurs* . . . who batten on them like leeches to extract from them their last farthing. If, as formerly, they could turn to their white man! How would they dare if this white man himself employs these chiefs, these judges, these *greffiers*, who follow him everywhere to enforce by fines and imprisonment of *corvées* and the still greater demands of the war effort? How would they even think of having recourse to this white man?[2]

Grévisse, for his part, speaks of

this crowd of unfortunates who swarm in front of the rest-houses. 'Give me a note to recommend me to the court of a neighbouring *chefferie* and show the judges that I am not abandoned. Give me a

[1] Rubbens, 'La Grande pitié du paysan indigène', *Dettes de guerre*, pp. 46-47.
[2] 'P.G.', 'La Carence des tribunaux indigènes', *Dettes de guerre*, pp. 30-31.

word of introduction to the neighbouring *chef de poste*', an elderly
African, who had travelled a hundred kilometres to find him, said
to an administrator. 'But why do you want this introduction? The
chef de poste will receive you, will listen to you, will understand you
and will help you to obtain justice.'—'You believe that, you do, but
on several occasions I have made the journey in vain. I presented
myself for the first time and was sentenced on the pretext that I was
dreaming of starting a palaver before having completed the prescribed work on my farm. I returned there later and the white
man told me that he did not wish to concern himself with my case
because it was a matter of *musendji* [this term means that which
pertains to a man still living in traditional society and is usually
used pejoratively, with the flavour of primitive about it].[1]

Some will see such an episode, portrayed by Grévisse as
frequent, as nothing more than a tenacious African concern to
enlist the support of a (powerful) European, but if paternalism
had the sort of meaningful psychological basis that has already
been argued for it, then episodes like this involved a real
sense of deprivation. Given the frequent inability or unreadiness of administrators themselves to give time to their
people's difficulties and disputes, and the deficient supervision
of the native court system and of the chiefs, there must too often
have been just such a distancing between the administrator and
the ordinary African, and a related alienation of the administered from their invested chiefs. A similar distancing must
also have resulted when medical facilities became less readily
available as the shortage of doctors increased.

The most obvious impact of the production policy on the
African in the village was that it made him work much harder
than he was wont to work. There was, behind the policies of
the colonial powers, the assumption that it was a good and
necessary thing for the African to work, and direct or indirect
pressure, especially the imposition of a tax obligation, was
used to make him do so. In the case of wartime Congo, however, it is clear that these pressures were much greater than was
on any reckoning desirable. The 120-day annual maximum may
be rationalized as little more than two days of the working week.
But quite apart from the fact that the notion of a 'working week',
of work beyond that necessary for subsistence, was still strange,
the allotted stint, in hectares or kilograms, was often not

[1] Grévisse, *Juridictions indigènes*, p. 75. See also Gille, 'Politique indigène', p. 731.

completed within the prescribed 120 days.[1] It was not so much that the administrator was so susceptible to the demands of production as to overestimate what could be done, though this must frequently have happened, as that the work was performed reluctantly and therefore slowly,[2] whilst poor organization of work tasks meant that they took longer than they should have taken. A failure to take account of a deficiency of men in a village, for example, would mean that the ability to make new clearings in the forest for cultivation—the men's work —was overestimated; through administrative rigidity a whole village might trek for miles to harvest wild rubber, and be away for weeks, whilst in their own village was an abundant cotton crop;[3] a prescribed length of road would take longer than estimated to build because the work could not be properly supervised. With sheer overburdening was often coupled unfairness, consisting principally in the inequitable distribution of work by a bad or inadequate chief but also, for instance, in the command to grow a particular cash crop, only for it to be discovered that the harvested product could find no purchaser. Mottoulle's description of the operation of the system seems all too likely. The need of an enhanced production suddenly becomes more acute—

The Administration wakes up; orders fall in torrents right down to the native chief who, fearful of appearing the accomplice of his subjects' inertia, does not dare to make clear to the authorities the excessive obligations weighing upon his community and, through ignorance or stupidity, at random or unjustly, divides up the work; the villager, who sees himself obliged to double or triple the extent of his ordinary plot, has neither the time nor the strength to open up a new clearing: his land is exhausted and eroded; his harvest is mediocre and does not correspond to his considerable but unsystematic work; he is blamed by the Administration which has had neither the time nor the means to guide and direct him; he has seen laid down as the common task so many *ares* of cotton or of groundnuts, so many kilograms of palm produce or of rubber, and without preliminary inquiry about his physical condition, the age distribution in the

---

[1] Rubbens goes further: 'It is . . . certain that no native in the Congo has, in fact, succeeded in doing so.' ('La Grande pitié du paysan indigène', *Dettes de guerre*, p. 47.)

[2] Ibid.

[3] An instance given by 'P.G.', 'L'Administration des indigènes', *Dettes de guerre*, p. 30.

community, his status (with a married man it is the women who do the work), the fertility of the soil, about the distance away from the settlements of the palm trees or wild rubber creepers. . . .

It is scarcely surprising that such a situation should often find a radical solution—migration. Mottoulle, in fact, goes on to portray a cyclical pattern:

Finally the brave villager reckons that it will be best for him to flee from the unbearable life of the rural community where, moreover, one is sad, where the dances are no more; he flees to the industrial cities and the *centres extra-coutumier*, thus increasing still more the weight of *corvées* on those who remain who, they also, will go [eventually]. Such is the cycle culminating in the flight of the rural population to the anarchic environment of the cities.[1]

At one level, then, a result of the war and the policy of production was to encourage emigration from the villages to the towns. To some extent this can be measured, though census figures relating to this period, drawn up on the basis of information supplied when a man came to pay his tax, must be seen for the approximations that they are. Between 1939 and 1944 the *population coutumière* dropped from 9,356,502 to 8,896,721, a decrease of about 4½ per cent. (By the end of 1946, however, it had climbed back to 9,097,892.)[2]

These brute figures do not indicate a catastrophic decline, but when estimates from other sources for individual regions are considered the picture could sometimes be alarming. For instance, between 1940 and 1945 there was a 23 per cent. decrease in the number of cotton-cultivators in the COTONCO (a cotton-purchasing company) zone in Lomami-Kasai, which was attributed to migration to the towns.[3] Between 1939 or 1940 and 1944 the population of the *territoire* of Befale, in Équateur, fell from 53,000 to 43,000, whilst in the *territoire* of Lodja, in Kasai, where there were in 1940 20,000 peasant farmers, by 1943 only 16,000 remained. In another area close to the B.C.K. railway there was a decline in the number of

---

[1] L. Mottoulle, 'Pour la protection et l'amélioration des conditions d'existence des populations rurales du Congo belge', *Dettes de guerre*, pp. 63-64.

[2] *Congrès colonial national*, 6th Session, 1947 (Éditions Techniques et Scientifiques, 1948); L. Mottoulle, 'Rapport sur la démographie', p. 97, Tableau 1.

[3] G. Malengreau, *Vers un paysannat indigène: les lotissements agricoles au Congo belge* (Brussels, I.R.C.B., 1949), pp. 8-9.

farmers from 20,737 to 15,729 between 1940 and 1944.[1] Certainly over the colony as a whole the drop in the male population of the rural areas was more pronounced than the general decline—as one would expect. The actual decrease was from 2,572,667 in 1939 to 2,403,218 in 1944, a decline of about 6½ per cent., and it was, of course, the healthy youths and younger men who tended to leave the village—Doucy gives a figure of 19·23 per cent. for able-bodied adult males in wage employment in 1940.[2] Looked at in another way, in 1939, 441,634 out of a total of 3,014,301 men, about one-seventh, lived outside the sway of custom: in 1944 the dwellers in the towns were 625,677 out of 3,025,895; that is, about one-fifth.[3]

It is worth remembering that the 1925 Native Labour Commission had recommended that only 10 per cent. of the adult *able-bodied* males should be allowed to work outside the village, and of these one-half should be no farther than two days' journey (a further 15 per cent. could be employed by European enterprises provided they continued to live in their villages). Even if one accepts as reasonable the subsequent official acceptance of 25 per cent. of *all* adult men, an indeterminate proportion of whom were to be working 'locally', then it is, on the figures, likely that some areas were exceeding what was reasonable. In fact, no one disputed that this was happening.

As far as the social pathology of customary life is concerned, it is perhaps even more important to see what happened to the ratio of women to men. On the general statistics it appears satisfactory (a ratio of 1–1·20 women to 1 man being regarded as demographically desirable),[4] moving from 1·18 to 1 in 1939 to 1·14 to 1 in 1944.[5] But it is interesting to see that by 1947, in the case of two provinces, Leopoldville and Katanga, the ratio was 1·27 and 1·25 to 1 respectively,[6] whilst in a much more accurate census carried out by FORÉAMI in six *secteurs* of Leopoldville province, in connection with a health programme, the 1939 ratio was 1·28 to 1 and rose to 1·30 to 1 in

[1] A. Rubbens, 'La Grande pitié du paysan indigène', *Dettes de guerre*, p. 45. See also J. Van Wing, 'La Situation actuelle', p. 585. 'I know *de visu* and from witnesses worthy of credence that in many regions a good number of villages scarcely contain any young people.'

[2] A. Doucy, 'Politique indigène', *Livre blanc* (Brussels, A.R.S.O.M., 1962), I, p. 360.

[3] L. Mottoulle, *Rapport sur la démographie*, p. 97, Tableau 1.

[4] Ibid., p. 93.   [5] Ibid., p. 97, Tableau 1.   [6] Ibid., p. 98, Tableau 2.

1944.[1] In short there is some sort of statistical evidence of an overall drop in the rural population during the war years, and of a more pronounced general drop in the rural male population. Whilst these decreases were not, over the colony as a whole, catastrophic, there is pretty clear evidence that in some areas there was a serious decline in the male population and to a level unacceptable by criteria which had earlier been admitted, and, as a consequence in these same areas, an undesirable preponderance of women over men. Finally there must be a presumption that the major cause of these movements in the rural population was the varying, burdensome implications of the wartime policy of production.

At the psychological level, an assessment of the impact of the wartime policy on the rural African population must be more impressionistic. But at least it can be said that because in almost all areas a heavy burden of labour was imposed; because in some areas that burden was left to be shouldered by a declining number of effectives; because the delicate balance of the community by sex and age-group was being upset, because the chief less and less fulfilled his office as father of his people; because cloth, blankets, pots and most other things not produced in the village became scarce and dear; because the paternalism of the administrator was less often seen and medicines were less easily available, for all these reasons, there would often be a presiding sense of oppression, of weariness, and of gloom. As Governor-General Ryckmans put this last important point, in a phrase which also testified to the migration from the villages, 'At each full moon, the circle of dancers grows smaller'.[2]

This consideration of the impact of the wartime policy of production has necessarily raised the question of the migration from the village to the town—indeed, what has been said so far possibly gives the impression that the forces behind this movement were purely negative. Attention has earlier been given to a notable 'pull' away from the village—the recruiter. However, from about 1930 onwards organized recruiting decreased considerably[3] (though as late as 1947 the Commission

---

[1] Ibid., p. 99, Tableau 3.
[2] Quoted in P. Joye and R. Lewin, *Les Trusts au Congo* (Brussels, Société Populaire d'Éditions, 1961), p. 82.
[3] Denis, *Le Phénomène urbain*, p. 167.

pour la Protection des Indigènes noted that recruiters were still occasionally paying a gratuity to chiefs who gave them particular help[1]), a change which was doubtless partly due in the short run to the slump and in the longer run to the increasing adoption by the big firms of the labour-stabilization policy. Recruitment therefore ceased to be a major influence pulling men away from the village, save in the indirect sense that particular paths of migration opened up earlier on would continue to attract succeeding generations, drawn on in their turn by tales told by men returning to their village for visits. From the late thirties or early forties onwards this particular influence seems to shade off into a kind of folk-image of the town as the great source of wealth and opportunity.

A Congolese writer portrays it in this way. The hero of his story is fascinated by the road which passes through his village and which then disappears from sight behind a hill:

It is not just any sort of road. It is a question of the road which leads to Leopoldville. Leopoldville . . . this name alone in Fwala's ear has a kind of magic resonance which conjures up before his eyes a kind of indefinable, gilded existence. Ah! the pain of the mysterious! When will it be given him to penetrate it? Fwala has already seen many men, some on foot, others perched on the tops of laden lorries, joyfully going to Leopoldville. Why should he not therefore also go? . . . The next day, in the morning twilight, Mama Anna calls her son. But it is in vain. For furtively, during the night, a little bundle under his arm, Fwala has set out along this irresistible road. [2]

It may well be that the town began to be seriously attractive only as the conditions of life in the bush began to decline— as they did during the war. But this said, there is a good deal of evidence from tropical Africa in general and the Congo in particular that the town had definite and positive attractions. For instance, Richelle, a social psychologist, in a study of urbanization in Elisabethville, found amongst his informants a general insistence not only on the way in which the Administration made life in the village difficult, but also on the attraction of the town as the place where education, or better education, could be had for one's children and oneself, where

---

[1] Report of C.P.I., 1947, *Bulletin officiel*, 1947, I, pp. 822-3.
[2] J. Lutumba, 'Histoire de Fwala', *Présence congolaise*, 21 December 1957, quoted in Denis, *Le Phénomène urbain*, p. 168.

medical care was available, and where one could earn money—though Richelle is careful not to accept avowed motives as necessarily a sufficient explanation of migration to the town.[1] Denis, in his more general study of urbanization in the Congo and Central Africa, likewise couples with the negative factor of repulsion a range of attractions similar to those enumerated by Richelle.[2] It is hardly necessary to add that the considerable growth of industry during the war years postulated a voracious appetite for labour. No new arrival from the bush needed ever to lack work.

The foregoing analysis of the effects of World War II in the Congo, when studied in the context of the process of change already in motion, presents the war as essentially a catalyst. What it did was to give urgent reinforcement to the whole process of economic and social change. The existing predominance of European industry, private and para-statal, was strengthened and its sway extended: the nascent movement to bring the Congo peasant into the cycle of production for the market really got under way. The effect of both these forces was further to weaken an only slowly evolving customary society and, in particular, further to undermine traditional authorities. At the same time the necessities of wartime led to a weakening of that European tutelage which was the more necessary in a period of rapid change.

By contrast, the war did nothing to bring about political change. Administrative decentralization to Leopoldville there had to be, for the Belgian Government in exile had not the means to exercise centralized control, but the war did not result in the birth of political hopes or of political life. With the end of hostilities the old pattern of colonial government was re-imposed—though in 1947 an attempt was made to systematize wartime decentralization to Leopoldville—but with no suggestion of any place for political life. With one exception, political aspirations do not seem to have dawned to any extent amongst the Congolese themselves. The exception was that many adherents of Simon Mpadi's *Mission des noirs*, or 'khaki movement' (see pp. 133-4 above) had the 'political' hope that Germany would be victorious in the conflict. Here, clearly, is a

[1] Richelle, *Aspects psychologiques de l'acculturation, passim* and especially pp. 147-59, 169. Richelle's field-work was done in 1957-8, but the experience of his informants went back over a varying number of years.

[2] Denis, *Le Phénomène urbain*, pp. 155-73.

perpetuation in a more emphatic form of the role of political protest in Kimbanguism.[1] But with this exception, Belgium, preoccupied with her own recovery, was not subject to the first surgings of nationalism which, as one of the harvests of war, other colonial powers had to face in 1945.

[1] Andersson, *Messianic Popular Movements*, p. 199; Balandier, *Sociologie actuelle,* pp. 462-3.

IX

AFRICAN ADMINISTRATION BETWEEN
1945 AND THE LATE 1950's:
SETTLERS AND THEIR INFLUENCE

THE economic and administrative policies of the war years
were essentially developments of existing practice rather than
new departures; continuity is also the hallmark of the post-war
period. As stimuli, the economic demands of war were
succeeded by the ravages suffered by Belgium during hostilities
and the need to make them good, and the high world demand
for many of the raw materials which the Congo could supply.
A continuation of the economy along wartime lines was therefore likely. Some lessening of effort there was, but it related
to products such as wild rubber—the compulsory harvesting
of which was stopped on the day the Japanese war ended—
for which in peacetime there was little demand. But minerals,
especially copper, and some natural products, were at a
premium by reason of their export and foreign exchange value,
and during the immediate post-war period Belgium stood to
gain an appreciable improvement in her foreign exchange
position by the maximum exploitation of these resources.

Again, the whole process of increasing the gross product of
the Congo demanded acceleration and not slackening. This was
a goal to which both the varied business interests active in the
Congo and those, like Ryckmans, who believed that only thus
could the poverty of the masses be alleviated, could subscribe.
'The Congo' he said, 'produces little because she is poor: she is
poor because she produces little.' The Congo, too, was unique
amongst the colonies of the European powers during the post-
war period in that her own (economic) exertions were the only
source of capital investment. From 1950 onwards Belgium
did contribute substantially to the economic development of

Ruanda-Urundi, but there was no contribution to Congo economic development, no equivalent to the British Colonial Development and Welfare Fund, still less to France's very considerable colonial effort. The Congo therefore had to raise money for development either from her own resources or, by an implicit appeal to the strength of the Congo economy, on the world money market.[1] To complete the catalogue of pressures impelling the Congo to produce more and more was the simple and understandable concern of the multifarious European business interests in the Congo—and we have noticed the exceptional importance in the Congolese economy of private commerce and industry—to make money.

Post-war Belgium economic policy in the Congo was crystallized in the Ten-Year Plan, adopted in 1948. This envisaged the expenditure over the period of some £183 million (with an equivalent expenditure in the private sector), but whilst the Plan is significant by reason of the sums involved, and in virtue of its being *planned* development over the long term, it is not otherwise a landmark, still less a change of course. The assumptions behind the plan were basically the time-hallowed ones as modified by the traumatic experience of the slump—a continued development of the European sector of the economy and of the services necessary for its further expansion, but a simultaneous lessening of the colony's dangerous dependence upon the export market which the slump had so pointedly revealed. This was to be done by the encouragement of an internal market through such means as the encouragement of native agriculture, including the really business-like promotion of the *paysannat indigène* programme. Associated with this purely economic programme, the plan also provided for a large expenditure on education and welfare, not only in the bush but also in the towns.[2]

This being the framework of Belgian policy in the Congo during the post-war period—and economic policy clearly set the pattern for policy as a whole—it will be convenient to follow its working out, first in the rural areas and subsequently its tremendously important urban implications. The five or six years following the war—probably because of the prevalent

---

[1] Stengers, *Combien le Congo a-t-il coûté à la Belgique?*, pp. 359-70.

[2] Pierre de Wigny, *A Ten-Year Plan for the Economic and Social Development of the Belgian Congo* (New York, Belgian Government Information Center, 1950), *passim*.

sense of the need to reconstruct—witnessed a steady flow of comment on Congo affairs from the pens of liberal-minded, constructive critics of the Congo Administration, possibly in part a reaction against a certain tendency on the part of the authorities to propagate a kind of 'Intourist' history, to adapt a term used by one of those critics. Samples from those reports make it quite clear that in this early post-war period what was happening in the villages was essentially what had been experienced during the war. Writing of the situation at the end of 1946, Van Wing, from experience of two provinces— Leopoldville and Equateur—says that 'in general, compulsory labour [*les travaux obligatoires*] continues as in the past', whilst 'the exodus from the rural areas continues at the same pace as during the war'.

An element in this process was the policy of maintaining low prices for native foodstuffs on the urban market, which meant that every young man who wanted to improve his situation, or obtain money for a dowry payment, had to seek work outside his *milieu*. Whereas in 1911 (Van Wing had gone to the Congo in the early years of the century) an African needed to bring to the market only fifteen kilos of *chikwanga* (cassava made up into a kind of cake) to obtain the price of a good loin-cloth, in 1945 he would have to bring seventy or one hundred kilos to procure a cloth of much inferior quality.[1] A magistrate, one of Malengreau's informants, speaking of the same period, indicates in more detail, and in a way reminiscent of *Dettes de guerre*, the way in which life bore too heavily on the African in the bush.

What makes the life of the natives in the Bush unhappy is above all the *corvées*, the multiple and diverse burdens which are imposed upon them and which leave them no respite; the innumerable prescribed obligations and prohibitions, with a severe penalty always attached, which wear them out, the bullying, the pestering by every kind of authority, European as well as traditional, and their subordinates, *moniteurs* or policemen, before whom they are defenceless; the excessive punishments inflicted without discernment by the European *agent*, the *juge de police*, and also by the *tribunal indigène*. These improper annoyances, which in large measure have their origin in our policy of production, inevitably result in the discouragement of the native, in making him live in an atmosphere of insecurity

[1] J. Van Wing, 'Quelques aspects de l'état social des populations indigènes du Congo belge', *Bulletin des séances de l'I.R.C.B.*, XVIII, 2, 1947, pp. 186-8.

M

and uneasiness; they bring him to hate his environment and to flee from it, breaking thereby the bonds, customary and social, which bind him to it and which our civilization has already rendered fragile.'[1]

Malengreau fills in the picture himself, speaking of 'certain villages, gloomy and half-abandoned, where I had formerly received a joyful welcome and attended interminable celebrations', and of how the mass of Africans in the bush 'continue to vegetate in a poverty which would prevent him from being other than miserable if the black man had not been long accustomed to content himself with the absolute minimum.'[2]

The *Commission pour la Protection des Indigènes*, meeting a little later, in 1947, can ring only slight changes on the same theme. 'The native flees from the bush', a man can rarely earn a living by cultivating the soil, and is constantly in fear 'of an unexpected, extra *corvée*, interrupting his normal occupations'. He loses the courage to live, seeing himself 'subject to incessant taxes and obligations'. The chiefs are no longer the fathers and protectors of their people but simply transmit—in an exaggerated form—the orders of the Administration. The *tribunaux indigènes*, being insufficiently guided, do not mete out justice, and not a little part of police activity is concerned with the non-fulfilment of compulsory labour tasks,[3] and infractions of this kind were an important reason why each year some 10 per cent. of the male population was condemned to a term of imprisonment[4]—a staggeringly high percentage.

Two years later Malengreau still discerned too many of the old tendencies at work. This time he was reporting on the first attempts to give full expression to the *paysannat indigène* policy, which had been accepted as desirable back in 1933. Starting in 1942, a number of agricultural resettlement schemes had been initiated whereby peasant cultivators were given land, supervision and advice in the hope that they would develop into prosperous communities and, by example and subsequent

[1] Malengreau, *Le Congo à la croisée des chemins*, pp. 15-16.
[2] Ibid., pp. 11-12.
[3] Report of the C.P.I., 1947, *Bulletin officiel*, 1947, I, pp. 827-45 *passim*. The inadequacy of *chefs de secteur* in the post-war period has been stressed to me in various interviews. For a similar opinion in regard to the Kwango district of Leopoldville province, see J(ean) K(estergat), *André Ryckmans* (Brussels, Charles Dessart, 1961), pp. 110-11.
[4] *Rapport de la mission sénatoriale*; J. Pholien, 'Le Fonctionnement de la justice', p. 68.

extension of the policy, set in train a reinvigoration of the rural areas. But too often, through a mixture of inadequate preparatory work and refuge in authoritarianism, the schemes had not really taken wing, and were kept in being only by a considerable stretching of the sixty days' labour stint prescribed in 1933 and to which, since the war, the Congo had reverted. In one scheme, a purely geometrical division had meant that good and bad land was inequitably shared: more often, settlement had been set up on land over which a near-by tribe claimed rights, and the newcomers, sharing their reluctant hosts' view of land rights rather than that enshrined in colonial legislation—whereby unoccupied land belonged to the State—did no more work than coercion could enforce, fearing that the land and their improvement of it must eventually revert to its rightful owners.

Again, too little thought had sometimes been given to the question of who was to buy the harvested crops. Cotton was the only really good seller, groundnuts, rice and maize were uncertain, whilst manioc and bananas usually rotted for lack of buyers. But at least as important as these various errors was the general reliance on a constraint of doubtful legality. A thriving peasantry could never be built up on a basis of coercion. 'What the native most suffers from today is a lack of liberty!' Nor did the experiment give adequate financial returns to the cultivator. The highest average annual income was about £35 14s. 0d. in the Gandajika scheme, whilst the overall average return was about £14 6s. 0d., and this at a time when an ordinary labourer in the town could command twice as much.[1]

When Van Wing shared his impressions of an extensive journey through the Congo in 1951, the burden of his remarks about customary society was essentially the same as in 1947. They are epitomized both in his title—'Le Congo déraille'—and in his reference to the frequent occasions when he asked town-dwelling Congolese, who bitterly complained of their hunger and their bad living conditions, why they did not return to their villages. They replied,

'Certainly in the village one eats and sleeps better; but there are the *corvées* of Bula Matari, and the constraints of the chiefs and the demands of the elders.' Others added: 'In the village there are no

[1] Malengreau, *Vers un paysannat indigène, passim.*

longer any young people and no longer any pleasures. Here at least one can be happy some days.'[1]

The 1950s, none the less, did see a limited improvement as far as the rural areas were concerned. Certainly migration away from the villages was still endemic, but despite this there was now a steady increase in the rural population such that, from the low point of an estimated 8,896,721 in 1944, it had attained 10,460,000 by 1958. It is reasonable to assume that the eventual augmentation of the *service territorial*, of the medical services and of various other specialist services must have contributed to this improved social health of customary society. (In all the literature already cited on the general condition of customary society in the early post-war years, the continuing paucity of administrators, of doctors, etc., and the way in which they were overburdened, too frequently moved, obliged to spend too much time on office work, was a recurrent theme.)

The mode of recruiting the first emergency replacements for the attenuated administration, which would have been admirable if it had been précis-writers who had been wanted rather than men possessed pre-eminently of character and initiative, may possibly have produced some odd results. (The method adopted was to call together all the applicants to hear a talk on legislation concerning the Belgian Press, of which they were then called upon to write a summary. The results were classified; the first forty were exempted from all training and sent straight out to the Congo, the next forty were entered for the next session of the *École Coloniale*, and the remainder, though they might have had a variety of more relevant abilities, were in effect turned away.[2]) But by the mid-fifties the numerical improvement was considerable. Whereas in 1946 there were fewer than 700 administrators, by 1950 there were 1,062, against an establishment of 1,187, whilst by 1954 the establishment had been increased to 1,370 and appears to have been completely filled.[3] On one view, however, much of the benefit of this increase for native administration in the strict sense of the term was cancelled out by continual growth in the administrator's responsibilities, not least his participation in the

[1] J. Van Wing, 'Le Congo déraille', *Bulletin des séances de l'I.R.C.B.*, XXII, 2, 1959, p. 616.

[2] Malengreau, *Le Congo à la croisée des chemins*, p. 9 n.

[3] P. Quinet, 'Quelques considérations sur les problèmes du service territorial', *Problèmes d'Afrique Centrale*, 1955, I, p. 10.

execution of the Ten-Year Plan.[1] No less an authority than M. Vanhove, an *Inspecteur Royal des Colonies*, asserted early in 1954 than only some 5 per cent. of the activity of an administrator was devoted to native administration in the proper sense. 'Native policy', he said 'is at the point of death.'[2]

Right up to the end of Belgian rule, the element of human, personal contact continued to be squeezed out to a greater or lesser degree, but it does appear that during the fifties Belgian policy could record at least two significant achievements of importance to the life of the rural areas. Firstly, the *paysannat indigène* policy really did begin to produce results. Despite its sometimes unfortunate beginnings, there was enough confidence in the potential merits of the project for it to feature prominently in the Ten-Year Plan. No fewer than 385,000 families were to be settled during the Plan's currency, and as a result of the initial successes this total was raised to 500,000. It is claimed that two of the elements of weakness in the original mode of allocation were avoided. Preliminary inquiries and preparations were much more careful—most of the original allocations had been made by officers of the agricultural service, whose qualifications and experience were purely technical—and the necessity of involving administrative officers in the process was recognized. The vexed question of land rights was to some extent sidestepped, so it is claimed, by appropriating land only in respect of its usufruct, whilst it is likewise asserted that care was taken to see that the new settlers really were volunteers.

If mistakes were still made, they seem to have been substantially fewer, and while the aim of half a million peasant holdings was not actually attained, the results of the venture were none the less impressive. By the end of 1952, 86,418 peasant families had been settled; by 1955, 136,981; and by the end of 1958, 197,155. By the time of independence, over 200,000 peasants with their families, some 8 per cent. of the rural population, had been installed, whilst many others had independently made the transition to peasant producers. That the whole operation was better founded is suggested by the much higher incomes which the holdings were now yielding. Whilst in 1954, in the Uele *paysannats*, where it was apparently the lowest, the average income, including the value of what

[1] Ibid. [2] Ibid.

was consumed by the producer, had only attained £31 6s. 0d. Elsewhere there had been notable increases. Whereas in 1950 the Kasai *paysannats* produced incomes ranging from £3 12s. 0d. to £27 3s. 0d., by 1954–5 the range was £46 9s. 0d. to £121 9s. 0d., and the average £104 4s. 0d. These later figures must, however, be considered in relation not only to the earlier income yields, but also to the fast-rising level of urban wages. In 1954–5 an unskilled labourer, with allowances due to a single man, could command a minimum annual income ranging from about £42 17s. 0d. in Albertville to about £57 17s. 0d. in Leopoldville. It is also relevant to point out that, by an estimate of the reasonable requirements of a family of four in Luluabourg in 1956, it should enjoy an annual income of between £94 4s. 0d. and £102 12s. 0d.[1] It goes without saying that the cost of living was cheaper in the countryside.

Since the aim was to bring to birth 'a numerous and satisfied class of cultivators, attached to the land, tilling their own soil and deriving from their work resources sufficient for all their needs' (Ryckmans) success would be achieved when a peasant's income at least equalled that of the ordinary labourer in the town.[2] That such an approximation does check the drift to the towns is shown by the case of two regions in Katanga (Sandoa-Dilolo and Albertville) during or just after the War. When agricultural production proved more lucrative than work in the mine or other European enterprise, the rural exodus was in the former case reversed and in the latter checked.[3] But this was not typical: on the contrary, whereas in 1940 19·23 per cent. of able-bodied adult males were in paid employment, the percentage had grown to 38·95 by 1956[4] (paid employment was not only to be found in a town or other centre, but almost always involved subtraction from the traditional *milieu*).

For all the success of the *paysannats*, the essential population movement was not altered during the years after 1945, was still towards the towns. Denis indicates the striking achievements of a co-operative founded at Kisantu, achievements which

[1] Denis, *Le Phénomène urbain*, pp. 260-3.

[2] This section is based on: P. Staner, 'Les Paysannats indigènes du Congo belge et Ruanda-Urundi', *Bulletin Agricole du Congo belge*, XLVI, 3, 1955, pp. 468-549; idem, 'Paysannats et vie rurale', in *Livre blanc* (Brussels, A.R.S.O-M., 1962), I, pp. 413-24; *African Survey*, pp. 799-800.

[3] A. Doucy and P. Feldheim, *Problèmes du travail et politique sociale au Congo belge* (Brussels, Les Éditions de la Librairie Encyclopédique, 1952), pp. 64-65.

[4] A. Doucy, 'Politique indigène,' *Livre blanc*, I, p. 360.

included the halting of the rural exodus from that region. But it does not appear that the Administration seriously encouraged co-operatives. This particular one owed its origin to missionary inspiration and support.[1]

The second achievement was the post-war improvement in the already relatively good medical services of the Colony, and the further development of public health policy and preventive medicine in particular. The achievement is graphically typified in the further strides made in the eradication of sleeping sickness. The principle of action was the systematic examination by mobile teams of the entire population of villages in threatened or afflicted areas, and the regular treatment thereafter of any sufferers. The effectiveness of this was such that whereas, in 1926, 1·2 per cent. annually, and in 1935–9, 0·302 per cent. contracted the disease, the rate of new infection by 1960 had been reduced to 0·25 per cent. The claim is quite justified that:

It is the incontestable achievement of Belgian doctors to have been the first to create a mobile organization to fight the endemic diseases of Central Africa. The number of people who were thus examined each year in the Congo exceeded six millions, that is to say, in round figures, a half of the total population and almost the whole of those living in the affected areas.[2]

But whatever the reasons for intervention in customary society, the fact remains that Belgium rule was characterized by such intervention to an exceptional extent. And the greater the intervention, the less were traditional institutions and customary ways able to retain their integrity. Governor-General Pétillon, addressing the Colonial Council in 1952, gave a most revealing commentary on the operation of Belgium native policy.

Our old conception of indirect rule—timid and attenuated as it has been from the beginning—has not ceased to grow weaker. Under the pressure of economic circumstances and wartime demands, from a praiseworthy concern to do things more quickly and better, we have wanted to take everything in hand and direct the Congolese masses, willy nilly, to a happiness conformable to our ideas.[3]

[1] Denis, *Le Phénomène urbain*, pp. 361–2.

[2] J. van Riel and P. G. Janssens, 'Lutte contre les endémo-épidémies', *Livre blanc*, II, pp. 917–19.

[3] *Conseil de Gouvernement*, 1952, Speech of Gov.-Gen. Pétillon, p. 37, quoted in *African Survey*, p. 223.

This being so, the character, conduct and attitude of administrative officers became more rather than less important in the closing years of Belgian rule. It is possible to form some idea of the quality of the administrative service in the fifties, not only from written sources, but also from inquiries made on the ground after independence.[1] It appears that there was a significant distinction between *fonctionnaires* on the one hand and *agents* on the other, between the professionally trained and the subordinate ranks of the administrative service. It will be remembered that both Rolin and Van der Kerken—and the latter's experience was very considerable—were critical of the harm done by entrusting delicate administrative functions to *agents* in the early period of Belgian rule. Because their training and education were limited, and because they were often in the job for predominantly financial reasons, they were too often inadequate or did positive harm (see pp. 53–55 above).

By the fifties the wheel seems to have turned full cycle and there do seem to have been a number of very poor-quality men in the *agent* class. One informant, an American missionary, went so far as to say that in his experience in Orientale province, seven out of ten of the Europeans working in the Government service in the bush were of poor quality. He was not, it should be said, differentiating between men of the administrative service and members of the medical, agricultural and other services, but his experience must necessarily have been more of men of the *agent* level since these were thicker on the ground, and more frequently seen.

A similar distinction was made, if somewhat ingenuously, by the president of an *évolué* group giving evidence to the Senatorial Commission of 1947. When asked what Europeans were guilty of striking Africans, he replied, 'Agents of the Administration and in the private sector. In general they are always agents of a lower grade. From the administrator to the Governor-General, the whites are generally good.'[2]

It has been seen that in the administrative system itself the *territoire* had, so to speak, adjusted itself to the amalgamations of 1933 by subdivision into a number of units, usually between four and six, each under the immediate control of an adminis-

[1] My principal sources here are *évolué* Congolese, Protestant missionaries and (in England) European visitors to the Congo.

[2] *Rapport de la mission sénatoriale*, 'Procès-verbal de la visite au cercle des évolués, à Paulis', 7 September 1947, pp. 268-9.

trative officer who would in most cases be of *agent* status (see pp. 80-81 above). Another informant, who was in general pro-Belgian, after relating a number of episodes in which gross injustice had been done to Africans, suggested that in her experience of Orientale province, *agents* in the Administration fell into two main categories. There were those who contented themselves with a pidgin *kiswahili*, did the minimum, committed various abuses, solaced themselves with African women and, possibly in some cases, bribes, and in this way passed the period of their African service. The second category set itself the goal of promotion at least one stage up the ladder and to this end a man would apply himself—but legalistically and woodenly. There were, of course, exceptions.

This last judgement may, if generalized, be too harsh, but at the same time the frustrations and limited insights and ability of men with only a limited preparation, seeking refuge in the Congo perhaps from unemployment, perhaps from military service, and motivated primarily by the opportunity of earning a relatively high salary, must often have produced unsatisfactory results. Amongst men of this kind the patient unravelling and resolution of 'palavers' was hardly to be looked for: much more likely a refuge in legalism or arbitrary punishment, in procrastination or in a refusal to become involved in matters pertaining to custom, with positive achievements restricted to the material and the measurable—such as ensuring the production of a good cotton crop.

It would be foolish to suggest that a clear-cut distinction can be drawn between *agents* and *fonctionnaires*, between the crude harshness of the one and the inviolate professional virtue of the other—there was too much deviation from each of these supposed norms. But for a mixture of reasons (his better ability to take the broad view, a more firmly implanted sense of vocation and professional conscience, a less detailed involvement with the African), it seems more often to have been the *administrateur* or the *commissaire de district* who became, in so far as this happened, an object not only of respect but also of veneration and affection.

The career of André Ryckmans, a son of the former Governor-General, who entered the administrative service in 1954, is a remarkable and moving testimony to all that was best in Belgian administration. Certainly Ryckmans' letters, which form an important part of M. Kestergat's tribute to their author, contain strictures on the failures and foolishness of the Administration. But positively, in their uncalculated testimony to what Ryckmans himself achieved, and negatively, by the way in which Ryckmans almost agonized over lost opportunities, they reveal the vital response that could be evoked by a devoted, gifted and unpatronizing paternalist.

To Ryckmans, the necessary work of the census and of tax collection should be made into more than a chore, backed by police activity, in which the administrator acted purely as the impersonal arm of *Bula Matari*: this was, rather, an opportunity which the administrator should use for getting to know his people and which should be followed by some sort of get-together of the village, with dancing and general celebration. In a bitter and intractable dispute about land, instead of following the advice given him that he should deliberately encourage the matter to blow up into violence, so that all the parties might be put in jail, and the problem be 'solved' in that way, Ryckmans made further painstaking inquiry and eventually reached a solution acceptable to both parties. Instead of taking refuge in a prestigious remoteness whose corollary was incomprehension of traditional life, Ryckmans simply went into the village chatting and joking—but certainly not allowing anyone to take advantage of him.[1] Here one comes not merely to the essential reason for Ryckmans' success as an administrator, but also to the necessary condition of real success for any administrator and any native policy. Ryckmans himself is quite clear about the importance of this sort of contact:

I remain convinced that any administrator whatsoever, if he wants to, can in spite of everything find the time and the opportunity to apply himself to *kikongo* [Ryckmans was writing during his service amongst the Ba-Kongo], can find one or two evenings a week which he can pass in the villages, and can find the leisure to read, from time to time, a book or a journal. . . . These solutions are too simple for anyone to have thought of putting them into practice; it makes one despair. . . . ([but] I am only putting into practice a teaching implicit in all the instructions, in all the courses of instruction for new recruits).[2]

It is clear that André Ryckmans was a man of exceptional gifts (so tragically squandered when he was murdered, on the

[1] 'J. K.', *André Ryckmans, passim,* and especially pp. 106-7, 114-16, 155-9.
[2] Quoted in 'J.K.', op. cit., pp. 159-60.

approaches to the bridge carrying the Leopoldville–Thysville road over the Inkisi river, by Congolese mutineers in July 1960), and it may be unreasonable to imply that Belgian African administration would have been incomparably better if the Ryckmans approach had been more commonly followed. The Ryckmans approach, it may be objected, demands a Ryckmans to apply it, and men of his quality are rare at any time, in any country. But it is no less true that the exceptional degree of intervention in traditional life which Belgian policy involved demanded exceptional men in exceptional quantity if paternalism was to be meaningful. Such a wealth of talent is, indeed, scarcely to be looked for. Belgian African administration seems never to have realized this contradiction.

It was perhaps in the post-war years that the Belgian settlers in the Congo came to have their greatest importance. Their economic significance was of the same order as it had been in the inter-war period; they continued to add their own labour demands to the pressures on customary society and its limited manpower resources; and their very presence was an obstacle to the growth of a Congolese entrepreneurial class. But included in their ranks were also some natural and, no doubt, uncalculating paternalists whose value was a genuine, if rough-and-ready, concern with their labourers. But commensurate with their growth in numbers (with their families they numbered some 15,000 by the early fifties) they became more forceful in their demands, speaking especially through FÉDACOL (the *Fédération des Associations des Colons du Congo et du Ruanda-Urundi Belges*). When they gave evidence to the Senatorial Commission in 1947, the old grievances had predominated, and especially the shortage of labour, its poor quality, and the various legal restrictions which made it difficult for the settlers to 'handle it properly'.[1]

But soon FÉDACOL and kindred organizations also began to make political demands. 'A hundred thousand Belgian settlers in ten years or the Congo will cease to be Belgian', ran a slogan formulated by FÉDACOL, though the illogicality of

[1] *Rapport de la mission sénatoriale*, Appendix, 'Réunion des colons à . . . Stanley-ville', pp. 241-5.

this demand, when laments at the labour shortages were as strong as ever, does not seem to have been realized. An implication of this attitude was a demand for political rights for Belgians in the Congo and opposition to the extension of political rights amongst Africans who were, it was asserted, quite unready for them. Indeed, said a settler leader in 1957:

Nothing IN THE HISTORY of the Congolese justifies any sort of rights for them over the country as a whole. They have never created anything, not a motor, not a wheel-barrow, nothing. We have lifted them from cannibalism and slavery. It is we who have unified, pacified and organized the country.[1]

But it would be wrong to suggest that the Belgian settler was merely a wonderful Aunt Sally for untested, armchair liberalism. As the fifties progressed, FÉDACOL opened its ranks to the Congolese middle class,[2] probably out of a mixture of principle and realization that here was a horse likely to find more backers. As successive Belgian Governments refused, by simply doing nothing positive, to go beyond assistance to colonization on the existing scale, and as during the fifties mild eddies of the Wind of Change—but oh-so-mild—began to flutter in the Congo, the settlers took up the defensive position of equal representation of the two groups, Europeans and Africans, in any new political institutions.[3] Whilst during 1959 and 1960, to anticipate, the majority of settlers adopted distinctly illiberal attitudes, others saw that the Congo was going to be governed by Congolese and that this must be accepted.[4] At any rate they avoided the mistake of supposing that the ordinary Congolese had a statement of adhesion to Western democratic principles carefully folded in his loin-cloth.

But in essence the major political importance of the settlers was negative. They had a small group of sympathizers in the Belgian Parliament,[5] but though their political strength was never strong enough to obtain the settler's positive political aims, it may well have been an important factor in dissuading the Belgian Government from taking positive action in regard to *Congolese* political emancipation. Especially is this likely

[1] See A. Maus and others, *Le Peuplement européen au Congo belge* (Brussels. FÉDACOL, 1952), *passim*. The quotations are from pp. 5 and 24.
[2] Slade, *Belgian Congo*, p. 37.
[3] See *Congo 1959*, ed. J. Gérard-Libois (Brussels, C.R.I.S.P., 1960), pp. 23, 26.
[4] See ibid., pp. 29-34.   [5] *Congo 1959*, p. 23.

when it is remembered how few and faint were the voices seeking to push the Government in a positive direction at a time when a policy aiming at gradual emancipation would have made every sort of sense.[1] Nor, for all the real success of some of them in dealing, as paternalists, with their labourers, were they any more welcoming to the *évolués'* pathetic (in the true sense) desire for acceptance into the European world. Indeed, the reverse was true. But with the rapid urbanization of the post-war years this was to be the crucial problem.

[1] Jean Stengers, review of *Congo: Background of Conflict* in *Journal of African History*, 1964, V, I, pp. 145-6.

X

THE BIG CITY (1)

WHEN reduced to figures, the increase in what might loosely be called the urban population of the Congo in the years after 1939 is quite unambiguous. The population living outside the sway of custom increased from 971,907 in 1939 to 1,569,195 in 1947 and 3,240,000 by the end of 1958. This last figure represented nearly a quarter of the total Congo population. As in earlier periods by no means all those living outside the authority of custom lived in towns—for example substantial numbers were to be found in the camps of the *Force publique* or in mining camps. Notwithstanding, it was in the towns that the most pronounced growth took place. The figures for Leopoldville indicate especially rapid growth, but Matadi and Stanleyville were not far behind.[1]

	1938	*1950*	*1955*
Leopoldville	40,000	190,000	c. 325,000
Matadi	12,500	37,000	c. 66,000
Stanleyville	12,500	34,000	c. 55,000

It may be useful to follow the fortunes of a youth newly arriving in the big city. We will call him Jacques. The first thing to notice is that despite the magic in the name of Leopold-ville or any other big city, Jacques may well not have made the transition from village to large city in one jump, unless he happened already to be living near to it. In a case noted by V. G. Pons at Stanleyville in the early fifties, and regarded by him as typical for Stanleyville, Pascal, a youth of twenty, had spent seven years in lesser centres, getting a little schooling, holding for a part of the time such jobs as houseboy and driver's mate, and living either with his employer or with a 'brother'

[1] Figs. cited in Gille, 'Politique indigène', p. 736 n., and Denis, *Phénomène urbain*, pp. 95, 100 (graphs).

(that is, both in this case and generally not a son of his own parents but another member of his family, clan or even tribe).[1] Just as Pascal had sought out a brother on arrival at a centre, so Jacques would do the same as he entered Elisabethville, Bukavu or wherever it might be. Unless the brother lived in the servants' quarters attached to a European household (servants' quarters were on the whole not thus attached) he would be found in the African city.

Such *cités indigènes* in the earlier years of Belgian rule consisted simply of a number of plots of land on which the new—and few —town-dwellers were left to build as best they might. As one might expect, traditional modes of construction were used. A common pattern was a framework of sticks as a basis for mud walls and thatched roof, but urban conditions gradually led to the incorporation of manufactured materials for roofs, windows etc. and, in some cases, and to the extent that hygiene regulations did not prevent it, to an increasing slumminess as habits acceptable in the interior revealed serious disadvantages in the new *milieu*.

A feature of the stabilized labour policy of concerns such as the *Union Minière, Huileries du Congo Belge,* and OTRACO was, from its inception in the thirties, the provision of much improved types of housing, but a really dynamic approach in the Congo as a whole had to wait for the end of the Second World War, which had so augmented the population of the towns. A number of important measures then followed. In 1947 a colony-wide system of house-construction loans was initiated, and by the end of 1956 some 23,000 loans had been made. The number of loans was particularly high in industrialized Katanga where 8,301 loans were approved in Elisabethville alone in the seven years 1950-6.

This Katanga achievement was due to the particular steps taken by M. Grévisse, the *commissaire de district* in Elisabethville in the immediate post-war period, to concert the action of the provincial and local administration with that of employers so

[1] V. G. Pons, 'The Growth of Stanleyville and the Composition of its African Population' in D. Forde (ed.), *Social Implications of Urbanization and Industrialization in Africa South of the Sahara* (Paris, UNESCO, 1956), pp. 255-7. In Stanleyville in 1952-3 a little over two-thirds of the African population had previously lived in a lesser centre.

Use has been made in this chapter and the next of various studies of Stanleyville, of which Pons' is one, made under the auspices of the International African Institute in 1952-3, and published as part of the work cited above.

that, with close State attention to preparation of sites, road-building, water supply, and so forth, and the provision of housing allowances by employers, the self-help of the intending householder, strengthened by a loan, could achieve the best results. Indeed, greater or lesser attention was given throughout the colony to providing the means whereby the urban African could obtain good-quality materials at an economic price, or even have a house built from a choice of plans, as could be done in Coquilhatville.

The third stage in the dynamic approach of the post-war years was the foundation, effectively in 1952 though it had initially been created in 1949 as part of the Ten-Year Plan, of the *Office des Cités Africaines*, entrusted with the construction as rapidly as possible and according to European standards of 40,000 dwelling units together with all the necessary services, the the properties to be purchased by instalments. By the end of 1946, 27,000 units had been built, but the relatively high standards of construction and equipment meant that despite their undoubted contribution to the housing problem, their cost was beyond the pocket of the more poorly paid. They could also look rather dull and uniform unless imaginatively sited.[1] Having found shelter, Jacques would be under no immediate obligation to find his own accommodation and would in fact probably stay with his brother for months rather than weeks. Nor would there be any compulsive obligation to find work, though, during the period of full employment which lasted until the mid-fifties, the great majority of new arrivals would both seek and easily find jobs. The jobs they would find would depend largely on their education, training and experience, and fell into one of four categories. At the bottom were the unskilled wage-earners, men in occupations demanding nothing more than a brief initiation, such as those of labourer, night-watchman, driver's mate. Above them was the body of the semi-skilled and skilled men performing tasks which evidently demanded significant training or, more frequently, experience; for instance, those of chauffeur, mason, carpenter, houseboy. The aristocracy of wage-earners, the *évolués*, were the white-collar employees, consisting chiefly of clerks, but also including professions such as those of school-teacher and medical

[1] Denis, *Phénomène urbain*, pp. 282–98, 302–10.

orderly. The fourth class consisted of a wide variety of self-employed—traders of all descriptions, master-craftsmen such as shoemakers, and so on. At Stanleyville in 1952-3 the percentages of all adult males in these four categories were 36·7, 42·5, 9·5 and 4·7 respectively, whilst 6·6 per cent. were not gainfully employed.[1]

The physical well-being of the Congo town-dweller naturally depended to a considerable extent on the size of his income. During the war considerable hardship seems to have been caused to wage-earners by the greater success of the Administration in keeping down wages than in stabilizing prices, and the Senatorial Commission in 1947 was quite sure that in general the wage-earners' position 'was not an enviable one'.[2] From 1949 onwards, however, the Administration responded to the plight of the employee by facing up to the need for a progressive increase in wages. The method it chose was periodically to establish a minimum daily wage, the wage perforce for unskilled labourers, and to assume that the wages of the skilled and semi-skilled, and of the white-collar workers, would increase correspondingly. The minimum rates were to be assessed regionally and with reference to a theoretical wage calculated in accordance with the local prices of about thirty commodities, excluding foodstuffs, considered necessary for a single man embarking on his first job. However, at the inception of the policy the gap between the lowest wages being paid and the theoretical level was usually such that it was resolved to close the gap gradually in order not to disrupt the economy.

None the less by 1950, the second year of the policy's operation, 30 per cent. of the seventy-eight regional minimum rates had attained the level of the theoretical minimum, whilst in the case of Stanleyville, for example, the legal minimum as a proportion of the theoretical minimum increased from one-third to two-thirds between 1949 and October 1952, a movement in cash terms from about 14s. 4d. to about 30s. a month. In addition to wages and lodging, or an allowance in lieu, rations according to a prescribed scale, or a locally assessed equivalent in cash, were also mandatory, as (from 1951) were wife's and children's allowances, determined by a scale proportional to the husband's ration allowance. The value of

[1] Pons, 'Growth of Stanleyville', p. 268.

[2] *Rapport de la mission sénatoriale*, 'Rapport général', pp. 24–25; A. Spreutel, 'La Condition des travailleurs autochtones', pp. 179–81; Appendix, p. 283.

N

these was such that, for example, at Stanleyville in 1952 the monthly total of income and extras for a man on the minimum wage was rather over twice as much for a man with wife and six dependent children as for a single man (£7 6s. 0d. compared with £3 9s. 11d.).[1]

Bearing in mind that the minimum wage and allowances were geared to prices, one can obtain an idea of the upward movement over the whole post-war decade by seeing how the minimum wage, together with allowances due to a single man, increased in two major centres and one lesser. In Leopoldville between the beginning of 1946 and the end of 1956 the increase was from about 39s. 5d. to about £6 8s. 7d.; in Elisabethville from roughly 21s. 5d. to roughly £4 18s. 7d.; and in Albertville from approximately 21s. 5d. to approximately £4 0s. 8d.[2] Evidently there was a substantial increase in real, as well as in the face value of wages, though some critics, doubtless basing their conclusion on such factors as alleged errors in cost-of-living indices, deny that such a substantial real increase actually took place as the figures and the system would suggest.[3]

Reverting to the question of the adequacy of the minimum wage, Denis has published figures of the minimum desirable budget for a family of four at Luluabourg in April 1956 and shows that they ought to have disposed of an income of between £7 17s. 0d. and £8 11s. 0d. a month. In fact, at that time the minimum wage plus the relevant allowances came to only £4 14s. 0d.[4] During the fifties it appears that a percentage of wage-earners (varying between thirty and fifty according to locality) received only the minimum wage (together with allowances, of course). It may be that the figure of 43 per cent. revealed by an inquiry at Stanleyville in the early fifties is not untypical. (This inquiry by a factory inspector also revealed that 2 per cent. did not receive this statutory minimum.)[5]

For the artisans and white-collar workers the situation was naturally better. Whereas the minimum wage, together with allowances for a single man, in Leopoldville in 1956 has been

---

[1] Nelly Xydias, 'Labour: Conditions, Aptitudes, Training' (Stanleyville Survey) in *Social Implications of Industrialization and Urbanization in Africa South of the Sahara*, pp. 291–5.

[2] Denis, *Phénomène urbain*, pp. 260–1.

[3] See W. Ugeux, 'Recent Developments in Belgian Africa', *Africa Today*, ed. C. G. Haines (Baltimore, Johns Hopkins, 1955), p. 360.

[4] Denis, *Phénomène urbain*, pp. 262–3.

[5] Ibid., p. 260; Xydias, 'Labour' (Stanleyville Surrey), p. 295.

seen to have been some £6 8s. 7d. a month, an artisan in that city would receive between £14 and £32, whilst a white-collar worker would receive not less than £21 and in a few cases as much as £71.[1] Interestingly, at least one major private employer, the *Union Minière*, set an opposite value on the artisan in relation to the white-collar worker. In the spirit of a slogan displayed in 1962 on a wall in the Company's main workshops at Jadotville—'It is as useful to be a designer as it is to be able to read and write'—the highest wage range was reserved for artisans.

Through this study of housing and wages, two important determinants of the physical conditions of living in the town, we have sought to show important ways in which Jacques' life altered when he came to the town. But there were also changes of an even more important kind, namely in Jacques' relations with other Africans. In a word, everything stemmed from the fact that his world was no longer restricted to the clan, the village and the tribe. Life in the town involved a whole new series of relationships and together they did much to make his outlook different from that of his brother still in the Bush.

The most significant change of all was in the marriage relationship. Under customary law, marriage, by A. Sohier's definition, was 'a combination of a contract between two persons of different sex, creating between them a common life, with reciprocal rights and duties, and a contract between groups of relatives which makes the union valid for them, assures their support of it and legitimizes the children'.[2] As one might expect, unions between persons of the same lineage, as well as marriages between couples joined by certain degrees of affinity, were forbidden, but sometimes only conditionally, so that, for instance, a son might be able to marry his father's widow provided she was not also his mother.

A major element in marriage was the payment made by or on behalf of the man to the family of the woman. The purpose of the marriage payment probably varied a good deal, but it

[1] Denis, *Phénomène urbain*, p. 260. When the sources give wages, allowances, etc. on a daily basis, I have multiplied this figure by twenty-five to arrive at a monthly figure. (The theoretical daily wage was arrived at by determining total annual expenditure on the specified products and then dividing by 300.)

[2] Quoted in P. Clément, 'Social Patterns of Urban Life' (Stanleyville Survey) in *Social Implications of Industrialization and Urbanization in Africa South of the Sahara*, p. 383.

seems that it included all or some of these roles: it was proof
of the families' consent and thus an attestation of alliance; it
was a compensation for the loss of the daughter, and not
necessarily for loss of a purely economic kind; and it was a
compensation for the sacrifice by the wife's family of certain
rights over her. This was especially the case amongst patrilineal
people, where rights over children of the union fell to the
father. Although an element of choice by each of the partners
was often present, the purpose of the union was the perpetuation
of the group by procreation.

The preliminaries of the marriage, betrothal, and the
marriage ceremony itself were usually of some complexity
and characterized by a rich symbolism. Divorce was justified,
provided certain procedures were followed, if either of the
partners failed to perform the duties involved in marriage.
With the extension of missionary activity following the advent
of European rule, Christian marriages became more and more
common, though they often included many of the forms and
procedures of custom. They differed from customary marriages
principally in that they were essentially monogamous and
made no provision for divorce. Civil marriage was only an
occasional phenomenon.[1]

A most thorough survey of marriage in urban Congo was
carried out at Stanleyville in 1952–3, and its conclusions,[2]
based mainly on seventy-seven case histories in two sociologic-
ally different quarters of the African city, are an indication of
how marriage could undergo major modifications in the town.
At the same time there was an obvious respect in which the
Stanleyville situation differed from that in some other parts of
the Congo—the tribes represented there were patrilineal.
Of the cases studied, 76 per cent. were unions contracted at a
European centre of some kind. Initial acquaintance was in an
important number of cases (40·5 per cent.) a casual encounter
between adults of a kind which rarely took place in traditional
society or which, if it did, would not be a preliminary to any
development of the relationship—meetings on the road, in a
shop, at the Mission, at a bar. As the nature of such encounters
suggests, they could often be between people of different tribes,

[1] Clément's summary in 'Social Patterns of Urban Life', pp. 378-89
[2] This whole following section is based on Clément, op. cit., pp. 378–438. Other
sources will be specifically indicated.

and in fact 32·5 per cent. of the cases were inter-tribal marriages.[1] It is significant that the percentage of inter-tribal marriages was higher in that part of the sample situated in the more advanced, more *évolué* of the two districts from which the samples were taken—45·9 per cent. as opposed to 27·1 per cent.

In regard to the forms and procedures of marriage and its preliminaries, in twenty-two out of seventy-four cases either a lover's relationship or a trial marriage preceded formal marriage, in each case with the approval of the woman's parents. In another eight cases there had been elopement as a prelude to marriage and in another five cases clandestine sexual relations. In all of these cases the marriage payment had sooner or later been made. The largest single category in the sample had a traditional appearance. It was that of marriage after betrothal with not only the marriage payment but also, it is implied, a prolonged preliminary dialogue. But the appearance was in many ways deceptive. One or both parties might not have their parents with them in town and in such a case a 'brother' acted for the party concerned in the negotiations; again, in urban marriages, including those of this apparently classical type, the responsibility for finding the marriage payment rested increasingly with the husband. In the Stanley-ville sample, in 47·3 per cent. of the cases the husband alone provided the payment, in 21·6 per cent. he was helped by one or more members of his family and in 29·8 per cent. the family alone found the payment. Family assistance was very much more marked in first than in subsequent marriages. Where the marriage negotiations were carried on by only a vague 'brother' of one or both participants, where the man's family had a lesser role in the provision of the marriage payment, and where the arrangement was between two 'nuclear' families, the marriage was much less of 'a contract between two groups of relatives'.

Finally, in all types of urban marriage, the function of the marriage payment was changing, especially in so far as it was a compensation for the loss of the woman's economic value. City-dwelling Yoruba of Western Nigeria may divide their time between town and country, and in such a case the wife still has a traditional economic value as the one who does all but the heavy agricultural work. But in Stanleyville, and generally in

[1] See also Richelle, *Aspects psychologiques de l'acculturation*, p. 161.

the Congo, it was exceptional for a town-dweller still to be an active cultivator. Consequently a wife was no longer an economic asset in this basic, traditional sense. However, except in the case of the wives of some white-collar workers, a wife would frequently undertake some form of economic activity, usually petty-trading of some description. Indeed the gap between the income and expenditure of the lower-paid men would often be closed in this way. For all that, the economic role of the wife was no longer central, and when to this is added the higher level of marriage payment demanded in the town, it would seem likely that the persistence of the marriage payment was due not only to the strength of custom but also to the cupidity of fathers and guardians and their concern to make a profit out of the happy circumstance of having a bride to bestow.[1]

It has been said that customary marriage was only incidentally monogamous but implied that urban marriage was unfailingly so. In fact, in earlier times most village marriages were polygamous, for to the man polygamy is clearly consistent with such aims of traditional marriage as the fathering of numerous children and the enhancement of wealth and status. European influences, and especially the missions, gradually decreased the incidence of polygamy so that too sharp a distinction between the rural and urban areas of Belgium's colony should not be drawn. It was rather that the factors working against polygamy were appreciably stronger in the town.

We have already seen that the marriage payment tended to be considerably higher in the town: it was therefore more difficult to acquire a plurality of wives. Again, few town-dwellers could afford accommodation sufficient for more than one wife, whilst it must also be remembered that under urban conditions a wife was not so great an economic asset. For some of the more sophisticated évolués there was also, no doubt, the feeling that polygamy was not compatible with European ways, especially as in the town the purely sexual gratifications of polygamy could easily be experienced by recourse to a concubine or prostitute. Furthermore, mission influence was of course present in the town whilst polygamy had long been discouraged by the Administration through such measures as a supplementary tax on additional wives. Finally, by a decree

[1] But see also Richelle, *Aspects psychologiques de l'acculturation*, p. 160.

of 4 April 1950, polygamous marriages contracted after the end of that year would not, subject to certain reservations, be recognized as legally valid. However, although the number of overtly polygamous marriages was small, many men had additional wives in the villages.[1]

According to the Stanleyville survey, urban conditions also affected the nature of marriages in another way. Whereas traditionally a good wife was one who was fertile, wholly submissive to her husband and whose work contributed to the prosperity of the household, it appears that in the town the ideal wife was seen as one who above all ran the house well, who was a good manager and able to cater for the husband's relatives and friends. Beyond this she should add to the household resources by her own pursuits, as far as she could, and should take proper care of the children. If she was unfaithful, then she should at least be discreet about it, and if the old rigorous subordination was no longer demanded, a wife should be unremitting in her care of her husband when sick. The fertility of the wife sometimes, indeed usually, continued to be valued, but not all men rated it amongst the three or four most necessary qualities, preferring a wife who might be divorced or no longer a virgin, and thus in common estimation be unlikely to bear children, but who, it was supposed, was more likely to have some poise and knowledge of managing than the girl fresh from the Bush who was more prone to be quite bowled over by the new and unfamiliar situation.

Most students of marriage in the towns of the Congo agree that through the manner in which initial acquaintance was often made, through the manner in which the marriage was frequently concluded, because of the varied discouragements to polygamy, because of the enhanced ability of the more *évolué* to desire a wife as a companion, the emphasis in urban marriage was beginning to be on the husband and wife and their children, on the nuclear family. In Clément's words:

the idea of the 'couple', of the husband and wife as team, is beginning to gain a foothold among married people and also, though more slowly, among their families. And this marks an important

[1] See summary of S. Comhaire–Sylvain, 'Food and Leisure among the African Youth of Leopoldville' in *Social Implications of Industrialization and Urbanization in Africa South of the Sahara*, p. 116.

change of custom. . . . Marriage is tending to become simply a union of two persons, rather than an alliance between two groups.[1]

Concrete evidence of this is found in the increasing extent to which at least a part of a deceased's estate went directly to his wife and children rather than the whole of it going to a brother or other member of his family. The Stanleyville survey team published nothing on this point, but Richelle found in a test given to a sample of 254 *évolués* in Elisabethville in 1957–8 that only about 15 per cent. were prepared to see custom followed purely and simply, that about 50 per cent. favoured a division, and that some 35 per cent. were prepared to break completely with custom and bestow the man's possessions wholly on the wife and children.[2]

There seems to be a good deal of evidence, though necessarily of a less precise kind, that the *évolué*, though frequently still attracted by the many conveniences of polygamy, was more and more seeking in a wife someone with enough poise and education not only to be a good manager but also something of a companion in his partially westernized environment. It can be argued that a wife competent to fulfil this role would, almost by definition, not be such as would accept polygamy, and that from the man's point of view polygamy *and* a wife who was a companion were sensed as mutually exclusive alternatives.

The ideal qualities which the town-dwelling woman wanted in a husband are much more unambiguously the qualities which imply a centripetal, monogamous household—he should stay at home with his family in the evenings; should not frequent bars, squander his money or contract debts; should regularly give his wife enough money for food and household necessities, together with a dress allowance for herself, and should trust her discretion in the use of it; and he should be kind and understanding. He should not allow himself to be led astray by women, but if he did keep a concubine he should not insult his wife by bringing the concubine into her presence.

It has already been seen that the African population of Stanleyville came almost entirely from patrilineal tribes. Clearly a matrilineal tradition would be a much greater obstacle to the emergence of the nuclear family. The tension

[1] Clément, 'Social Patterns of Urban Life', pp. 422–3.
[2] Richelle, *Aspects psychologiques de l'acculturation*, pp. 163, 166.

between the nuclear family and the matrilineal system has been summed up in this way, albeit from a European perspective:

The matriarchate effected the dislocation of the family, properly speaking, by depriving it of its natural head: the father. The latter, of different blood from his wife and children, had to remain an outsider, forced to abdicate his responsibilities before a representative of his wife's clan. The latter would see in her uncle or her brother her habitual support. Each of the partners would preserve their own ancestral cult, their customs, lineage, mode of living and separate possessions. Authority over his children is snatched away from the father. How could it be tolerated that this outsider should bring up the true members of the clan? The uncle, the mother's brother, will claim authority over the children, harshly demonstrating to the father that nature intended his [the uncle's] line to be continued in them. The father, for his part, seeing his sons escaping his influence, becomes alienated from them and will turn towards his nephew, his future heir. It is the latter to whose upbringing he will devote special care, to whom he will attach himself, whom he will enrich and for whom he will seek marriage. It is he who will continue the participation in the life of the ancestors.[1]

Madame Comhaire-Sylvain has something to say of the impact of town life on the matrilineal system, on the evidence of an inquiry she conducted in 1945 in Kinshasa, a quarter of the African city in Leopoldville, where about 70 per cent. of the inhabitants were from matrilineal tribes. She believed that, in the important matter of the care of children, the matrilineal system was holding its own, but that as a result of urban life the parents had become more important, the father gaining more authority over his children. The father would usually pay for his children's education but on the other hand there was no case where the maternal uncle had relinquished care of the children.[2] For what a single instance is worth, there could be a more marked weakening of the compulsions of matrilineal society. A Mukongo master-joiner, living in the same *secteur* as his own village but not in the village itself, had only limited contact with members of his clan, and no longer paid the customary tribute to his maternal uncle. On the other hand the

[1] A. Storms, 'Famille chrétienne et société matriarcale au Katanga', *Zaïre*, XI, March 1948, p. 245.
[2] Comhaire–Sylvain, 'Food and Leisure among the African Youth of Leopoldville', p. 115.

joiner would give his uncle hospitality and visit him if ill, and would include him in the disposal of his estate, as he would include his own nephews. But the greater part would go to his own wife and children.[1]

There was, then, a marked tendency for the varied conditions of urban life to discourage polygamy, and there was, amongst *évolués*, and especially amongst women, some positive desire for marriage to subsist in the context of the nuclear family, but it would be quite wrong to suppose that the transition was taking place smoothly. During the war years and after there were increasing laments over the moral and spiritual failings at any rate of the *évolué* members of the town populations, and to many, such as Van Wing writing in 1945, it was the disorder of their private lives which was the root cause of instability. In the big cities he reckoned that 90 per cent. either had no regular union or were unfaithful, and quoted from an article by Joseph d'Oliveira, a mulatto, in the first number of the *évolué* periodical, *La Voix du congolais*, which drew attention to the progressive embitterment and corruption of the *évolué* as he went from one grasping concubine to another in fruitless search of a permanent partner.[2] Madame Comhaire-Sylvain estimated that at the time of her survey one-third of the female population of Kinshasa was living in concubinage, either as a second wife, or as a partner in a temporary union. However, in some instances the relationship might be more or less permanent or eventually result in marriage. Amongst the most prosperous, concubines had replaced the frowned-upon plurality of wives, and divorce at all levels was easy.[3]

On paper the situation revealed by a survey of the composition of the African population of Stanleyville was much more regular, even allowing for exaggeration, at least in Van Wing's impressionistic estimates, and for reasons which are obscure. The Stanleyville survey divided its large sample of 1,607 women into five categories. 69·7 per cent. were married, only 4·3 per cent. lived in concubinage, 11·5 per cent. were divorced and living singly, 9·1 per cent were widowed and living singly,

[1] J. M. Domont, *La Prise de conscience de l'individu en milieu rural Kongo* (Brussels, A.R.S.O.M., 1958), pp. 40–42.

[2] Van Wing, *La Situation actuelle des populations congolaises*, pp. 590–3.

[3] Comhaire-Sylvain, 'Food and Leisure among the African Youth of Leopold-ville', pp. 116–17.

whilst 5·4 per cent. were spinsters.[1] Here is an immensely different picture, but how far it is to be explained by the differing factors of patrilineal and matrilineal influences, by other less obvious differences in custom, by improvements in living conditions between 1945 and 1952, by more precise study (the Stanleyville survey was based not on registers but on actual house-to-house visits), or by other factors, is not clear.

However, this was not all the story for, as in Leopoldville, and for that matter throughout the Congo, the ending of customary marriage by divorce was an easy matter. A divorce could be given by the *tribunal du centre* according to customary law, with little delay, expense or trouble. Of a sample of 352 persons who were or who had been married, 201, or some 57 per cent., had been divorced once or more. The reasons offered by the parties for wanting a divorce are the conventional sad components of domestic discord, but it is worth drawing attention to various causes of marital instability particular to urban, part-westernized Africa.

First, of course, was the traditional understanding of marriage as an agreement which could be terminated, albeit under certain conditions. Secondly, the suppression of polygamy on the one hand and the continued prevalence of such customs as the prolonged feeding of a baby and sexual abstinence until weaning, of lengthy visits to parents (though the more urbanized the wife, the less common the visit), deprived the husband for long periods of a legitimate sex partner. Either then, or indeed, as a matter of course, the husband might have relations with some other woman; opportunities for this abounded in the town, with the absence of the tight communal moral code and constraints of customary society. Certainly it appears that few of Clément's Stanleyville subjects believed that their spouses were absolutely faithful.

Lastly, there is the important factor, amongst *évolués* at any rate, of the very limited number of girls with the level of training and education which *évolués* more and more desired in a wife. The relative neglect of girls' education, attributed by *évolués* to the Administration, but also no doubt due to parental neglect to send girls to school, was a great source of grievance. 'In civilizing the Congo, the Belgians have forgotten the

[1] Pons, *Growth of Stanleyville and the Composition of its African Population*, p. 264.

women', Stanleyville *évolués* said bitterly,[1] whilst the article of D'Oliviera, already quoted, was a *cri de cœur* for the better education and training of future *évolué* wives. In this problem are crystallized many of the tensions and distortions resulting from the decline of customary marriage in face of western, Christian ideas of marriage backed by the mild constraints of the ruling power. A corollary of this emerging type of marriage was that it was less and less a significant bond of union between two groups of relatives, whilst in so far as the marriage was between persons of two different tribes it was an association transcending the bounds of traditional relationships.

If the nature of the most intimate of all social relationships was affected by residence in the town, where European pressures and influences were most marked, so also were relationships with other people generally.[2] In the Bush, even after effective European penetration, relationships rarely extended beyond the tribe, the exceptions being those members of a particular tribe who might trade over a distance in some commodity, dried fish, for example. The most limited modification of traditional relationships is suggested by the link which the new arrival in the town first established. This, we have seen, was with a 'brother' (usually in the extended sense of member of the clan or tribe rather than in the strict sense of the word). Bearing in mind the traditional dependence on the support of the group, what more likely than that associations as close to the original as possible in respect of composition and function should appear in the town? In Stanleyville, for instance, the survey suggested that each tribal group represented in the city had its own tribal association, sometimes officially authorized, sometimes not, frequently subdivided by region, *territoire* or *chefferie*, and Clément believes that the tribal association of this kind was essentially a society for the mutual aid of its members.

At the same time the limitations of the link of tribal affinity, when it was no more than that, are indicated by the responses to questions put by Richelle in Elisabethville in the questionnaire which we have already noted. Certainly only 7 per cent. of his sample approved the complete abandonment of obligations of hospitality to tribal brothers, whilst 42 per cent.

---

[1] Clément, 'Social Patterns of Urban Life', p. 436.
[2] Clément, op. cit., pp. 439–92, is the source for this section, save as otherwise indicated.

believed in unconditional acceptance of the obligation. But it is significant that 51 per cent. approved the giving of hospitality only in the case of real need and for a limited time.[1] Of course, the tribal association could not simply be a reproduction of customary society, whilst at the same time it was something of an anachronism in an urban society of which so many of the norms and guide-lines were inter-tribal. But these associations did play an important role in maintaining some links with customary society and attitudes whilst at the same time somewhat assisting the process of adaptation.

Just as Stanleyville harboured a significant percentage of inter-tribal marriages (32·5 per cent. of the overall sample)— especially amongst *évolués*, so also it nurtured a number of voluntary associations whose basis was other than tribal— again, especially amongst *évolués*. Some might be residents' associations like the *Association Progrès Social Rive Gauche*, or 'old-boy' societies, such as ADAPES (Association of Former Pupils of the *Pères de Scheut*), almost by definition an *évolué* association, or a straightforward *évolué* group, the Association of *Evolués* of Stanleyville. Groups such as these appear to have provided some satisfactions for individuals lacking the supports of traditional society, yet for whom the purely tribal urban groupings were not sufficient. Membership of the one type of association did not preclude simultaneous membership of the other—indeed the membership of the same tribal association by the clerk and the labourer was a counter to the apparent development in urban society of embryonic class-groupings.

The importance of other than tribal relationships amongst Stanleyville *évolués* is further indicated by an inquiry concerning choice of friends and neighbours. Certainly the sample was small (nineteen), and one was not an *évolué*, but the results were in a broad way confirmed by a similar inquiry (concerning classmates, playmates, and so on) conducted amongst a much larger sample of schoolchildren. The adults interviewed were asked to name those whom they would choose as next-door neighbours, and to name their best friends and their wives' best friends—all in order of preference. It was discovered that 52 per cent. of the desired neighbours, 41 per cent. of the friends, and 39 per cent. of the wife's friends belonged to the chooser's tribe. When the desired friends and neighbours were categorized by

[1] Richelle, *Aspects psychologiques de l'acculturation*, pp. 160, 164.

socio-professional class, however, a more telling picture emerged, the percentages in the same class being: desired neighbours 79 per cent., friends 82 per cent. and wife's friends 77 per cent.

A final indication of the differing importance of tribal bonds amongst *évolués* and non-*évolués* is given in a study by Pons of settlement patterns in the three divisions into which the African city in Stanleyville was divided.

Conditioning factors were that plotholders held title to the occupation of their plots, mobility was possible through wide-spread sale of titles, and administrative action was no longer a significant factor in determining the pattern of settlement. It emerged that each division of the African city contained a more and a less westernized area (type of employment or occupation was the criterion), the portions of each division closest to the European city and commercial quarter containing a higher proportion of *évolués* than the more remote. A steady transition was apparent as one moved outwards from the European city, but there were no neighbourhoods exclusive to the more westernized inhabitants. Considered tribally, throughout the African city as a whole there were areas in which one or more tribal groups were significantly over-represented, though the reasons for this appear to have been partly extraneous. More important was the tendency in the less 'civilized' areas for members of the same tribe to be found in clusters, whereas for the more 'civilized' this implied ethnic affiliation was less important.[1]

An important non-customary type of association found in the towns was that of the Christian Churches, but little work has been published on the position and role of the Church in an urban setting as far as the Congo is concerned. However, some analogies may tentatively be drawn from *Christians of the Copperbelt*, the discerning work of John V. Taylor and Dorothea Lehmann. The authors of this study reckoned that, in a particular Rhodesian mine township in 1958, up to 25 per cent. of the adult population had at least occasional contact with one or other Christian denomination. It is reasonable to suppose, if only because of the wider spread of a primary education

[1] V. G. Pons, 'The Changing Significance of Ethnic Affiliation and of Western-ization in the African Settlement Patterns in Stanleyville (Belgian Congo)', *Social Implications of Urbanization and Industrialization in Africa South of the Sahara*, pp. 638–66.

provided largely by the missions, that this percentage would have been higher in the Congo cities, whilst the relatively greater numerical strength of the Roman Catholic Church, with its insistence on regular attendance at mass, might also have served to raise the percentage.

In the Congo, as in Northern Rhodesia, the fact that different missions evangelized different areas often meant that a particular mission had gathered together principally the people of one tribe or of a small number of tribes often speaking related languages. This phenomenon would in a measure be reflected in urban congregations. Thus in Stanleyville, partly because the B.M.S. had been the Protestant mission most concerned with the Lokele, its congregations would in some cases have a predominantly Lokele component. A missionary with experience of Stanleyville and the region to the west added that 'the Church became a real community for the town-dweller largely to the extent in which the Church coincided with tribal and kinship groupings'. In short, the Church, as an integrating force, often worked through the tribal group.

The quality of Church life must have varied a good deal, and if Europeans are ready to criticize such characteristics as too formal worship and a conception of Church membership too closely linked to status, they should remember the fragility of their own glasshouse. There are indications that, at the very least, Church membership often gave a real moral structure and reinforcement to the lives of members, and it seems likely that, as a class, it was the genuine Christians who best endured the searching experience of life in the town.[1]

A factor affecting the depth and extent of an immigrant's relationships in the town must surely have been the strength or absence of links with his village. In his Elisabethville questionnaire, administered in 1957-8, Richelle posed three groups of questions relating to this problem. To questions concerning frequency of visits to the ancestral village, the attitude approved by the great majority (75 per cent.) was a return to the village on each holiday, and full participation in the village's life. In the matter of sending gifts or money for the support of parents in the village, 33 per cent. approved the dispatch of money

---

[1] Based on Taylor and Lehmann, *Christians of the Copperbelt*, pp. 59, 271, and *passim*. Derived also from p. 95 above (Turnbull's verdict); Drake, *Problems confronting the Protestant Church, passim*; and personal information.

every month in a situation where the parents were not in fact poor, whereas 63 per cent. approved of help being given only in the event of financial difficulties. Only 4 per cent. favoured the denial of any such obligation. Approved attitudes towards the desirable place for retirement broadly reflected attitudes towards visits, 77 per cent. favouring a return to the village. 18 per cent., however, approved retirement in the town.[1]

It must be remembered that Richelle's tests were basically tests of approved attitudes as distinct from firm statements of actual conduct or intentions. Pons, in regard to Stanleyville in 1952-3 (albeit in a numerically much more restricted survey of thirty-eight men which did not include any white-collar workers), also introduced the important factor of the continued existence or the absence of links with the village of origin. He found that as many as 31·6 per cent. had no continuing rural contacts but that in addition to this category, who understandably proposed to end their days in Stanleyville, a further 36·8 per cent., who did claim continuing links, none the less regarded themselves as permanently urbanized. The figure of 31·6 per cent. who envisaged a complete or partial return to the village, in some cases before old age, indicates a much more limited enchantment with the village than a superficial reading of Richelle's results would suggest.[2]

It is appropriate to have devoted more attention to the modifications in his relationships with other Africans which the town-dweller must make than, say, to the changes in his material environment, if only because of the primary importance of the group in traditional society. Despite the fact that Congo townships were by and large the neatest and most hygienic in tropical Africa, the casual European visitor to the African quarters of any Congo city is prone to see in its physical limitations the root of all the spiritual and moral ailments of urban society. In its congestion and occasional squalor he sees the causes of disease, drunkenness, depravity and destitution, contrasting the whole unfavourably with some idyllic vision of a village peopled by Rousseauesque Negroes rejoicing in a state of nature. Only if alliteration chances to lead him on to 'detribalization' does he begin to come near to the real problems of urban living,

---

[1] Richelle, *Aspects psychologiques de l'acculturation*, pp. 161–5.
[2] Pons, 'The Changing Significance of Ethnic Affiliation and of Westernization in the African Settlement Patterns in Stanleyville', pp. 667–9.

and even here this overworked word is not very illuminating unless closely examined. In so far as it is a useful term, it is so because it may imply that tribal life is life essentially in a group whereas in the town collective attitudes and responses have often to yield to individual ones.

This can perhaps most clearly be seen in regard to morality—indeed in our consideration of marriage, for example, we have seen the considerable differences between customary marriage, with all its collective qualities and overtones, and the Western type of marriage, with its emphasis on the individual partners, which was increasingly common in the towns. That the canons and criteria of customary morality were essentially those of the closed group seems certain. De Cleene puts it in this way, in his *Introduction à l'ethnographie du Congo belge*:

The actions of the individual are regarded as good or bad according to their conformity with the rules of conduct, with usages and traditions sanctioned in the bosom of the community since time immemorial by the ancestors and spirits of the clan. Morality has no general or universal bearing. Conditioned by the relations of the group, it knew all the limitations of group morality.[1]

The consequences of this are, as it has been elsewhere expressed, that

in a primitive community . . . the moral objection to stealing is largely confined to stealing from members of the extended family, village or tribe. The moral obligation to support the extended family is held to condone theft from others.[2]

To go farther, morality, as the first clause of the last sentence implies, is essentially social—but social within the context of the group. Taylor and Lehmann imply both of these points when reciting various canons of Ba-Lunda morality, for the situations envisaged are those of small communities.

A good person is not quarrelsome, but peaceful; he does not use abusive words, he shares his food with others and is hospitable; he keeps secrets told to him, and tries to reconcile families who hate each other; if he sees a person developing bad habits, like stealing, he stops him and talks to him but not in front of others.[3]

[1] N. de Cleene, *Introduction à l'ethnographie du Congo belge* (Antwerp, De Sikkel, 1957), p. 68.
[2] J. Mars in M. Perham (ed.), *Mining, Commerce and Finance in Nigeria*, quoted in J. S. Coleman, *Nigeria, Background to Nationalism* (Berkeley, University of California Press, 1958), p. 148.
[3] Taylor and Lehmann, *Christians of the Copperbelt*, p. 88.

o

Understanding, then, that morality is by tradition integrally related to the more or less restricted group, an important psychological and moral problem is presented to the town-dweller. It may well be that a strong subconscious motive for membership of some urban association is a feeling of inadequacy in face of the lack of moral bearings in the new, more individualist *milieu*. If it is assumed for the moment that education in some degree imparts the notion of the general truth, the general standard, the idea of general validity, then the position of the more *évolué* town-dweller is likely to be psychologically more secure. None the less, it was from educated as well as uneducated inhabitants of the Copper Belt that Taylor and Lehmann repeatedly heard the statement, 'In the village I was a better man', the testimony of the speaker that he 'feels . . . he is a victim of the moral conflict between village standards and town ambition'.[1]

Turnbull's verdict is more positively pessimistic. In the town:

the rural African . . . quickly discovers that here he is no longer a member of a family, even of a tribe; that his neighbour is not bound by the same beliefs that bind him, and so cannot be relied on to behave as a reasonable man. The only sensible and safe thing to do is to mistrust one's neighbour, to think for oneself alone, to have no consideration for others.[2]

A similar adjustment from a collective world to an individualist one was required in the field of work. Work with a strong communal element gave place to work which, sometimes at any rate, was the subject of a mere contract and which to the eye of the labourer, at least, might well appear to serve no comprehensible purpose. But work, like so much else in the town, was primarily conditioned by Europeans' initiatives, and it is to the impact of European influences on the urban Congolese that we must now turn.

[1] Loc. cit.   [2] Turnbull, *The Lonely African*, p. 107.

XI

THE BIG CITY (2)

IT has been seen that in the early thirties urban administration had been organized on the basis of the *centre extra-coutumier* (pp. 115-16 above). By an ordinance of 20 July 1945 something of a change of course was indicated by the creation of a new unit of urban administration, the *cité indigène*. In theory it was to be adopted when the community was insufficiently mature to sustain the more complex, more autonomous structure of the C.E-C., and when more direct administration was in consequence desired. In practice, however, it seems that the rapid urbanization of wartime had proved the element of self-government in the *centres*, the fostering of which was in any case of considerable inherent difficulty, to be unworkable, with the result that the *centres* had in practice been administered by administrative officers. What the 1945 ordinance did, therefore, was to extend existing practice to new urban agglomerations by tidying up its legal basis. Henceforward the creation of new *centres extra-coutumier* virtually ceased and direct administration of *cités* and *centres* was the general rule.[1] Significant African participation in municipal government began only when from 1957 certain urban areas were designated *communes* in which members of the municipal council were for the first time elected.

While in administration the European role predominated, the judicial system of the *centres*, according to Grévisse, was sometimes one in which ill-tutored and ill-supervised Congolese judges faced two daunting tasks. On the one hand they had to administer justice according either to custom or equity in situations in which custom might have little to say because the situations were not comprehended by custom, and when their training and ability might be insufficient for them to grasp the criteria on which equity must be based. On the other hand, the

[1] *African Survey*, pp. 222-3, 557; Gille, 'Politique indigène', pp. 734-7.

tribunaux de centre had as a second major task the enforcement of a whole code of police regulations mostly related to the preservation of law and order. Necessary as they mostly were, they were European laws and not such as to command instinctive endorsement in the judges called upon to administer them. The result might be either an extraordinary degree of arbitrariness in the penalties imposed, or alternatively a quite ludicrous uniformity. In consequence it would command no confidence as a court for the settlement of a wide range of matters, but was, rather, feared for its extensive activity in the enforcement of police regulations. In the words of a generally applauded complaint about a *tribunal de centre*, quoted by Grévisse:

Our tribunal has become an instrument for the application of the law. People fear it, but they do not any more esteem it. People no longer have sufficient confidence to take a civil case to it. To resolve differences in matters which we consider vital nothing is available any more.

It is interesting that when confidence in the tribunal was thus lacking, people would often take their disputes to some trusted senior member of their tribe living in the town.[1] The success of the *tribunaux de centre* may have been greater in places other than Elisabethville, Jadotville and Kongolo, where Grévisse obtained his evidence, but it does not appear that much success was ever claimed for them.

While urban administration and urban courts were impersonal, as far as his work was concerned the urban African could have a widely varying relationship with his boss, almost invariably European. At one extreme was the kind of situation which generally prevailed at Stanleyville by the early fifties. Here, it would appear, the exercise of paternalism was, by most employers, limited to that prescribed by law—principally the provision of all the various allowances such as family and housing, partial payment during illness or, after 1949, for incapacity caused by accident, and so forth. In a word, the essential element in the relationship was the contractual, the agreement to provide a given wage and other benefits in return for labour. By European standards there is nothing more than the usual type of relationship between employer and employee, but there are strong grounds for believing that this is

[1] Grévisse, *Juridictions indigènes*, pp. 45–61.

a relationship which an African finds unsatisfactory, at least when he has recently left a tribal environment.

It was suggested in Chapter V (pp. 98-100) that paternalism, defined as a combination of authority and concern, was a European attitude which often met a real need in the African when he was removed from his traditional way of life and habits. There is abundant evidence, right from the early days of European rule, of African attachment to a European in this kind of way, and psychological bases for the relationship have been suggested by writers such as Mannoni and Tempels. Relating this concept to town life, I was very much struck by the remark of a thoughtful—and eminent—Congolese, that what the first-generation urban African ideally needed was the positive, personal concern of a European.[1] Carrying the concept farther and relating it specifically to the attitude of the employer, Tempels points to the rude shock when the employee, who wants a relationship with his employer which he would sum up in that common declaration 'You are my father and mother', meets only with the response, 'I am ignorant of your interests; I do not know your rights; I only think of one thing: if this evening there are three hundred bricks here, I will give you two francs.'[2] Rubbens develops this theme of pseudo-filiation, and the rupturing of it, in this way:

In engaging his services, the African does not believe that he is simply selling his labour. He sees in the labour contract something more than the *do ut facies* which is the European party's reason for making the agreement. In the mentality of the African, to engage himself is to choose for himself a new master, it is an act of adherence to such a master. From this master he expects, beyond the legal salary and the benefits stipulated in the agreement, help and protection in every circumstance.

Henceforth he will call himself the man of such and such a European, of such and such a company, he will use and abuse this name like a passport. He feels naïvely proud to share in the wealth, in the importance and in the power of his lord. . . . Over a bottle of beer he will boast with jealous pride of 'his firm', not hesitating to make disparaging comparisons with others. For all that he will not stop himself from obtaining from his master all the benefits possible at the price of the least effort, his scruples will perhaps not prevent

---

[1] Personal information.
[2] P. Tempels, 'La Philosophie de la rebellion', *Dettes de guerre*, p. 22.

him from stealing [from his master], but he will not permit a third party to do moral or material harm to 'his house'.

The labour contract for the African is therefore essentially a contract of loyalty, and involves a change of personal status.[1]

'But', Rubbens continues, 'the day when he realizes that the other contracting party has not meant to engage himself in a pact of fidelity, he is deceived and dismayed.' When his master will not listen to his palaver, he feels deceived, when his master refuses to support him before the judge, he feels deserted, and when finally, at the end of his resources, he seeks his master's help in vain, he is convinced that he has been betrayed. Here then, on this analysis, is the source of many of the ills of urban society. At the very least it is a potent source of racial disharmony and may have the further outcome of strikes, or of an animosity always prone to erupt in violence.[2]

Whilst rebuff of this kind could be a common experience for the ordinary labourer, rebuff of a more complex type was often the lot of the white-collar worker. By virtue of his attainments, the clerk, for example, might feel that he merited acceptance into the administrative grade in the firm for which he worked. But until the later fifties, and even then only on a small scale, there was no possibility of promotion to the managerial administrative class, and so a resentment at this block might be coupled with the residual disappointment at the narrowly contractual nature of the relationship with the employer—a disappointment which even an évolué could still feel. Moreover, resentment at the artificial block would be felt not only by those who were in fact competent to overcome it, but also by those who were not, but believed they were. If there is anything in the view that a common évolué failing was to identify the expressions and symbols of managerial activity with its essence, to believe that knowing how to write, to dictate letters, to confer, to telephone was to understand the process of management,[3] then there would be many who would feel rebuffed.

[1] A. Rubbens, 'L'Indiscipline des travailleurs', *Dettes de guerre*, pp. 104–5.

[2] Ibid., pp. 105–9. Note the comment of an eminent industrialist following a tour of the Congo in 1946–7: 'It is striking to see . . . the lack of concern of many European *agents*, especially those at the bottom of the hierarchy, for the native workers for whom they are responsible.' (E. Van der Straeten, 'Quelques réflexions à la suite d'un voyage dans la colonie', *Bulletin des séances de l'I.R.C.B.*, XVIII, 1, 1947, p. 214.)

[3] See, e.g., Rousseau, *Relations entre chefs d'entreprises blancs et employés autochtones*, p. 630.

The attitude to the European, and to European authority, of the third main category of male Congolese town-dwellers seems usually to have been different. It is certainly the common European opinion in the Congo that the skilled and semi-skilled workers were the most contented and least restless (personnel officers of the *Union Minière*, for example, believe this in the light of experience). Amongst the reasons for this may be the fact that the prolonged training necessary for, say, a lathe-operator or pattern-maker inevitably involves a close association between European teacher and his pupil with (on the pseudo-filiation theory) attendant satisfactions.

Underlying such harmonious relationships there was, it would seem, a real element of contentment and fulfilment. The craftsman is heir to the esteem and prestige which a craftsman, the iron worker, for instance, often enjoyed in traditional society, whilst there is also all the evidence of traditional African craftsmanship to suggest that skilled and, only less, semi-skilled work command the satisfaction of creativity. Railway engines in the Congo follow the regrettable Continental practice of remaining unnamed: I was greatly struck on one occasion to see written in chalk on the smoke-box door of a locomotive, presumably by a proud driver, 'Marie-Thérèse, la plus belle machine du monde!'

A more substantial insight into attitudes to skilled manual work is given by the results of a test given during the Stanley-ville study. In reply to the question 'If you had a son who was now ten to twelve years of age, what trade would you like him to follow, and why?', occupations involving skilled manual work commanded nearly half the votes of a sample consisting of clerks, motor drivers and unskilled workers. Of the clerks, only 13 per cent. chose the same calling for their sons, and whilst 33 per cent. chose the more exalted profession of *assistant-médical*, 25 per cent. wanted their sons to be mechanics. Of the drivers (a category representing moderately skilled work), the occupations of clerk, teacher and male nurse accounted for only 36 per cent. of the votes, whilst that of mechanic claimed 23 per cent. and that of carpenter, 38 per cent.[1] It should

[1] N. Xydias, 'Labour: Conditions, Aptitudes, Training', *Social Implications of Industrialization and Urbanization in Africa South of the Sahara*, pp. 359–60. In the published results of the test, occupations obtaining less than 5 per cent. of votes were ignored: those remaining were mechanic, carpenter, clerk, medical assistant, teacher, male nurse.

be remembered that white-collar workers were the best paid.

So far we have spoken of the relationship with European authority, in its various manifestions, entered into by the three main categories of men dwelling in the towns. The framework of the relationships studied was one whose main basis was a European-type employer–employee relationship. A major departure from this pattern now falls to be considered—the highly developed paternalism of some of the big Congo companies. We have already spoken of the inception of the policy of labour stabilization and of its striking results during the thirties, with particular reference to the *Union Minière*. During the post-war period the results of the policy were yet more impressive. For instance, the male mortality rate, which had already dropped from 39·1 per thousand in 1925–9 to 7·1 per thousand in 1935–9, had declined further to 2·74 per thousand by 1956 and increased only to 3·03 by 1960. Infant mortality rates over the same stages were 161·0, 43·1, 12·71 and 6·82 per thousand, whilst the demographic balance also improved with a continuation of the increase in the ratio of women to men—they totalled 26 per cent., 54 per cent., 84 per cent. and 85 per cent. of the number of men. The child population, as one might expect, also increased markedly; indeed, the increase in the ratio of live births to total deaths was from 23·6 per cent. per thousand in 1935–9 to 54·18 in 1950 and 60·22 in 1960. Finally the figures for re-engagement improved, 47 per cent. of all workers in 1959 having served ten or more years. In 1940, of those who had completed one three-year term, 25 per cent. had been with the company for more than ten years.[1]

These brute figures do not only testify to the continuing success of the *Union Minière*'s medical and social policy: they also indicate that the employer–employee relationship was much more than a narrow contractual one. Indeed, the defenders of the policy—whose principal initial and continuing inspiration was of course economic—contend that a company like the *Union Minière* gives to its employees the kind of employment relationship which they desire; that is, one in which the employer assumes responsibility for the general welfare of the employee. This is apparent in, for example, the physical

[1] *Notice sur le statut du personnel* (Elisabethville, *Union Minière du Haut-Katanga*, duplicated, 1961), pp. 2–5. See also pp. 118-20 above.

facilities of one of the 'workers' cities' at Kolwezi. It contains a social club, close to which is a semi-circular amphitheatre for film shows, a market, a sports ground, a church. The more detailed concern of the company for the individual workman is seen in the record card kept in the office of the European *chef du camp*, whilst an important part of his functions was to settle palavers. 'I am at their disposal', said one *chef du camp*, and one believed him.

A corollary of the assumption of general responsibility for the worker was that a paternalist company took over some of the roles of government. It had to have its own police whilst a *chef du camp* would also have his own trusted *hommes de confiance*, usually, one gathered, long-serving employees and respected members of the various tribes represented in a camp, who would either nip any unrest or disturbances in the bud or else forewarn the *chef du camp*. A somewhat different system seems to have prevailed in the camps of *Plantations Lever* (successor to *Huileries du Congo Belge*). There a petty dispute between members of the same tribe would be left to be settled by a tribal elder (i.e., an elder in the context of the camp). An inter-tribal dispute in civil or petty criminal matters would be put to the Congolese *chef du camp* (elected by the workers but paid by the company) to resolve with the aid of a tribunal consisting of members of different tribes. If this was unsuccessful, then the personnel department of the company would intervene (as it would right at the beginning if the issue was one directly affecting the company, such as theft of its property). Only if all these 'domestic' resources failed would the matter be referred to the State.

If the paternalist company assumed responsibility for the life of its work-people as a whole, it no less assumed responsibility for their families. The expressions of this responsibility are summed up in schools, kindergartens (attendance at both of which was sometimes compulsory), training in housecraft, comprehensive medical care, ante-natal and post-natal clinics. In short, a man's family shared in the various social services just as he did himself. Random indications of the scale of the social services provided by the *Union Minière* are given by pointing to the forty-one doctors which it employed and the 1,417 hospital beds which it provided in 1960, whilst the total personnel employed in general and technical education and in the non-medical social services in the same year was 805. This was for a labour force of some 22,000 and a total community of some 95,000.[1] Moreover, the hospitals and other facilities appear to be most attractively built and well equipped; it was not for nothing that the Senatorial Commission of 1947 drew attention to the better-quality facilities provided by the big companies, as compared with the State.[2]

In short, the paternalistic company not only made the relationship with its employee much more than a contractual one, by concerning itself with the whole of his life; it also acted in the same fashion towards his dependants. An important corollary of such a policy was that the introduction of the Congolese to European culture and technology was regulated and smoother. Not the least implication of this was that some of the tensions and evils of town life were mitigated or avoided. To take two examples, Maria Leblanc, as a result of her study of the female personality in an urban setting, suggests that amongst women cultural change took place more as a result of education in the domestic arts than of academic education:[3] such *éducation familiale* was more readily available in the camp or *cité* of the company than elsewhere. In November 1960, apart from those women who had received instruction of this kind as children, who were many, some 3,000 out of 18,500 women in *Union Minière* camps were attending adult courses of this sort.[4]

Again, because control over residence was strict, there were not found in company communities the vagabond boys and youths who, increasingly, and especially after the slackening of the economic tempo in the mid-fifties, were a problem in the cities. As early as 1945, a time of over-full employment, Van Wing wrote of a group of such at Lusambo who, having completed primary school and finding no acceptable place in society, lived by theft.[5] Here was a growing urban problem—

[1] *Notice sur le statut du personnel*, pp. 18, 24.

[2] *Rapport de la mission sénatoriale*, E. Van Eyndonck, 'La Dêfense de la santé publique', p. 167. My personal impressions of the operation of the stabilized labour policy are based on visits to *cités* or camps of the *Union Minière* at Kolwezi and Jadotville, of the B.C.K. at Elisabethville, and of *Plantations Lever* at Elisabetha (Orientale), in 1962, and on discussions with officials there.

[3] M. Leblanc, *Personnalité de la femme katangaise: contribution à l'étude de son acculturation* (Louvain, Publications Universitaires, 1960), p. 280.

[4] *Notice sur le statut du personnel*, p. 24.

[5] Van Wing, *La Situation actuelle des populations congolaises*, p. 586.

and for that matter rural as well—and in it were the origins of the *jeunesse* problem of the period after Independence. The testimony of some of those who saw the phenomenon developing in Katanga[1] is essentially the same as that of an Inspector of Technical Education in regard to Orientale province, writing, it would seem, in the early fifties, and quoted and amplified by Nelly Xydias in the Stanleyville survey report.

'Some of the young people from country districts, immediately their primary studies are finished, move into the European centres, where they work only on a casual basis, after a varying spell of vagabondage. Others remain in the country areas, but refuse agricultural work and live as parasites. As for the young people in the towns, most of them also are familiar with long periods of idleness.

'After five or six years at a primary school the boy feels he has a claim to a post as a junior clerk. But he cannot find it and spends months, sometimes years, in looking for an unobtainable situation. It is only under pressure of dire necessity that he will finally take a job as an unskilled labourer—since he has no specialized knowledge, he considers himself worthy of something better, because he has been to school.

'The principal cause of the critical situation of native youth, in my view, is the excessive disproportion between the number of primary schools ending nowhere and that of post-primary schools (ratio of 60 to 1). The former pupils of the primary schools will be a breeding-ground for unemployed, for loafers and gangsters, of no use to the community, disappointed, discouraged and to-morrow in revolt.'[2]

There has been a good deal of criticism of the paternalism of the big companies on the grounds that the workers are treated like cattle, that this is 'Big Brother' and *1984* in anticipation. Much of the criticism, one suspects, is because paternalism, to the European trade unionist or progressive, is a dirty word, or stems from Western notions of class structure and class struggle, or is informed by excessively developed Western ideas of the autonomous individual for whom a dependent relationship is indecent. A more substantial and here more relevant criticism is that this benevolent paternalism hinders rather than helps the process of acculturation, because it treats the worker

[1] I am particularly indebted to conversations with Dr. Th. Theuws and Mlle L. Centner.
[2] N. Xydias, 'Labour: Conditions, Aptitudes' (Stanleyville), p. 325.

as sub-human, giving him every comfort but denying him liberty and initiative.[1]

Clearly this is a danger which may not always have been avoided, but this line of criticism invites a number of responses. First of all, the allegedly suppressed yearning for a freedom hitherto denied them did not result in major eruptions from within the camps and *cités* of the big companies at those times following independence in which there was all too much opportunity. Indeed, there was frequently a surprising loyalty to the firm and a general relief when conditions approached normality again. Secondly, there were from within the system itself significant developments countering its admitted dangers. These were such modifications as the promotion of Africans to the administrative grade in the later fifties (by the end of 1960 the *Union Minière* had eighty-three African *agents du cadre*);[2] the decision of the *Union Minière* in 1959 to give the value of rations and family allowances to all its workers in cash.[3] (Hitherto the lower-paid and more junior had resented the fact that they received their allowances in kind and thus had no free choice in what they consumed.)

Again, from 1948 many of the Katanga companies began to grant housing loans to approved employees who wanted to build their own houses outside the *cités*, a move which did something to meet a grievance of the more sophisticated. Finally, it should be remembered that those responsible for running the policy were not those responsible for production. Moreover, they were, in my experience, intelligent and devoted people, so that in consequence the system could develop into something in a sense better than it deserved to be, bearing in mind the mainly economic reasons for its inception and continuation. With the exception of some of the (great majority of) *évolués* not admitted to administrative rank, who were often discontented, the general African content with the system, to which there is a good deal of testimony from Africans themselves, may well have been the response to an initiative which met a real need in the African passing out of the exclusive sway of his traditional culture. It remains true that even enlightened paternalism is not an appropriate attitude in regard to Africans at all stages of their development.

[1] See, e.g., Malengreau, 'Le Congo à la croisée des chemins', pp. 100–1.
[2] *Notice sur le statut du personnel*, p. 1.   [3] Ibid., p. 7.

Although the urban African's relationship with his employer was obviously one of considerable importance, it was no less obviously not his only relationship with Europeans and with European rule and laws in their urban setting. The legislation underlying the relationships between Europeans and town-dwelling Africans changed little between the early days of Belgian rule and its closing period. On the one hand it reflected the failure of the theory of colonial policy, such as it was, ever to come to terms with the fact that rapid economic development was creating a large urban population, on the other hand, that legislation expressed pragmatically the practical need to make some sort of legislative provision for governing inter-racial relationships in urban areas of mixed racial composition. That legislation therefore imposed measures of separation between the two communities—measures which were reasonable when initiated, given the markedly unequal development of European and African, but which came to bear an increasingly restrictive and repressive air when they were maintained in face of a growing town population, which was more and more permanently urbanized, and which came to include men of standing and attainments comparable with Europeans.

Take first the case of housing. A law of 14 September 1898, obliging the Administration to set aside land for separate areas in new townships for Europeans and non-Europeans, continued in operation under Belgian rule, and was confirmed by an ordinance of 12 February 1913. This legislation was strengthened by an ordinance of 29 May 1926 compelling Europeans to reside in their own separate locations, but permitting non-Europeans to live in these areas if granted a permit by the administrator. The beneficiaries of this last proviso were exclusively domestic servants and their families.[1] The result of this legislation was to stamp a predominant characteristic on the towns of the Congo, with their African areas separated from European areas by a neutral zone consisting of, say, a park, hospital or military camp. In the case of Leopoldville, for example, this neutral ground consisted of the golf course, police camp, Zoological Gardens, a park and the commercial quarter; Leopoldville was also typical in that Portuguese and Greeks, those most involved in retail trade with Africans, had

---

[1] Brausch, *Belgian Administration in the Congo* (London, O.U.P. for the Institute of Race Relations, 1961), pp. 21–22.

their establishments along the Avenue de Gaulle; that is, as close as possible to their African clientèle.

Here, then, was the Belgian variant of the physical, urban pattern general in colonial Africa, a pattern which only began to be modified in the last eighteen months of Belgian rule. Legislative action then was certainly draconian, for an ordinance of 14 February 1959 abolished all discriminatory legislation in housing. Due, however, to the great disparity in income which obtained between European and African there could hardly be any immediate widespread effect: but Government departments and some private firms made it possible for African staff doing work similar to that of their European staff to move to European residential areas.[1]

For a long time the educational provision for European and African children reflected the starkly physical division between black and white areas in the towns. The beginnings of a change in this segregationist policy came in 1948, when legally recognized or adopted Euro-African children were admitted into schools hitherto reserved for European children. By degrees this bridgehead was broadened to include other categories, with the result that by the end of 1959 the annual number of admissions of non-European children into European primary schools had risen to 1,493.

Further and more radical departures from segregated education came in 1955 with the creation of inter-racial *athénées* (high schools) and the opening of Lovanium University. The foundation of this Catholic University was followed in 1956 by the creation of a State University at Elisabethville, both being inter-racial. In 1959 all the special regulations governing the admission of non-European children to European (now re-named Metropolitan) schools were abolished, and by 1960 all schools were officially inter-racial.[2] Change here had certainly been radical and rapid, but there had not been enough time to shake off the legacy of earlier years with their emphasis on making *primary* schooling available as widely as possible and the relative neglect (originating, it is claimed by apologists, in a fear of creating an *élite* separated from the mass) of secondary education. The outcome was a marked constriction in the educational pipeline for Congolese children at the end of primary schooling, a constriction which, in turn, meant

[1] Brausch, *Belgian Administration in the Congo*, pp. 22–23.   [2] Ibid,, pp. 26–28, 88.

that the number of Congolese qualified to enter university was very small indeed. In 1959–60, including students from Ruanda-Urundi, there were 344 African students at Lovanium and seventy-seven at Elisabethville.[1] At the time of Independence, as we all know, there were only seventeen Congolese university graduates.

Housing, education—chronologically the pattern was similar in the hierarchy which included political and administrative power, the civil service. Here again, until the fifties the situation was uncomplicated. The higher branch of the service could be entered only by those who had completed the metropolitan secondary school course, or who had taken a degree, and who were of Belgian (or Luxembourg) nationality. Thus Africans were, whilst these rulings obtained, excluded—just as Europeans were excluded from the African preserve, the lower branch of the civil service. As long as Africans could not meet the professional requirements of the higher branch, this two-tier system was more or less accepted. From 1953 onwards, however, a growing number of African civil servants had acquired the necessary professional standing for admission to the higher branch of the service, but were denied it because they were not Belgian nationals, only subjects.

Eventually, in the spring of 1958—that is to say, after a delay which disappointed the growing number of Africans with a stake in the matter—and after an initial, abortive decision which alienated European civil servants by laying down unified salary scales lower than those they had hitherto enjoyed, the decision was taken to integrate the civil service, as from the beginning of 1959. In consequence, in the first eight months of the operation of the new law, 742 Africans were appointed to grades previously reserved to Europeans.[2] Judged by this result the measure may appear radical indeed: none the less an observer like Grévisse believed that

Its general orientation signified a concern to preserve the level of efficiency of the public services and, by this bias, to safeguard the acquired rights of Europeans, much more than a desire to see the administrative *cadres* rapidly reflect the political imperatives of the country and the respective importance of the two racial groups.[3]

[1] R. Lemarchand, 'The Bases of Nationalism among the Bakongo', *Africa*, XXXI, 4, October 1961, p. 352.
[2] Brausch, *Belgian Administration in the Congo*, pp. 29–30.
[3] F. Grévisse, 'Évolués et formation des élites', *Livre blanc*, I, p. 401.

Furthermore, in August 1959 Vice Governor-General Schoeller observed that the incorporation of African *assistants médicaux* and *assistants agricoles* into the fourth grade of the higher civil service had not involved any marked change in their responsibilities.[1]

In accordance with the pattern of change which we have seen to have been emerging in the fifties, and especially the later fifties, the original system, whereby the civil status of Africans and Europeans was different, also underwent modification. Two measures were taken to extend to two categories of Africans—*évolués* and those in process of evolution—certain privileges enjoyed by Europeans. Thus by legislation of 1948 any African who was literate, who was not a polygamist and who had not within the previous five years been convicted of certain specified offences, could apply for the *carte du mérite civique*. This entitled the holder, notably, to be judged in the *tribunal de territoire*, the point being that that court was presided over by a European, and to a special position in regard to the acquisition of real property. An attempt to meet the case of Africans who had adopted a more definitely European mode of life was made by the revival in 1952 of the process, defunct since the time of the Congo Independent State, of *immatriculation* (registration). The essential condition for *immatriculation* was that the candidate should be able 'to justify by his education and his way of life a state of civilization implying the ability to enjoy the rights and fulfil the obligations laid down in written law'. The reward for the successful candidate was that he should be subject to European and not customary courts, have all rights under the Civil Code and have similar treatment with Europeans on public transport vehicles.[2] An extension of the rights of members of both of the above categories came in an ordinance of 1 July 1955 by which they were allowed to buy all categories of alcohol in restaurants[3]—a right which was effectively a precondition of the patronage of European restaurants.

The common characteristic of the measures taken in these four directions is that they constituted only a late and limited departure from the original segregation. 'Limited' is a key

[1] Schoeller to Minister of the Congo, 13 August 1959, in *Congo 1959*, p. 103.
[2] *African Survey*, pp. 224–6.
[3] Brausch, *Belgian Administration in the Congo*, p. 24.

word, for what seems to have impressed the Africans who stood to benefit by these reforms was not so much the benefits they obtained, but the fact that those benefits did not in the aggregate come near to constituting full social equality with Europeans.

The denial of this equality took various forms. In 1951 a Congo missionary wrote that

Contempt increases with the considerable number of *petits blancs* ['Poor Whites' is a possible, but too pejorative translation] who feel the possible competition as soon as they set foot on Congo soil.

The Congo is becoming rather colour-bar and in Leo[poldville] one feels that an increasing gulf is separating White and Black.[1]

Alan P. Merriam, the American anthropologist, on the basis of residence in the Congo in 1951–2 and again in 1959–60, comments that his own observation

led me to believe that those Belgians who truly felt friendship for the Congolese on an equal basis were few and far between. Belgians in my experience seldom had true African friends, seldom invited Africans to their homes, seldom felt that Africans were their intellectual equals. On the contrary, the sentiments most often expressed were that the Congolese were, in truth, savages, and I could not count the number of times that their differing cultural behaviour was explained to me in terms of the 'fact' that 'they were up in trees just fifty years ago'.[2]

André Ryckmans, in 1958, was much disturbed by the indifference, or worse, of most Leopoldville Europeans to the African population, and especially the *évolués*,[3] whilst Marc Richelle, whose socio-psychological inquiry has already been made use of, goes farther. In his experience, gained in parts of Katanga in 1957–8, Europeans who attempted to establish with Africans social relations similar to those they maintained with other Europeans would run the risk of being ostracized by many fellow Europeans.[4] It is also significant that Georges Hostelet, the title of whose book, *L'Œuvre civilisatrice de la Belgique au Congo . . .* , published in 1954, suggests a basic sympathy with Belgium's Congo work, can very much regret

[1] Quoted in 'J.K.', *André Ryckmans*, p. 95.
[2] A. P. Merriam, *Congo: Background of Conflict* (Evanston, Northwestern University Press, 1961), pp. 57–58.
[3] 'J.K.', *André Ryckmans*, pp. 185–90.
[4] Richelle, *Aspects psychologiques de l'acculturation*, p. 84.

P

that 'all Belgians continue to believe in the Congo, that they belong to a race of medieval Seigneurs'.[1]

The ways in which an attitude of determined racial domination expressed itself were various; a number of incidents build up a picture. There was the European who forced his way to the front of the queue of Congolese at the Post Office; there was the Belgian proprietress of a butcher's shop who refused to allow two Congolese accompanying a European lady themselves to enter the shop to make their own purchases—they had to wait outside and be served there; there was the refusal of the European members in Equateur parish to accept their priest's wish that chiefs and évolués should be allowed to sit on chairs during Mass, along with the Europeans, instead of on benches; there was the restaurant manager and clientèle who, after it was no longer possible to exclude évolués from restaurants, insulted a European and his Congolese guest—as it happened, the future General Mobutu.[2] Just such an incident seems to have had a profound effect on Patrice Lumumba himself. He first came to Leopoldville as an immatriculé and expressed a positive pride in being Belgian after a visit to the much less sophisticated Brazzaville across the river. A month after his arrival, when walking in a daydream in the European residential area, he bumped into a European woman. 'Can't you take care, sale macaque [dirty ape],' was the response, before he could apologize. This, the supreme injury for a Congolese, turned hopes into illusions.[3]

Against actions such as these the Belgian Administration took such action as it could, both specifically, by, for instance, appeals to shopkeepers to abandon discriminatory practices, backed eventually by a strong ordinance on 1 October 1959,[4] and more generally. In July 1956, for instance, Governor-General Pétillon declaimed that the time was approaching when the Congolese would be saying 'Brother' instead of 'Father' to the Whites, whilst in December of the following year a decree was promulgated laying down penalties against anyone who 'showed racial or ethnic aversion or hatred'.[5]

---

[1] Hostelet, L'Œuvre civilisatrice de la Belgique au Congo, I, p. 498.

[2] It is unnecessary to indicate sources for such everyday incidents, but all are particular episodes of the fifties, published or told to me.

[3] P. de Vos, Vie et mort de Lumumba (Paris, Calmann-Levy, 1961), pp. 30–31.

[4] Brausch, Belgian Administration in the Congo, p. 25.

[5] Slade, The Belgian Congo, pp. 20–21.

But, in sum, it would seem that the actions which the Government did take—we have seen what it did in the representative, once-segregated fields of housing, education, the civil service, and civil status—either came too late to make much practical difference (the first three), or were from the start rejected as inadequate (*immatriculation* and the *carte du mérite civique*). There seems to have been particular disappointment at the mouse which the commission on *immatriculation* eventually brought forth. 'Juridical assimilation', writes Dr. Slade, 'was in fact the least interesting of any form of equality from the African point of view.' A reason for this particular disappointment was also that *évolués* had hoped for what the Commission had indeed actively considered giving, full social and economic assimilation.[1]

'Social and economic assimilation'—here, indeed, was the crux and crisis of Belgian tutelage. If the will was lacking at governmental level to take drastic action in good time, it seems to have been lacking even more amongst Belgians in the Congo generally. And, of course, it was upon the attitudes of these that the inter-racial and inter-cultural experience of urban, and especially *évolué* Congolese largely depended. Ruth Slade sums up the general Belgian attitude and the *évolué* response in this way (she is writing of the post-war period):

[The *évolués*] were turning their backs on traditional Bantu society, and saw their best hope for the future in assimilation to the Western way of life. It was an overwhelming disappointment to them when they became aware of the attitude of the great majority of the Europeans towards their aspirations, expressed in such modified forms of the colour bar as were beginning to make themselves felt in the Congo, especially in the sphere of social relations. They became aware that while the Whites had taken seriously their task as 'tutors', had striven in various ways to introduce new and Western forms of culture, and to a certain extent to Europeanize the Africans, there was a point at which they seemed determined that the process should stop. When it came to inviting Africans to a meal, to buying meat at the same butcher's shop, to travelling next to an African in the train, to letting their children sit on the same school benches as young Africans, to the great bitterness of the *évolués* the Europeans objected. All had been well as long as the Africans had remained

[1] Slade, *The Belgian Congo*, pp. 22–23; *African Survey*, p. 226; personal information.

as children who were to be taught and encouraged and gradually persuaded to change what appeared to the Europeans to be the more barbarous of their habits. But the limit was reached at the adolescent stage, when Africans began to want to be treated on terms of equality, as adults, to be regarded as brothers rather than as sons. . . .[1]

The reasons why the attitudes of many Belgians in the Congo —which were similar to the attitudes of many Europeans in colonial Africa—were what they were remain obscure in the sense that no systematic work has been done upon racial attitudes amongst members of this group. But there are useful pointers from work done in comparable situations in other areas. Richelle, for instance, believed that Katanga Europeans applied to Congolese the general European stereotype of Africans, as it has been summed up by Carothers, whose experience had been in East Africa. This stereotype certainly attributes to Africans a number of virtues, but these very virtues—cheerfulness, stoicism, self-confidence, loyalty, lack of rancour, etc.—are commonly of a kind which are consistent with a dependent status, whilst the (longer) list of failings—lack of foresight, perseverence, judgement and humility, an incapacity for objective thought, instability, and so forth—is such as to underline the African's unsuitability for a relationship of equals.[2]

Richelle makes the further point that many Europeans in the Congo were not in a situation where their everyday contacts involved relationships which challenged the stereotype.[3] There may also be an additional reason for not abandoning the stereotype—which may not have given a wholly incorrect picture of the 'primitive' African—when confronted with an évolué. It is that the maintenance of the stereotype, which shades off insensibly into the maintenance of prejudice, justifies advantages for the European—for example, the superior rewards that go with greater innate abilities, or with a privileged position. At the same time, the abandonment of the stereotype in favour of a more receptive attitude to évolués runs counter to the racist ideas widely held amongst Europeans: for example, that there are basic physical and mental differences between groups which are due to hereditary biology and which nothing

[1] Slade, *The Belgian Congo*, pp. 11–12.
[2] Richelle, *Aspects psychologiques de l'acculturation*, p. 81.   [3] Ibid., pp. 81–82.

can change; or that biological crossing of the species involves degeneracy in the offspring.[1] Furthermore, most social psychologists would probably agree with the point put by the authors of the classic in its field, *Frustration and Aggression*, in this way: that the existence of an obviously distinct group, in this case distinguished by colour, is an instigation 'to aggressive responses which are prohibited within the group and must be either directed towards the self at the price of great discomfort or displaced to groups of persons outside the society'.[2]

But whatever the causes of European reserve, prejudice or aggression, there is no doubt of the effect these attitudes had upon Africans, and especially *évolués*, just at the point when *évolués* at any rate were hoping for acceptance. It was marked enough at the level of the ordinary wage-labourer. Commenting on an examination of works' council minutes undertaken during the Stanleyville survey, already referred to, Nelly Xydias points out the frequency with which ordinary workers display an 'anxiety to win respect for their dignity as human beings'. In one case protest was made at the hurtful insults of European supervisors; in another, more simply, 'the workers asked that their foreman should treat them as men'.[3]

Somewhat more precise were the results of a test designed to measure racial attitudes. The test was given to a group of primary-school girls and secondary-school boys, and included requests to name the three best and three worst qualities of white people. Nelly Xydias found it striking that in the case of white people's good qualities 40 per cent. of the replies enumerated qualities manifesting themselves essentially in relation to Africans, whilst, of the bad qualities specified, 69 per cent. of the replies were also in relation to Africans. In the latter category, 65 per cent. were accounted for by such qualities as 'unjust, harsh, ill-natured, unkind, cheating the Blacks . . . insulting, contemptuous, humiliating the Blacks (calling them niggers, etc.)'[4]

---

[1] See Arnold Rose, *The Roots of Prejudice* (Paris, UNESCO, 6th impression, 1960), *passim*.

[2] J. Dollard, L. W. Doob, N. E. Miller, O. H. Mowrer and R. R. Sears, *Frustration and Aggression* (New Haven, Yale University Press, 9th impression, 1957), p. 90.

[3] N. Xydias, 'Labour: Conditions, Aptitudes, Training' (Stanleyville Survey), *op. cit.*, p. 301.

[4] Ibid., pp. 362–4.

Whilst all Africans resented being treated in ways which offended their human dignity, the *évolué* felt such treatment the more precisely because he felt himself more on a level with the European and because he wished not merely not to be insulted but to be positively instructed and befriended. There is an almost pathetic implication in the editorial in an early number of the *évolué* journal, *La Voix du congolais*:

And as the white man in fact enjoys a superior education to ours, is it not up to him to incline towards us to read what is in our hearts and to learn better how to know us? What difficulties would be flattened out and suppressed if our civilizers knew us better, and tried to understand us more.[1]

More surprising, to some at any rate, is a passage in the one book which Patrice Lumumba wrote, the manuscript of which was completed before the end of 1956.

It appears to us that the better formula would consist in personal relations, whence follows the necessity of every Congolese who aspires to a certain ideal to make a serious effort to draw closer to every European with whom he is in contact. It is this European who would be at the same time his friend and his guide or his 'god-father'.[2]

Evidence is abundant of this *évolué* yearning to be treated at least with a proper human respect and regard. In 1958 A. R. Bolamba returned to the plea he had made ten years earlier in *La Voix du congolais*. The first duty of Belgians is 'to take account of the human dignity of the black man',[3] a plea which I heard echoed as a lament when talking to a schoolteacher one night in 1962 in a village on the banks of the Upper Congo. 'If only they had treated us as human beings', he said. But just as the words of my acquaintance soon faded away in the darkness, so the hope which they expressed usually found no responsive echo. The major, officially sponsored move at this level was the creation of *cercles d'évolués* up and down the Congo, which were also frequented by Europeans. But unless the European membership included men of rare tact, perception and sympathy, this venture usually did little as far as a

[1] *La Voix du congolais*, February 1948, p. 54.
[2] P. Lumumba, *Le Congo, terre d'avenir, est-il menacé?* (Brussels, Office de Publicité, S.A., 1961), p. 126.
[3] *La Voix du congolais*, November 1958, p. 670.

mutual enrichment of personal relations was concerned. At some point in his experience the *évolué* usually came to realize that further progress along the European way was denied him.

So far the *évolué* has been painted as a genuinely pathetic figure and worthy of compassion. That he got little compassion or even understanding was due not only to European blindness or arrogance but also to the many infuriating qualities which he often exhibited. The remark so frequently on the lips of Europeans in colonial Africa, 'Give me the raw African straight from the bush', was merely the reflection of a dislike of the *évolué* which was inspired by his real and alleged deficiencies. How arrogant he was, treating his compatriots, when he could, much more harshly than would a European; how little his pretensions to promotion were matched by his abilities; how bound to routine tasks and how incapable of initiative; how mediocre at clerical work but how contemptuous of manual labour; how avid for the certificate but how ignorant of real learning; how ardent his professions of civilization, how real the actual grip of sorcery and witchcraft; how moral his professions, how immoral his conduct! The list could be lengthened and some or all of it might be true of many cases. But quite apart from the fact that the actions and omissions of his rulers might have done much to bring about his condition, nothing that has been said relates to or limits the traumatic shock which the *évolué* experienced when he came to understand that there was a point beyond which he could not pass, that although they would lead him a certain distance, European Government and Europeans individually would eventually rebuff his wish to go yet farther.

Twenty years ago, on the basis of study in British East Africa and South Africa, Malinowski propounded the thesis which first enshrined this very point. The 'selective giving', as Malinowski termed it, of the colonial power in respect of physical power, political mastery, economic resources and the withholding of social and perhaps even religious equality has already been elaborated (p. 138), and is of the utmost importance. In more recent years scholars such as the anthropologist Balandier[1] and the psychologist Mannoni[2] likewise have been concerned to emphasize the fact that any study of colonial society must start from the recognition that there is a

[1] Balandier, *Sociologie actuelle.*   [2] Mannoni, *Prospero and Caliban.*

'colonial situation'. It follows that the presence of such a situation, where all the instruments of power are in the hands of the colonizer, must by definition be one in which the colonizer must hold back some part of his power—or else he ceases to be a colonial power.

From the viewpoint of those amongst the colonized who have been admitted to a share of the colonizer's power and thus, necessarily, of his culture, there is therefore a block in his attempts to assimilate himself to the white man, to acquire the secret of the European's power. And the confronting of this line, the line of integral rebuff as Malinowski was pleased to call it, could be a devastating experience. In terms of the Belgian Congo a man might make the difficult ascent of the educational ladder through primary and secondary school, undergo lengthy professional training and become an *assistant médical*, probably the *évolué* occupation which carries most prestige; but he could not become a doctor. He might none the less do much the same work as a European doctor: but he was paid less. He might be a respected and able member of his community: but he could enjoy even a measure of administrative authority only if European authority nominated or permitted. He might make it possible for his children to equal the attainments of European children: but he could still find that they were refused admission to a European school. He might have impeccable manners, personal hygiene and poise; yet he might never be invited by a European to his house. He becomes an *immatriculé*: but in the best hotels his *carte d'immatriculation* can command only grudging admittance, being proffered like a passport at a hostile frontier.

One can not improve on Malinowski's description of his progress, though of course that had South and East African overtones.

The Native in a way enters into a new covenant. For value received and hopes inspired, he has to abandon some of his old allegiances and ways; he has to forswear some of his old faiths and convictions. He takes up new ways of life and even a new disguise in dress, manner and personal habits. He enters this avenue, fascinated by the qualities, power, wealth, and general prestige of things European. The ultimate goal implied, if not explicit, is to become, if not European, then at least a master or part-master of some of the devices, possessions, and influences which in his eyes constitute

European superiority. How far and in what way is he ever allowed to approach this goal? ...

In the life-story of every assimilated African, and in the development of any African detribalized community or group, there comes a moment in which . . .[a] line or barrier makes its inevitable and inexorable appearance. We may call it the Line of Integral Rebuff from total assimilation. Concretely, it exists as colour-bar legislation, the principle of racial discrimination, the fundamental rule of the Grondwet; or the policy of permanent segregation. It separates as by a deep rift the community of partly assimilated Africans from that of their white neighbours.[1]

Of course in the Belgian Congo certain of the barriers began at the last to be removed. But it *was* at the last: it will be the burden of the next chapter to argue that the reaction of Congo *évolués* to rebuff, to their failure to obtain acceptance and assimilation—the eventual removal of some long-standing barriers coming too late—was not so much to turn back and take refuge in traditional systems of value and belief, as in Malinowski's thesis, but rather to draw from the example of other parts of Africa and establish their leadership of the masses, urban and rural. With this new strength they could make an outright bid for political mastery and independence.

[1] Malinowski, *Dynamics of Culture Change*, pp. 157–8.

XII

THE REVOLT OF THE ÉVOLUÉS AND THEIR LEADERSHIP OF THE MASSES: (1) TO THE BEGINNING OF THE ROUND TABLE CONFERENCE

WE have seen that in earlier eras of the history of the Belgium Congo, the various messianic movements had had as one of their functions the expression of political protest. In the postwar period this element, in Kimbanguism at any rate, recedes, and when that sect assumed a more stable and, in terms of its own foundation and early development, orthodox form in the mid-fifties, its character was essentially religious. There is no reason to doubt its new leader, Joseph Diangienda, Kimbangu's third son, when he asserted to the Administration in 1959 that 'political questions are the concern of the parties', and it is reasonable to suppose that the more liberal attitude of the Administration towards Kimbanguism, which was first demonstrated in 1955 and which culminated in the ending of the ban on the sect in December 1959, was a reflection of this more acceptable character of later Kimbanguism. (The fact that Kimbanguism in its later form of 'The Church of Jesus Christ on earth by Simon Kimbangu' was also less unorthodox theologically may also have swayed the Administration.)[1] Thus although the continued existence throughout the whole postwar period of messianic movements was a factor encouraging an attitude of expectancy, political as well as religious, we can not discern in these movements any seed-bed of political protest in any more precise sense.

Such a seed-bed is rather to be found, in the first place, in the Belgian trade-union movement. After the Second World War the Christian and subsequently the rival Socialist Trade Union Federation, each with a distinct political affiliation, were

[1] 'Le Kimbangisme', *Courrier africain*, 8 January 1960, pp. 9–21.

allowed to open offices in the Congo. Initially their activities were directed towards Europeans and were a consequence of the right accorded to Europeans generally in 1942 to form trade unions and professional associations. The example of European trade-unionists in striking on occasions during the war was perhaps not lost on at any rate a few Congolese, but the principal influence of European trade unions in the Congo was in their nurturing of the Congolese trade-union movement. European trade unionists in the Congo, let it be said, could not always decide whether the solidarity of all workers was appropriate in the Congo. Facile sentiments such as 'workers of the world, unite! . . .' could be expressed with great fervour in Belgium, but it might be another matter when it came to a collaboration which logically disavowed the privileged position of the European in the Congo. But certainly Belgian trade-unionism in the Congo never ran up the blind alley which, for example, the British and Afrikaaner miners of Northern Rhodesia so determinedly followed.

Formally, the result of this nurture of the Congolese by Belgian unions was unimpressive. By the end of 1956, after nine years of Congolese trade-unionism, there were only 8,829 unionists, and unionism, up to 1960, never became comparable to company and State paternalism as a force improving the lot of the Congolese worker.[1] But the experience of organization which trade-unionism gave to its leaders was an important factor in training them for political organization, whilst the use of a threat to gain concessions is a technique of obvious political application in a colonial situation. Such men as Cyrille Adoula, Arthur Pinzi, and Paul Bolya were launched on a career of political protest in this way, whilst the major agitation of the most effective Congolese union, the *Association du Personnel Indigène du Congo* (A.P.I.C.)—for the ending of the two-tiered status in the civil service—was political in its implications.

Direct political activity began in 1955 when both the Liberal and Socialist parties of the mother country founded fraternal organizations, called *amicales*, to which Africans as well as Europeans could belong. Although Africans do not appear ever

[1] For an account of trade-unionism in the Congo see R. Poupart, *Première esquisse de l'évolution du syndicalisme au Congo* (Brussels, Éditions de l'Institut de Sociologie Solvay, 1960).

to have dominated these *amicales*, they gave to some *évolués* their first introduction to European-type political activity. Lumumba, for instance, was for a period a member of the *Amicale Libérale* at Stanleyville; Adoula was very active in the *Amicale Socialiste* of Leopoldville. Disenchantment came when the parties made no effective moves to modify their programmes to fit an African context, and their attraction for *évolués* gave place in 1958 to a concern to start their own, Congolese, parties.[1] An incidental, but important result of this involvement of Congolese in Belgian-based political parties was that the *évolués* became very much aware that Europeans were divided amongst themselves on a number of important issues. None of these aroused more feeling than the extension to the Congo of the lay-schools controversy following the appointment of a Liberal, M. Buisseret, to the Colonial Ministry in 1954. A commission of inquiry blew hard on the anti-clerical trumpet and it was proposed to set up lay schools for African children and to reduce the subsidies to Catholic schools. The ensuing, hard-hitting debate extended beyond the relatively cloistered ranks of the *amicales* to the Press and to literate public opinion generally, indicating to *évolués* as a whole that two of the three pillars of Congo affairs—The Administration and the Roman Catholic Church (the third being the big companies)—were no longer in harmony, and that Belgians were even prepared to canvass *évolué* support for their particular viewpoint.[2]

Nor were these the only respects in which Congolese political protest was nurtured and encouraged from outside. In December 1955 Professor A. A. J. Van Bilsen published a proposal for the emancipation of the Congo in thirty years. In it he criticized the absence of any clear direction in Belgium's colonial policy, the over-emphasis on industrialization in the Congo, and the failure to provide Congolese with higher education. Since almost nothing in relevant directions had been done, it would take thirty years to prepare the Congolese for independence. When that independence was conferred, the form of government should be federal.[3] The Belgian reaction to Van Bilsen's proposals was mixed, but they generated great enthusiasm

---

[1] Brausch, *Belgian Administration in the Congo*, pp. 33–35.
[2] Slade, *The Belgian Congo*, pp. 39–42.
[3] Merriam, *Congo: Background of Conflict*, pp. 68–70.

amongst those *évolués* who had become aware of them, and provoked the first Congolese political manifesto, a statement published in *Conscience africaine* in the summer of 1956.

Conscience africaine was an occasional journal reproducing the views of a group of *évolué* intellectuals originally formed by an outstanding Congolese priest, the Abbé Joseph Malula (later Archbishop of Leopoldville), in 1951. Its editor was Joseph Ileo, who was soon to achieve eminence in Congo politics. The manifesto was essentially an appeal for political, social and economic emancipation, to be obtained with the co-operation of Belgium and Belgians, and a general endorsement of the Van Bilsen plan as the means for the attainment of these goals. It was a moderate document, and Europeans had had some part in its drawing up and also in its timing: a number of Catholic laymen in Leopoldville were concerned to time publication so as to steal the thunder of the Belgian Socialist Party's new declaration of policy for the Congo.[1] It none the less had a considerable effect amongst the African population of Leopoldville, whether or not they could read.[2]

A few weeks later came a further, more aggressively couched pronouncement, the Counter-Manifesto of the A.B.A.K.O. group. Whilst the counter-manifesto gave credit to *Conscience africaine*, much more did it damn it with faint praise. And it differed from the original manifesto not only in being more aggressive in tone, but also by its demand for immediate independence and by the fact that it was the production not of a group of intellectuals prepared to accept some European participation, and apparently contemplating a unitary constitution, but of a tight and intransigent tribal association advocating a federal constitution for an independent Congo. A.B.A.K.O. had been formed in 1950 as a social and cultural organization of the numerous Ba-Kongo people. Centred in Leopoldville in its early days, the association was concerned to prevent the swamping of Ba-Kongo traditions and language by the less sophisticated tribes flocking to the capital. A.B.A.K.O. also feared that the Administration would organize these more backward tribes against them and, indeed, resented Belgian rule generally.

[1] Slade, *The Belgian Congo*, p. 43.
[2] Merriam, *Congo: Background of Conflict*, pp. 70–75, 321–9 (English translation of the manifesto).

Distinguishing A.B.A.K.O. and underlying these attitudes was a profound sense of Ba-Kongo history, and the Counter-Manifesto drew heavily upon the fact that a Ba-Kongo empire had existed in the fifteenth century. Indeed a recurring motif was reunion with the Ba-Kongo of French Congo and Angola. Significant for the future development both of A.B.A.K.O. and the Congo was the appointment of an intellectual, Joseph Kasavubu, as president in 1955. Evidently political aims had always been implicit in the association, and the very publication of the counter-manifesto gave a further impulse towards development as a political party.[1] Certainly, and like *Conscience africaine*, the A.B.A.K.O. manifesto made use of Van Bilsen—indeed it concluded with a quotation from him[2]—but basically it represented the uncompromising political attitude from which A.B.A.K.O. never departed, and which, to look ahead, dominated Congolese politics from the middle of 1959 onwards.

What was the response of the Administration and the Belgian Government to these first cries of Congo nationalism? The traditional attitude to Congolese participation in administration, as far as the rural areas are concerned, has been seen to have been a form of indirect rule in which the element of European direction always overshadowed effective Congolese participation in government. In the towns, it was more rare for Congolese to share in effective government and in any case members of the *conseils* were nominated. It should be added that after the Second World War the nomination of Congolese was extended to higher echelons of Government. In 1947 African councillors were nominated to the advisory councils both of the Governor-General and of the provincial governors. At least half of the seats available to Congolese were in almost every case reserved for representatives of traditional authority rather than for *évolués*. A measure of change came in 1957. In the national and provincial councils the basis of representation was altered and, although appointment was still by nomination, more Africans, representing more varied categories, came to be nominated. At the same time councils, in which Africans might even have a small majority, were also created in the *chefferies*,

[1] For more detail about A.B.A.K.O. see *A.B.A.K.O. 1950–1960, Documents* (Brussels, C.R.I.S.P., 1962).
[2] Merriam, *Congo: Background of Conflict*, pp. 75–77, 330–6 (English text of counter-manifesto).

secteurs and *centres*. The same year witnessed the *statut des villes* which provided for the designation of *centres extra-coutumiers* as *communes* with a communal council appointed by the principal burgomaster of the *ville* (made up of a number of African and European *communes*), who was an administrative official. Each *commune*, in turn, had its burgomaster who, like the principal burgomaster, was appointed by the Administration, but who did not have to be a member of the Administration.[1]

The fact that these measures were instituted in 1957 might appear to indicate that they were a response to the two manifestos of the previous year, especially as in practice the designation of members of the communal councils and of burgomasters in the three *villes* created in 1957—Leopoldville, Elisabethville and Jadotville—was replaced by elections. In these elections, all adult males over twenty-five, with six months' residence and without a prison record, were allowed to vote.[2] But the appearance was deceptive, both because the *statut des villes*, at least, had been in gestation since 1948 and because of the limited powers conferred upon the new communal and other councils.

In fact a pattern made up of unfulfilled or only partly honoured promises of reform had already begun to be established, and is of significance when assessing Congolese responses to the *statut des villes* and to subsequent Belgian reforms. So far vain promises included the announcement in 1954 of an intention to review the less favourable conditions of the *contrat de travail*, regulating the African's relationship with his employer, in relation to the more favourable *contrat d'emploi* which in practice was reserved almost entirely for Europeans; and the amalgamation of the higher and lower branches of the Civil Service, promised since 1954.[3]

There is also abundant evidence of growing resentment at the disparity in salary and other respects between even highly qualified Congolese and Europeans of all descriptions. This theme is prominent in Lumumba's book, *Le Congo, terre d'avenir*, for example, whilst the A.B.A.K.O. manifesto had referred to the oft-cited case of the European sanitary inspector

[1] Brausch, *Belgian Administration in the Congo*, pp. 46, 48–49; A. Durieux, 'Institutions politiques (1908–1960)', *Livre blanc*, I, pp. 266–80.

[2] Merriam, op. cit., p. 78.

[3] *Documents parlementaires*, Chambre des Représentants, 1958–9, 3, 27 March 1959, report of parliamentary commission of inquiry into the Leopoldville riots of January 1959, p. 27.

earning much more than the Congolese *assistant médical*, who was only a little less highly qualified than a doctor. Add to this the whole complex of resentful frustrations which, the last chapter has suggested, was often harboured by the *évolué*.

If, then, *évolué* attitudes were as I have represented them, it was hardly to be expected that the very limited measures which the 1957 reforms were would have been accepted as a radical, new response to *évolué* complaints and aspirations. In the event, therefore, the 1957 reforms seem to have been seized upon not as significant in themselves but as an opportunity to flex the muscles of political organization and, by a demonstration of political power, to make a claim for more.

The communal elections were of particular importance in Leopoldville and Elisabethville. In the capital A.B.A.K.O. gained some two-thirds of the popular vote, seven out of ten burgomaster positions and 133 of the 170 seats on the communal councils.[1] The Ba-Kongo were certainly the largest single ethnic group in Leopoldville,[2] but at the same time A.B.A.K.O. success was striking, disproportionate, and achieved only through careful preparation. It brought Kasavubu to power as burgomaster of the Dendale commune—he made a strong attack on the Belgian Administration at his inauguration in April 1958[3]—and marked a further stage in the transformation of A.B.A.K.O. into a political party, ethnically based but nationalistic.

In Elisabethville the significance of the elections was less immediate but no less important. With no party organization, the cohesion of the Ba-Luba immigrants from Kasai, called Kasai Ba-Luba to distinguish them from the Ba-Luba of central and north Katanga, was sufficient to gain three of the four burgomaster positions *and* (the important point) within twelve months to bring about by reaction the grouping together of 'authentic Katangans', as its founders described the tribes which could claim longer residence in Katanga. As an extension of this general disposition, the 'authentic Katangans' were also concerned to prevent Belgian settlers in Katanga from dominating its affairs—though at the same time the

[1] Merriam, *Congo: Background of Conflict*, p. 79; *Congo 1959*, p. 265.

[2] See L. Baeck, 'Léopoldville, phénomène urbain african', *Zaïre*, X, 6, 1956, p. 628.

[3] Merriam, *Congo: Background of Conflict*, pp. 79–80.

moderation of its leaders earned the party a good deal of support from settlers—and to oppose the Administration in its alleged favouring of 'non-Katangan' Africans. Thus was born the *Confédération des Associations Tribales du Katanga* (CONAKAT), consisting mainly of Ba-Lunda, Ba-Yeke and Ba-Lamba but with some participation of Katanga Ba-Luba. Its principal original leaders were MM. Moise Tshombe, Kalenda and Munongo. Technically CONAKAT remained a federation of tribal associations, only becoming political with the registration of the *Rassemblement katangais* in July 1959. But the leaders were the same, and the name CONAKAT was the one usually used throughout, whilst CONAKAT right from its formation had had political aims.[1]

The Congo's first two parties then had ethnic foundations, being nationalistic but with a necessarily restricted vision and appeal; however, during the second half of 1958, outside events breathed a wider, more broadly based nationalism into Congo politics. The first such event, illuminating quite new horizons, was the Brussels International Exhibition, where the seven Congo pavilions were served by numerous Congolese, whilst many others were invited to the Exhibition as guests. Here for the first time Congolese were not only made aware of wider, less parochial perspectives generally, but were also brought into contact with other Congolese from all corners of the Congo—and the Congolese at the Exhibition included a number of emerging political leaders. Apart from seeing that Belgian metropolitan society was (naturally) different from Belgian colonial society, and experiencing such novelties as being served in restaurants by European waiters, they were, claims Dr. Slade: 'amidst their tribal factions . . . able to become conscious of the value of Congolese unity; they were able to discover that African problems and hopes were much the same in every part of the country. They returned with new ideas to continue the discussion at home.'[2]

Whilst the Exhibition was still in full swing, an event on the Congo's very doorstep had a more direct impact on Congolese opinion generally, at least in Leopoldville itself. This was

[1] *Congo* 1959, p. 279; J. Gérard-Libois and Benoît Verhaegen, *Congo 1960* (Brussels, C.R.I.S.P., n.d.), I, pp. 225–6; personal information.
[2] Slade, *The Belgian Congo*, p. 45. See also Merriam, *Congo: Background of Conflict*, pp. 80–81.

the visit of General de Gaulle to Brazzaville in August 1958 with his offer to the French Congo either of autonomy within the French community or of complete independence. 'Whoever wishes independence can have it as soon as he wishes.'[1] Here, then, were events which both quickened the pulse of Congolese nationalism and which at least sapped the ethnic basis which it had so far possessed. These new influences of 1958 were reflected in the foundation of a new political party in October, a party destined to be the most interesting and the most dynamic of all Congo parties, the *Mouvement National Congolais*. Its first platform demanded a rapid democratization of institutions, the grant of fundamental liberties, and of independence within a reasonable period, and promised strong resistance to separatism. The foundation of the party was the work of a group of *évolués* at Leopoldville; it is significant that this first committee of the party included men of varied political tendencies—Ileo and Adoula, for example—and of a variety of tribes. It is no less noteworthy that the committee included Gaston Diomi and Alphonse Nguvulu, Ba-Kongo who had come to oppose the exclusiveness of A.B.A.K.O. Its president was Patrice Lumumba.[2]

To begin with, the M.N.C. was a moderate party and one which the Administration favoured on account of its opposition to a separatism which was threatening to split the Congo. At the turn of 1958–9 Kasavabu was regarded as the extremist, and it may be that the fact that his health documents were not in order was used as a pretext for forbidding him to fly to the Accra Pan-African Conference in December. (It is equally possible that Kasavubu did not really want to go, conferences not being his favourite forum.) Originally the Governor-General had purposed to stop Lumumba and two other members of the M.N.C. central committee from attending, but is said to have changed his decision as a result of the intervention of Father Van Wing.

In fact, the Accra Conference was a third notable outside event influencing Congolese nationalism during 1958, not least because it played an important part in Lumumba's radical

[1] Merriam, op. cit., pp. 81–82. Slade, *The Belgian Congo*, p. 45–46.

[2] Ganshof van der Meersch, *Fin de la souveraineté belge*, pp. 99–100; C. Hoskyns, *The Congo since Independence* (London, O.U.P., for the Royal Institute of International Affairs, 1965), pp. 27–30. Miss Hoskyns very kindly allowed me to see the early chapters of her book in typescript.

progress. At Accra, it is claimed, he first came under Kwame Nkrumah's influence, was encouraged, indeed exalted by meeting other African nationalists, and came to see the expediency of adopting an anti-European line. On his return the effects of his pilgrimage were not long in making themselves felt. At a meeting on 28 December he rivalled the earlier extremism of Kasavubu. But there was more to it than this: the meeting was not a restricted affair in a bar or amongst *évolués*, but Lumumba's first triumph with a mass audience. 'We follow you! We will support you! Down with the Belgians! Long live the Congo! Long live the M.N.C.!'[1] Lumumba the demagogue was well in the making.

The elements of Congolese protest as they developed during 1957 and 1958 have been seen—an element of European nurture and encouragement, *évolué* initiative and leadership, the use of the tribal association as the basis of the political party, the reaction against ethnically based nationalism. During 1958, there had been important external influences—the Brussels Exhibition, the offer of independence to French Congo, and the Accra Conference. In the excited reaction to Lumumba's speech telling of the Conference, moreover, there was a first hint of a new element in the fabric of nationalism—mass enthusiasm. During 1959 and the first half of 1960 all these elements were to flow together into a restless and unstable but dynamic compound. In face of this explosive mixture Belgium, in successive stages, yielded, and yielded at a speed far beyond what Congolese radicals had hoped, or Belgian conservatives feared.

In the summer of 1958 Belgium had faced the need to formulate a policy for the Congo by appointing a study group which was to make recommendations aimed at resolving the political problems of the Congo. The commission visited the Congo in the autumn of 1958, and it was to make radical recommendations which were reflected in policy. But before that policy was due to be announced, serious riots took place in Leopoldville. It would be wrong to suppose that these riots of 4 and 5 January were of the simple *à la Bastille* variety, the work of political leaders imparting political consciousness to the mass and

---

[1] De Vos, *Vie et mort de Lumumba*, pp. 68–71, 75–77; Hoskyns, *The Congo since Independence*, p. 28; Jean Van Lierde, 'Témoignage: Patrice Lumumba, leader et ami', *Présence africaine*, XXXVI, 1961, p. 113; personal information.

launching it against the ruling authority, as in some Marxist textbook of revolution.

The parliamentary commission appointed to inquire into the riots, in summarizing the conclusions of its very critical report, placed the main emphasis on failures of the Administration, on underlying causes such as resentment at *de facto* segregation and the disparity of incomes, and the high level of unemployment which Leopoldville had experienced since the recession set in during the mid-fifties. The fact remains that rioting started a week after Lumumba's inflammatory speech and had as its immediate cause the disappointment of the crowd at the postponement of an A.B.A.K.O. meeting, and the apparently pugnacious words spoken when Kasavubu and other A.B.A.K.O. leaders subsequently did appear for a few minutes. It was not long before there were attacks on Europeans, before pillaging began and a large crowd began to march on the European quarters. The police opened fire and the *Force publique* was called in. According to the Commission's figures 241 Congolese and forty-nine Europeans were injured, and forty-nine Congolese killed.[1]

The whole ugly affair was a great shock to Belgian rule and to Belgian opinion and could scarcely have come at a more unfortunate time for the development of Belgian policy towards the Congo. The Study Group had submitted its report on Christmas Eve and it had been announced that an important policy pronouncement would follow on 13 January. The effect of the riots was apparently to bring two diametrically opposed pressures to bear on the Government. On the one hand there was radical pressure for an unambiguous enunciation of the goal of Independence: on the other, conservative pressure to stand firm in face of the same mob violence that had led the radicals to their opposite conclusion. The outcome was some confusion. After seemingly fierce discussion during the night of 11 January, the declaration came to speak of Belgium's resolve 'to organize in the Congo a democracy capable of exercising the prerogatives of sovereignty and of deciding on its independence'.

The king, on the other hand, had already recorded on tape a message based on an earlier, more radical draft, and the tape had been taken to Leopoldville. As a result the royal pronouncement

[1] *Chambre*, report on Leopoldville riots, *passim*, and especially pp. 34–37, 90–91.

was in one sense more radical than that of the Government. '. . . Our resolve is today to lead, without fatal delays but without inconsiderate precipitation, the peoples of the Congo to independence in prosperity and peace.' But even if the royal pronouncement was more positive, it was couched in guarded and unexciting terms, whilst the Government's longer declaration enunciated the distant goal only equivocally, with only the initial steps to it spelled out in any detail.

There were to be elections, based on universal (male) suffrage, to the councils of *communes* and of the rural *circonscriptions*. The most important of the latter, the *territoire*, would be administered by councillors, the great majority of whom would be elected, and the councillors of the *territoires* would combine with the communal councillors to form an electoral college to appoint the majority of the provincial councillors and, later, of a General Council of the Congo as a whole. From this General Council would develop a Chamber of Representatives, and from a new Council of Legislation, whose members would be elected in a similar way, would grow a Senate. The authority of these two bodies would be progressively increased. As regards timing, all that was said was that by March 1959 the existing (nominated) provincial councils would each appoint two councillors to the Council of Legislation, that the communal and territorial elections would take place at the end of the year, whilst the new provincial councils would follow in March of 1960.[1]

It may be that the most striking feature of the new policy announced on 13 January was a threefold ambiguity—about the precise meaning of independence, about the stages by which it was to be achieved, and in the circumstances of its enunciation, it being likely that many Congolese must have seen the new policy as a response to the riots. Of the reactions to the policy, those of the Congolese parties were the most important. Only A.B.A.K.O., theoretically dissolved after the riots, rejected it: more usual was the attitude of the M.N.C., which in February requested such things as modifications in the proposed electoral arrangements, and firm dates for the reforms announced in the higher echelons of government, but which accepted the new policy as a starting point.[2] But as the year

[1] *Congo 1959*, pp. 9–16, which include the texts of the royal message and the Government pronouncement.
[2] Ibid., pp. 43–51.

progressed most parties became more extreme. This was probably due to two main causes. In a situation of party rivalries, no party could afford to allow another to gain an ascendancy in what was increasingly coming to be termed a movement of national liberation, whilst there was also some suspicion that Belgium might go back on her promises.

During the Round Table Conference of January 1960, the moderate Joseph Ileo said that the Congolese delegates were striking a hard bargain because they remembered all the promises which had not been kept.[1] By this was presumably meant the various reforms which have been seen to have been promised in the early fifties or earlier, but these were years in a gestation which sometimes only produced a dwarf (see pp. 205-9). Strength may have been lent to this suspicion by the hostility shown to the new colonial minister, M. Van Hemelrijck (a *Parti Social-Chrétien*/Liberal coalition had come into power in December 1958), by various European organizations in the Congo; he was very popular amongst Congolese. During a visit to the Congo in June 1959 he was boycotted by the Federation of ex-servicemen and was pelted with tomatoes by Europeans in Bukavu, a group of whom also sent him a letter which almost deserves his own epithet 'racist'.[2] When it is also remembered that Van Hemelrijck and Governor-General Cornélis were widely known to have differing views on Congo policy,[3] and that Van Hemelrijck resigned in September 1959, it is not altogether surprising that such suspicions should have been harboured.

In fact, the Belgian failure during the greater part of 1959 fully to sustain the impression of their own sincerity seems to have been due first to the unsuitability of the traditional centralized control from Brussels[4] in a situation which every day was becoming more political and less administrative, and

[1] Cited in Hoskyns, *The Congo since Independence*, p. 32 n.

[2] *Congo 1959*, pp. 29-34, 37-39.   [3] Ibid.

[4] Minister Renkin had made an abortive attempt at decentralization in 1914 and so had Minister Godding in 1946-7. On the latter occasion the number of principal departments in the Colonial Ministry was reduced from six to three and as many functions as possible transferred to Leopoldville. But in 1952 the three disbanded departments were reconstituted and by 1953 there were almost twice as many employed in the Colonial Ministry as there had been before the reforms (Stengers, *Belgique et Congo*, pp. 224-5). It also appears that the new structure persisted in Leopoldville and so the last state was worse than the first with a vengeance!

which demanded 'on-the-spot' handling. Added to this was the possible unsuitability of the Governor-General for *political* leadership, which, after all, was quite foreign to all his training and experience, and his retention in office despite his own wish to resign after the Leopoldville riots. The reasons for his retention are not entirely clear. It is evident that the different groups in the Belgian Government were long unable to agree on a successor, and that when agreement was reached, the King refused his endorsement. But it may be that the King acted more from an unreadiness to abandon Cornélis than from objection to the agreed candidate, M. Raymond Scheyven.[1] The French journalist, De Vos, believes that the real pro-Cornélis influence in the Palace at this time was King Baudouin's father, the former Leopold III.[1]

Thirdly, the deficient training of the Governor-General was matched by that of the Administration generally. The professional spirit, the competence and the standards which the Colonial University had been very successful in inculcating, were not its only fruits. There was also too much of an authoritarian element in the training given whilst, intellectually, a questioning habit of mind and true intellectual development were discouraged. Nor did the majority of administrators expose themselves to new ideas in their reading, whilst, for reasons that are not altogether clear, there were no major influences at work during their home leaves to jolt them out of categories of thought suitable for the twenties and thirties, and confront them with the realities of European rule in Africa in the fifties. As a result the majority of the Administration simply were not attuned to a situation which demanded political rather than purely administrative handling, to a situation where their true role was self-effacingly and constructively to encourage political life and emergent nationalism and not solely to direct and to command.[2]

The months after January 1959 saw the ranks of Congolese political radicalism strengthened by the foundation in April of the *Parti Solidaire Africain* (P.S.A.). The creation of *évolués* from the Kwilu and Kwango districts of Leopoldville province, living in the city of Leopoldville, its leaders included Antoine

---

[1] *Congo 1959*, pp. 125–9; De Vos, *Vie et mort de Lumumba*, pp. 109–10; and personal information.

[2] Personal information.

Gizenga, C. Kamitatu and Pierre Mulele. From Leopoldville, its activities immediately spread to Kikwit, the administrative centre of Kwilu, and the almost missionary zeal with which the first party members began to establish branches throughout Kwilu, and to only a lesser extent in Kwango, makes fascinating reading.[1] It was a party whose initial relations with the Administration were sometimes cordial, and which in Kamitatu always retained a moderate component, but by the end of the year, as we shall see, it had entered into alliance with A.B.A.K.O. and others, and had come to share a part of A.B.A.K.O's conspicuous intransigence.

There was, however, on the Congolese side one counter-development to the increasing radicalism of the political parties. This was the foundation in November 1959 of the *Parti National du Progrès*, a federation of a number of small, local and tribal parties informed by disquiet at the growing extremism of the M.N.C. The party enjoyed the tacit support of the Administration and, given the value of this and the appeal of a moderate party to the sometimes still influential traditional authorities, it had a considerable potential.[2]

But this was not a characteristic development; more typical was the demand by the first congress of Congolese political parties, meeting in Luluabourg in April 1959, for a Government for the Congo in January 1961, a Government which was to decide when the Congo should advance to total independence. In the following month Lumumba urged the constitution of a Government for the Congo in 1959 whilst, altogether, there developed a strongly expressed demand that Congolese should participate in the planning and timing of their political emancipation and not merely accept it passively as Belgium thought fit to grant instalments.[3] By November Belgium had accepted this position but other factors contributed to this modification of her attitude, factors summed up in the term 'tribalism'.

The first of these was the attitude of A.B.A.K.O. It was not only that the party was the most extreme and intransigent, but also that it espoused a federalism so pronounced that it could sometimes pass over into separatism. Coupled with this

[1] *Congo 1959*, p. 266; M. Weiss and B. Verhaegen (ed.), *Parti Solidaire Africain* (*P.S.A.*) (Brussels, C.R.I.S.P., n.d.), esp. pp. 5–156.

[2] Ibid., pp. 269–70. Hoskyns, *The Congo since Independence*, p. 31.

[3] *Congo 1959*, pp. 129, 133.

was an ethnically based solidarity which sustained a policy, complete in some districts, of non-co-operation with the Administration. From the end of April 1959 A.B.A.K.O. was demanding that the new Congo be a federation of autonomous units,[1] whilst in a letter of 21 June to the Colonial Minister it went over the edge and coolly announced that as from January 1960 the then Leopoldville province (in which the Ba-Kongo were concentrated) would become the autonomous 'Republic of Central Kongo'.[2] The Minister, as one might expect, immediately rejected this letter,[3] but the policy of non-co-operation with which it was backed could not thus easily be shrugged off. In August, Vice-Governor-General Schoeller visited the Cataractes district of the Lower Congo and reported to the Minister:

All the people I met unanimously agree that, on the political level, contact with the population has become impossible. Directives, advice, efforts at persuasion, attempts at a dialogue, everything which comes from the Administration, from Europeans in general or from Congolese considered as collaborators of the whites, is rejected without discussion. They reply that one thing matters: immediate independence; that one person is competent to decide everything: M. Kasavubu. Although the latter was still almost unknown in the district on 4 January his personality is now veritably deified, and is the object of a blind and fanatical submission of the mass.[4]

In a dispatch written later in the month Schoeller described the situation in the Middle and Lower Congo regions (meaning, apparently, the *districts* of Bas-Congo and Cataractes) as 'pre-revolutionary'. There was not yet terrorism but he was convinced that it was very near.[5] From early in the previous month a deep-rooted dispute had also erupted in parts of Kasai, especially in Luluabourg, the provincial capital. The dispute had its origin in the movement of Ba-Luba into certain Bena-Lulua areas in the Luluabourg–Tshikapa–Luebo region of Kasai. The original movement had been encouraged by the Administration since, with the development of the area with the building of the Port Francqui–Katanga rail link, the Ba-Luba, with their quickness to learn European skills, were in

---

[1] *Congo 1959*, pp. 73–81.   [2] Ibid., pp. 81–86.   [3] Ibid., pp. 86–87.
[4] Schoeller to Minister of the Congo, 13 August 1959, *Congo 1959*, p. 100.
[5] Schoeller to Minister of the Congo, late August 1959, *Congo 1959*, p. 117.

demand. To begin with there was not merely plenty of land, but the Bena-Lulua were not interested in learning European ways. But when their interest did begin to quicken they found that in educational opportunity and jobs they had been pre-empted by Ba-Luba, and antagonism began to sharpen. Communal elections in December 1958 had shown the potential political strength of the Ba-Luba and then, on 6 July following, an administrative report on the Ba-Luba–Bena-Lulua rivalry, favouring the Bena-Lulua, was stolen and published in two newspapers.

At this stage M. Albert Kalonji, a leading Muluba politician and member of the M.N.C., returned to Luluabourg and began to arouse the Ba-Luba yet more against the Bena-Lulua until he was arrested on 3 August. His arrest sparked off rioting on the following day, and there was further, Bena-Lulua-inspired, rioting in October.[1] Thus in the summer and autumn of 1959 there was not only the primary Ba-Kongo threat to orderly progress towards independence, but a situation of growing seriousness in Kasai. And though this was as yet a cloud no bigger than a man's hand, CONAKAT had in July come out firmly in favour of maximum decentralization in preparation for a future system of federated states. Its simultaneous espousal of the project of a Belgo-Congolese community,[2] first canvassed in 1952, was less significant since the whole notion, once quite widely popular, had by that time lost much of its appeal because of the failure to give it any precise definition.

In this situation the acting Governor-General, broadly in accord with M. A. Stenmans, the *Secrétaire du Gouvernement*, began to urge upon the Minister for the Congo the necessity of initiating a dialogue with Congolese political leaders and of announcing not only a definite timetable for Congolese participation in power in the higher echelons of government but also a more accelerated timing then Van Hemelrijck himself was envisaging in the summer of 1959. The proposed new timing provided, notably, for the constitution of a Government for the Congo at the end of April 1960, Schoeller and Stenmans being particularly concerned at the threat of Ba-Kongo militancy going to the point of a secession which other regions

---

[1] Ganshof, *Fin de la souveraineté belge*, pp. 535–6; *Congo 1959*, pp. 185–90.
[2] *Congo 1959*, pp. 95–96.

would emulate.[1] But at this stage the Belgian Government would not budge. Van Hemelrijck had already had cause to resent the mysterious dispatch of the Count d'Aspremont-Lynden to Leopoldville, without his knowledge, to check that he was rightly interpreting Schoeller's reports. After a political crisis at the beginning of September, when Van Hemelrijck's wish for an accelerated timing could not prevail in the Cabinet, he resigned.[2] But to look ahead, by the end of the year the Government was none the less forced by events to concede more and more.[3]

In the early part of this next phase, Belgian policy expressed the view of the moderate party in the Belgian Cabinet, whose predominance had been reflected in Van Hemelrijck's resignation. This policy held good until the end of November and its essence was the naming of August or September 1960 for the constitution of the two central legislative assemblies, originally proposed in the Declaration of 13 January, with substantial powers in internal affairs. There was also a quite new departure —an executive authority, consisting of a council of ministers, nominated by the king and presided over by the Governor-General—to be set up at the same time. This first legislature would last for not more than four years (but also not less than three years, as a private Cabinet paper made clear) and before the expiry of its term its members would draw up a constitution for submission to the people as a whole.[4]

---

[1] Schoeller, Proposal for discussions with political parties, 4 August; Schoeller to Minister for the Congo, 29 July, 13 August, 14 August, end of August (n.d.), 2 September (Telex), and Stenmans, Report on Federalism, 24 August 1959, in *Congo 1959*, pp. 96–120, 148–51, 159–60, 181–4.

[2] *Congo 1959*, pp. 151–8, 160–2.

[3] Van Hemelrijk's own later comment, made to the Catholic Flemish club at Lier, is interesting. 'The drama was that those who thought I was busy losing the Congo were themselves contributing most towards the result.' After denouncing Freemasons and certain financial interests, he went on, 'I proposed immediate elections to establish a constitution with an African Government, with the proviso that the Congo need not become a unitary state but could become a federation. I came up against the opposition of former Ministers of the Colonies. Behind my back somebody was sent to the Congo to take the pulse of the people there. My dismissal provoked concern among the blacks. My successor, the best and [most] experienced of statesmen, was also of the opinion that my policy went too far. Since then, however, the most advanced opinion in the Congo has imposed its will. The extremists have come into power in place of the former leaders.' (Quoted in Colin Legum, *Congo Disaster* (London, Penguin Books, 1961), p. 63.

[4] De Schrijver, radio messages, 4 September and 16 October 1959; Belgian Cabinet paper, 7 October 1959, in *Congo 1959*, pp. 162–3, 166–74.

The new policy brought no Congolese welcome but only rebuff,[1] and matters worsened in later October and November, when the party which had now emerged as a substantial breakaway from the M.N.C., following internal cleavage in mid-July, and which took the name 'M.N.C.-Kalonji' (after its Muluba leader, who had been released from rustication in September), came out in favour of a federal régime for the Congo. Moreover, Kalonji was now recruiting support only from Ba-Luba and had in September even suggested the idea of a Republic of Kasai.[2] Then on 30 and 31 October there was serious rioting in Stanleyville, following a congress of the M.N.C.-Lumumba, in which, according to one of the various estimates, twenty-six Africans were killed and more than one hundred Africans and Europeans injured.[3]

At the Congress itself, the party had resolved to boycott the December elections and, in effect, rejected the new policy[4] which Van Hemelrijck's successor, M. de Schrijver, was attempting to carry through. As November progressed, the voices of first the M.N.C.-Kalonji and of the Belgian Socialist party and then others in a swelling chorus (and especially A.B.A.K.O., the M.N.C.-K., and the *Parti Solidaire Africain*, in concert), began to demand a full-scale dialogue with Belgium—a Round Table Conference. Such opposition, together with the espousal of federalism by the A.B.A.K.O./M.N.C.-K./P.S.A. alliance on 22 November, was too much for the Belgian Government, and on 26 November it announced that such a conference —though the Minister for the Congo refrained from using the name 'Round Table'—would meet in January 1960. Possibly as the result of yet further pressure from the M.N.C.-K./ A.B.A.K.O./P.S.A. alliance, the Belgian Government went further on 15 December when De Schrijver promised independence for 1960 as an outcome of the Conference.[5]

---

[1] *Congo 1959*, pp. 164–5, 196.   [2] Ibid., p. 120, 267.
[3] Merriam, *Congo: Background of Conflict*, p. 97.   [4] *Congo 1959*, pp. 196–7.
[5] Ibid., pp. 202–22.

XIII

THE REVOLT OF THE ÉVOLUÉS AND THEIR LEADERSHIP OF THE MASSES: (2) FROM THE ROUND TABLE CON-FERENCE TO INDEPENDENCE

The De Schrijver declaration expressed a genuine change of policy on the part of the Government, though certainly ministers hoped that Belgium might continue to exercise authority in fields such as foreign affairs after Congolese Independence. Thus, the promise of Independence in 1960 having been made, it might appear that it only remained for the Conference to fix the precise date and arrange the details of the transition. But, remarkable though it may seem, the significance of the ministerial declaration of 15 December simply was not realized, either in Belgium or in the Congo. The Minister himself—to avoid rousing a conservative hornet's nest perhaps—did not emphasize this vital part of his speech, whilst the newspaper reporters in the Chamber, and following them the Belgian Press, did not properly grasp its significance either. Yet more important, the Congolese political leaders do not seem to have grasped the purport of the declaration—so that in fact they arrived in Brussels for the Conference in a tough frame of mind when the Belgian Government had in fact promised them what they most wanted.[1]

In the Round Table debates first appearances suggested that the Belgian delegates might have the advantage. Their experi-ence and sophistication was greater, and the Congolese were not united. In particular there was the division between the A.B.A.K.O./M.N.C.-Kalonji/P.S.A. alliance and the M.N.C.-Lumumba on the one hand, and the moderate P.N.P. on the other. This last had been far and away the most success-ful party in the December elections and it might well appear to

[1] I am indebted to Professor Jean Stengers for clarification of this point.

Belgium that such success by a moderate party was indeed a rock to build upon.

In practice the Belgian position was on any reckoning weaker than this, for failure by the radical Congolese parties to get what they wanted would undoubtedly lead them to develop the non-co-operation, which A.B.A.K.O., in particular, was already so successfully practising, into general passive resistance or worse. In either case Belgium would then have to hold the Congo by force and there were already abundant indications that Belgian opinion, especially on the left, was not prepared for the use of metropolitan troops in Africa. The Belgian Government, moreover, was a weak one, a coalition of the *Parti Social Chrétien* and the Liberal Party containing very varying points of view, and which was faced with a strong socialist opposition. But worse was to come on the very eve of the Conference, due to open on 20 January. Virtually all the Congolese delegations met together in a series of meetings and, influenced by the Congolese students studying in Brussels, who had themselves recognized the weakness of the Belgian position, formed a Common Front with a radical programme. In a statement issued on the evening of the nineteenth, the Front demanded that the decisions of the Conference be binding and that the Congo should be given immediate independence. It was perhaps this unexpected unity which was the most disturbing. In Miss Hoskyns' words:

This statement shook De Schrijver and the Government delegation to the core. They had totally underestimated the extent of Congolese discontent and had never for one moment expected that the P.N.P. and CONAKAT would join the others in a demand for immediate independence. From that moment on [adds Miss Hoskyns], the initiative was out of Belgian hands.

It certainly was. When the Conference officially opened, the Congolese insisted, against the suggestion of the Belgian Government delegation, that the competence of the Conference should be decided before procedure was agreed upon. When the Government yielded on this, the Congolese immediately demanded a guarantee that the Belgian Parliament endorse the decisions of the Conference, and it was in vain that the Government delegation, supported by the delegation of the P.S.C. (*Parti Social Chrétien*), argued that this was not constitutionally possible. Eventually De Schrijver promised that he would present to Parliament a law based upon the resolutions of the Conference and that he would resign if it were rejected. Although Kasavubu continued to demand a more binding commitment, this promise satisfied the other Congolese delegates.

Belgium further succumbed to Congolese pressure in accepting that Lumumba, news of whose sentence to six months' imprisonment for his role in the Stanleyville riots was received early in the Conference, should be released. The Congolese, for their part, were not so much enamoured of Lumumba as apprehensive of the consequences of not binding him to the decisions of the Round Table. As M. Kashamura, the delegate of the *Centre de Regroupement Africain* (C.E.R.E.A.), a party in alliance with the M.N.C.–L., said, in pressing for Lumumba's release, 'He is a man who has a great, a very very great influence and to decide something without him would lose the confidence of the masses'.[1]

Symbolically (for Lumumba was undoubtedly the most outstanding nationalist leader of them all), it was on the very day that he took his place at the Conference that Belgium substantially accepted the already formulated Common Front demand for rapid independence by agreeing to 30 June; this was a date only one month later than the 1 June which the Front had wanted. Belgian withdrawal from her essentially untenable defensive position was complete when she withdrew her suggestion that, after Independence, Belgium should continue to have responsibility for matters in which, she claimed, the take-over could not be arranged in time. These were, notably, defence and security, foreign affairs, and certain financial questions. (It had already been decided that economic and financial questions should be reserved for separate discussion at a second conference to be held in April.) Here again the view prevailed that, in the words of Henri Rolin, one of the Belgian Socialist delegates, the Congolese must be given 'all the keys to their new house'.

With one exception the questions remaining to be discussed were such as to cause dissension between radical and moderate Congolese rather than between Congolese as a whole and the Belgian Government. By its very acceptance of complete independence at a date only five months ahead, the Belgian

[1] Free translation of Kashamura's verbatim remark as printed in *Congo 1960*, I, p. 30.

Government had somewhat withdrawn itself from the conflicts still latent amongst the Congolese delegations. Amongst those delegations the euphoria imparted by the success of their united demand for early Independence, their possible un-awareness of the real dimensions of many of the problems involved, and the fact that the proximity of the May elections for the national and provincial legislatures, and of 30 June itself, left little time or inclination for arguing, meant that on the whole they were prepared either to compromise or, more often, to record disagreements, to defer a decision on contentious matters and in this way to gloss over their continued existence. Another reason for this relative detachment of Belgium in the later stages on the Round Table was probably the real hope, based on its compelling success in the December local govern-ment elections, that the moderate *Parti National du Progrès* would again be successful in the May elections and so, whatever the machinery of government, sensible men owning a sense of their dependence on Belgian help and advice would be oper-ating it. (The total votes cast for the P.N.P. were far and away greater than those recorded for any other single party: more-over it had emerged as the strongest party in Orientale, Kivu and Kasai provinces and had only just failed to gain the ascendancy in Leopoldville province. It thus appeared to be shaping well as a nationally based party.)

The exception, the really contentious matter, was the ques-tion of whether a provisional Government should be set up to tide the Congo over the transition period up to the end of June. Both Kasavubu and Lumumba demanded this, but both the P.N.P. and the Belgian Government resisted this step from fear that, if such a provisional Government were set up on the basis of representation at the Round Table, then the extremists would simply refuse to relinquish power after the May elections—which, of course, were expected to result in a victory for the moderate P.N.P., supported by the traditional authorities. Eventually a compromise was reached: a central executive college was to be set up consisting of the Governor-General and six Congolese, nominated by the king, whilst provincial colleges consisting of three Congolese and the Governor were also to be created. With certain exceptions the colleges were to take over the powers hitherto exercised by the Governor-General, or Governors, alone.

The question of the constitution of the new State had, it has been seen, received different answers from different political parties. All points of the spectrum were represented, from confederalism through federalism to the unitary state; from CONAKAT to the M.N.C.–L. in this ascending order of cohesion. But the effective distance between these theoretically opposed positions was narrowed by the realization of, for example, A.B.A.K.O. that even a federal state needs a strong central government, and of the M.N.C.–L. that there must be considerable decentralization in a unitary state. Thus the Central Government was given control over foreign affairs, the *Force publique*, national finance, customs and currency, communications and public works of national importance, higher education, the organization of the judiciary, national security and economic planning. With some reservations mineral prospecting and exploitation, and general control of land policy also came within the purview of the central Government. To the provincial Governments—the six provinces were to remain, at least for the time being—was given control of the (local) police, of provincial finance, of communications and public works, and of primary and intermediate education, subject to inspection. There was provision for settling disputes over competence, and matters not specifically attributed were to be the responsibility of the central and provincial Governments jointly, though in the case of conflict in this realm a national law would override a provincial one.

The institutional expression of this quasi-federalism was, at the provincial level, a legislature and an executive elected by the assembly. At the national level there were to be two houses, a chamber of representatives elected by adult male suffrage on the basis of one member for every 100,000 people, and a senate containing fourteen members for each province and elected by the provincial assemblies. Provincial and national elections were to be held as soon as possible and, guided by the results, King Baudouin would choose a prospective Prime Minister who would form the first Government. This Government must include at least one member from each province and must be approved by each house. Enjoying a position in some sense above politics was a chief of state who was to be elected by the two houses.

The basic agreement on all these matters was contained in a

R

series of sixteen conference resolutions, and a political committee was appointed to put them into more precise and legal form. In doing so it contrived to strengthen the powers of the central Government and Chief of State in certain respects. The upshot constituted the most important part of *Loi fondamentale* and was passed by the two Belgian Chambers, and signed by the King, on 18 May. The emerging independent Congo had thus been provided with a constitution which was to remain in force until replaced by a constitution drawn up in due form by the Congolese themselves after Independence.

The Round Table was followed in April and May by the economic conference—the Economic Round Table, but its importance was much less since the major Congolese figures were too busy with the election campaign to attend, and the Congolese delegates were successful in avoiding many binding commitments. Indeed the centre of interest moved back to the Congo as the delegates to the political conference made their triumphal return with the Independence, which few of them had probably in their heart of hearts expected so soon and so easily to obtain, in their pockets.[1] In the remaining months of Belgian rule, much of the positive interest in the Congo is contained in the further rise and enhanced impact of the political parties, the negative interest in the demoralization of the Administration in particular and of Belgians in general.

Although certain parties—the P.S.A. and A.B.A.K.O., for example—had boycotted the December 1959 elections, the agreement reached at Brussels on the early granting of Independence, to be preceded by further elections, meant that all parties bent every nerve to obtain maximum success in those elections. It was lost upon none of the politicians that the results of those elections would largely determine who was to gain power, both in the provinces and at the national level. In the study of the intense political activity of this period it is useful to note the categories into which H. Weiss perceptively divides the Congolese parties of this era. Demanding least explanation is the ethnic party of which A.B.A.K.O. is possibly

[1] Some of those who mixed with the Congolese delegations to the Round Table Conference believe that few of them originally believed that they would obtain independence in 1960, and that possibly they were secretly apprehensive of such a rapid development. But given the competition between the parties, escalation was the result. In the whole of this section I have drawn heavily on Miss Hoskyns, *The Congo since Independence*, pp. 36–48, and on *Congo 1960*, I, pp. 11–84.

the most obvious and most successful example. Being the political expression, in the new world of parties and impending self-government, of a more or less homogeneous ethnic group, its growth was as obvious, given African categories of political thought, as the rising and the setting of the sun. A.B.A.K.O. had many smaller counterparts. Alan P. Merriam, living at the time in Lupupa, a small village in Eastern Kasai, points to the dominating element of tribal self-protection and assertion by quoting the words with which a new ethnic party was introduced in that village. The party, the *Mouvement Unitaire Ba-Songe*, had been founded by Ba-Songe *évolués* and was commended in the village on these grounds.

The Congolese have returned from the Round Table talks in Brussels. There were Ba-Luba, Ba-Kongo, Ruandaise, people from Stanleyville, and from Bukavu, all with their different languages. But there were no Ba-Songye there. Our people were forgotten. Here in our part of the country we have nothing. They say that at Leopoldville there is much money; at Luluabourg there are diamonds. . . . But the Ba-Songye have nothing. So we must unite.[1]

The response was positive. Within a few weeks fifty-six out of seventy party membership cards left in the village had been bought at the relatively large sum of about 7s. each, and there was lively interest in the party's plans for building such things as social centres and securing the means, for example, of paying for European help after independence.[2]

Where rival parties sought to enter the field the appeal might become more nakedly tribal, or perhaps tribal/territorial. To give an example, when the P.S.A. tried to extend its influence from Kwilu into Kwango, it encountered opposition not only from a rival *regional* party—to introduce the second of Weiss's categories—but also the trenchant opposition of an established tribal party. This was L.U.K.A., the *Union Kwangolaise pour l'Indépendance et la Liberté*, which was essentially the party of the Ba-Yaka. But it also claimed the right to be the sole party in areas dominated by the Ba-Yaka. In such areas people of other tribes must join L.U.K.A., whilst, certainly, a reciprocal right to other parties seems to have been admitted in areas in which they were dominant.[3] Thus, if the account of an official of the rival P.S.A. is to be believed, a L.U.K.A. meeting of March

[1] Merriam, *Congo: Background of Conflict*, pp. 186–7.   [2] Ibid.
[3] *P.S.A.*, pp. 211–21; Biebuyck and Douglas, *Congo Tribes and Parties*, p. 35.

1960 in contested Kenge, in northern Kwango, was announced by loud-speaker in these words:

Today at 2 p.m. there will be a public meeting of L.U.K.A. The P.S.A., being a party of the Ba-Mbala of Kikwit, ought to rule in Kikwit and the L.U.K.A. in Kwango.

Kwango is for the Kwangolese and each in his own district. . . . The P.S.A. in Kwilu, like the A.B.A.K.O. in the lower Congo, the M.N.C. in Kasai [sic], the UNILAC in Lake Leopold II. . . .

The officials of the P.S.A. have taken refuge in their house, which is tangible proof that the L.U.K.A. is stronger than the P.S.A.

We shall do everything to ensure that natives of Kwilu and of the Lower Congo return to where they came from.[1]

More of an achievement was the creation of the second category of party, the regional. The P.S.A. is the outstanding—and best-documented—example of this. The bare facts of its foundation have already been indicated: what has not been pointed out is that it was in principle a national party and in practice, because of its success in fusing together virtually all the tribes in Kwilu, and many of those in adjoining Kwango, a *regional* party. In the former region it gained the support of the Ba-Pende, Ba-Mbala, Ba-Kwese, Ba-Mbunda and Ba-Huana as well as of the minority of the Bashi-Lele and Ba-Wongo resident in the district: in Kwango it successfully organized the Ba-Mbala, Ba-Ngongo and a large proportion of the Ba-Suku and Ba-Sonde.[2] There may be some sort of affinity between at least some of these tribes: if so, here is part of the reason for the party's success. Its programme was also no doubt attractive—notice the poster reproduced in this book—but no more nor less so than that of most other parties.

My own conclusion is that the party was successful because it was first off the ground in much of the Kwilu-Kwango region and, to reverse the metaphor, the first *on* the ground. The actual programme may well have had only moderate drawing-power. What mattered to the villagers of Kwilu and parts of Kwango, as the teams of party speakers spread out from Kikwit into the bush, was that here was a party, commonly introduced to them by one of the better educated of their own number, whose leaders were at least from tribes which were not hostile. More than this, in collective support for the party lay the newly

[1] C. Kizika, Account of L.U.K.A. meeting, 21 March 1960, in *P.S.A.*, pp. 221–4.
[2] Biebuyck and Douglas, *Congo Tribes and Parties*, p. 36.

dawned hope of bringing to an end the inconvenient or oppressive demands of *Bula Matari*, an expectation of a better life for themselves, and a new guarantee of peace and security necessary now that European rule was evidently drawing to an end. The fact of collective adhesion and the circumstances that the P.S.A. was commonly the first party to appear must be emphasized. As a generalization it is fair to state that the political and social ideas of Congolese postulated the homogeneous action of the group. There was rarely a place for the individualist. The following excerpt from an account of an inter-party meeting at Kenge in January 1960 speaks for itself and is representative.

. . . All the members of C.R.I.K. (*Centre de Regroupement pour les Intérêts du Kwango*) or L.U.K.A. shout that whatever his origin everyone ought to belong to C.R.I.K. or L.U.K.A.

Objection from a C.R.I.K. member who concluded that each individual is free to follow whatever seems good to him, as in the case of a protestant and of a catholic. . . .

Unanimous objection from C.R.I.K. or L.U.K.A. supporters.[1]

Of this concern to act as a group the P.S.A., as long as it was the first party to appear, was the beneficiary. None the less, trouble might still lie ahead, for the newly awakened political consciousness could not always be harnessed exclusively and permanently to the P.S.A., and, in particular, friction, fear and rivalry might lead to tribal breakaways[2]. All in all, however, the success of the P.S.A. was remarkable and can be measured by its achievement in the May elections. As regards the central legislative chamber it gained eleven of a possible twelve seats in Kwilu, and two of a possible five in Kwango. In the provincial election the party gained thirty-two of a possible thirty-four seats in Kwilu, and three of a possible seven in Kwango.[3]

Only two of the Congo's parties could, on attainment, claim admittance to the category of national parties—the P.N.P. and the M.N.C.-Lumumba. In the May elections the former gained fifteen seats in the central legislative chamber, the latter thirty-three, or forty-one if its direct allies are included.[4] Such a disparity was not merely a disappointment to the Belgians,

---

[1] B. Labakuhana and C. Kizika, 'Report on Political Meeting', n.d., in *P.S.A.*, p. 220.
[2] *P.S.A.*, p. 6.   [3] Ibid., pp. 272–3.   [4] *Congo 1960*, pp. 262–3.

particularly as Lumumba's radicalism had increasingly antagonized them in the months after the Round Table,[1] but also reflected major differences between the nature and organization of the two parties. Despite its participation in the Common Front at the Round Table, the P.N.P. remained a moderate party. Indeed, it has been seen to have been not so much a party as a federation of local parties, with strong participation by traditional authorities. To take the most striking example, in Kwango, L.U.K.A., the party essentially of the Ba-Yaka, was strongly patronized by the Kiamfu, or traditional ruler of the Ba-Yaka, whilst the party itself was a component of the P.N.P.—and gained for it four of its fifteen seats.[2]

Although the power of the Kiamfu might be strong enough to keep the Ba-Yaka in line, this was not always the case, even with genuinely traditional rulers. When it came to those who were customary authorities only in official terminology, that is those who were essentially nominated by the Administration, their influence was much less. To the real traditionalists amongst their people, they were not proper chiefs anyway, and their eclipse was as natural as the eclipse of their European masters. It is perhaps also true that the very role they had played in the past had not furnished them with the horizons which the politics of the new Congo had in view—or it may have given them a greater sense of harsh realities! It could also be that the very fact of a chief's adhesion to the P.N.P., when his authority was weak or when he was disliked, was sufficient reason for his people to vote for the P.N.P.'s rival. It has also been suggested that the P.N.P. had an unhappy knack of backing the wrong people, and that it lacked able leaders. Indeed, it is in the realm of political organization and leadership that the differences between the P.N.P. and the M.N.C.– Lumumba were of crucial importance.[3]

The M.N.C. was, of course, the creation of Patrice Lumumba. Born at Katako-Kombe, in northern Kasai, in 1925, he owed his early opportunities in adult life to various Europeans, lay and missionary, who seem to have recognized in him a man

[1] Colin Legum, *Congo Disaster*, p. 87.

[2] *Congo 1960*, pp. 262–3.

[3] Biebuyck and Douglas, *Congo Tribes and Parties*, pp. 16, 27; Hoskyns, *The Congo since Independence*, p. 66.

of unusual gifts. Not the least of these gifts was a passion for reading. He read extraordinarily widely and sometimes at random—Voltaire, Rousseau, Agatha Christie, Victor Hugo, Molière, Jacques Mantain, Churchill, Simenon were all grist to his mill, but he did not anchor himself in any particular philosophy, certainly not Marxism. The fact and form of his reading indicates his concern to get to grips with the literature of Europe and is a concern which is related to his very real desire, which we have already remarked, to enter the European world at the all-important level of personal relationships. Rebuff at this level was of great importance to Lumumba's development (see p. 210). As a result of such episodes as his collision with the European woman in the European quarter of Leopoldville, and her infliction of the supreme insult by calling him *sale macaque*, he came to see that he could not enter European society as an equal, and thus could not fully participate in its culture, both of which he so admired.

This traumatic experience appears to have led to his parting from his clerical mentors both in anger and in sorrow at the realization that he could not in the event do as they had encouraged him to believe he could—enter the European world through the logic of his own attainments. But at no stage of his life did he end his involvement in and admiration for European culture; but repulsion none the less brought him a stark consciousness of what the French call *négritude*, of the fact that he was an African, and that Congolese independence should be the microcosm of a continent-wide assertion of the African personality. Whilst for many other Congolese leaders, the Brussels Exhibition, with all its opportunities for meeting other Congolese and analysing their situation, was the origin of political thought and calculation, Lumumba had by that time already formulated the project of a national political party.

He had also been found guilty of embezzlement. The facts are not in dispute; he had defrauded the Post Office, his one-time employers, of £900 and been sentenced to eighteen months' imprisonment as a result. His legal defence was that he was only borrowing the money and that the fact that, before his detection, he had returned about one-fifth of it, proved at least the honesty of his intentions! As a 'political' defence he was later known to argue that his theft was really restitution to the

Congolese of a small part of what the colonizer had taken from them. But interestingly, his biographer claims, he did not at heart ever get over the shame of having embezzled public money, of having transgressed one of the standards of the culture which he so respected.

But whilst he respected and admired the culture of Europe it was seemingly just his inability freely to enter the European world of the Congo that caused the element of violent antagonism to Belgian rule. Hence the suspicion of Belgium, the violent attacks upon her, the infuriating intransigence. Perhaps, also, it was from this starting-point that originated Lumumba's avidity for power, an avidity intense beyond what is common amongst politicians. With this was coupled a formidable ability to work hard. Jean Van Lierde has testified from first-hand observation that Lumumba could work for seventeen to twenty hours a day, for weeks at a time.

In the purely political period of his life it was not merely his self-acquired erudition and his capacity for hard work which were reasons for his rocket-like rise, but also his ability to weigh up and choose people, the compulsiveness of his private argument and the magnetism of his public word. I have been told of how in May 1960, after his own first attempt to form a Government had failed, and when Ganshof van der Meersch had then turned to Kasavubu, he was almost unanimously urged at an all-night cabal of the M.N.C. to assert his claim to power by revolutionary action in the streets of Leopoldville, to start at sunrise that very morning. For two hours, almost alone, Lumumba argued the folly of this course at that time. He gained the day. His public touch was no less remarkable and seemed to have the effect on his hearers of the oratory of Hitler or of Aneurin Bevan. But one of the things which made him unique was his use of his gifts and position to build up a national party aiming to make the Congo a nation and not an uneasy congeries of tribes.

It was in this that he also revealed his defects. At the risk of judging from the safe position of hindsight, he was ingenuous—ingenuous in supposing that there was even the bare minimum of experience, skills and the will to make the Congo into a nation, and that he in his person could make up any deficiency. At bottom he may have lacked an adequate definition of human nature and of the possible. But, in his defence, this was not mainly his fault, and in supposing that there was in the *Force publique* the ultimate conserver of the nation, he merely shared the near-universal opinion. And he certainly had not himself contributed to the undermining of military morale by building up amongst its ranks a personal praetorian guard, as many other Congolese politicians attempted to do.

Of course, Lumumba's failure and fall was caused by the mutiny of the *Force publique*, and the disappearance almost over-night of the great majority of those who managed the admin-istration and technical services of the nation; of course this occurred after Independence, and does not strictly lie within our consideration. But an overall assessment must take account of this, of the quite desperate problems which it presented, before reaching the possible conclusion that the wonder is not that he failed in the end as that he achieved so much.[1]

From his foundation of it in October 1958 Lumumba's gifts made his party, the M.N.C., into a remarkable phen-omenon. Inspiring it, in one sense, was Lumumba's own passionate conviction that the Congo must from the outset be a unitary state with a strong central Government. But it would be wrong to suppose that the party was sold to the electorate in these terms. It is very doubtful if more than a few initiates fully supported Lumumba's pan-Congo aims: what mattered was Lumumba's great political skill in appealing to the masses on a national scale, and his ability to weld together a national party. The explanation of this success is not entirely clear, but there are a number of valuable pointers, and in particular there are useful analogies with the P.S.A. There was the missionary zeal of the M.N.C. party evangelists (and to use the term in this bastard sense is entirely appropriate). The good news which the 'ward heelers' of the party—less inhibited than those of the P.S.A.—brought to the villages on, say, the banks of the Lomami, in Orientale, which is where this specific example comes from, was certainly of a new earth, if scarcely of a new heaven. Unfolding a picture of the skyscrapers constituting an American city—it was in fact a brochure for an

---

[1] On Lumumba see De Vos, *Vie et mort de Lumumba*; Lumumba, *Le Congo, terre d'avenir, est-il menacé?*; J. Van Lierde, 'Témoignage: Patrice Lumumba, leader et ami', *Présence africaine*, 36, 1961, pp. 112–19; J. Van Lierde (ed.), *La Pensée politique de Patrice Lumumba*, Preface by Jean-Paul Sartre (Brussels, Éditions Amis de Présence Africaine, 1963); Colin Legum, *Congo Disaster*, pp. 94-97. I have also drawn upon personal information.

encyclopedia—the party speaker declared that after Independence all the huts in the village could be pulled down and be replaced by buildings like those in the picture!

Promises such as these appear to have been the common currency of M.N.C. canvassers. More money, the cars and sometimes the wives of the white men, an abundance of work— or no work at all; these and numerous other extravagant promises were such as to confer a perverted religious dimension on Independence, to give to the hearers an almost apocalyptic sense of expectancy.[1]

A further useful comparison with the P.S.A. is that to all intents and purposes the M.N.C. was the first party on the ground in many of the areas where it operated, the earlier activity of the P.N.P., in connection with the December 1959 elections, having had much less mass impact, and its later activity being less extensive, and incomparably less effective than that of its rivals. To the extent that this was so, the same factors obtained, making for group adhesion to a new source of guidance and leadership in a period of waning European authority, as had obtained with the P.S.A. in Kwilu and Kwango (see pp. 244-5 above). One circumstance existing in many parts of Orientale, the heartland of M.N.C. power, seems to have been quite different. This was the presence there of a number of Kitawalists and some exiled Kimbanguists and the consequent dissemination of their ideas. The political significance of this was that, a lively sense of apocalyptic expectancy being common to both of these sects, there was both a disposition to see Independence in religious as well as political terms and, Professor Biebuyck suggests, a readiness to accept unrealistic promises. It is certainly the case that in parts of Orientale the graves were tidied in the expectation that Independence would be accompanied by a general rising of the dead, that in other parts word went round (and was widely obeyed) that all sheep, or all goats, must be killed as a condition of the successful realization of Independence. Finally, membership of Kitawala, with its emphasis on a supra-tribal (black) brotherhood, may well have been a factor making for adhesion to a national, as distinct from an ethnic, party.[2]

Along with extravagant promises, the M.N.C., of all the

[1] Personal information.
[2] Biebuyck and Douglas, *Congo Tribes and Parties*, pp. 27, 44; personal information.

parties, was most prone to coercion of its opponents, though its apologists maintain that threats and violence were reserved for officials and supporters of the P.N.P., which they saw as the tool of the Administration which itself (they continue) acted unfairly by persecuting the M.N.C. Certainly these bands of young toughs were a distinctly unpleasant feature of Congo politics at this time and were the precursor of much worse that was to come. But if one assumes a general disposition for political choices to be community choices, it becomes credible that coercion was not a determining factor of the M.N.C.'s success.

Indeed there was more to the M.N.C.'s success than the enthusiasm of party zealots, the first harvesters of a particularly favourable field. There was the personal magnetism and energy of Lumumba himself, which gave him an almost god-like image, and inspired an extreme devotion. And it was accompanied by a penetratingly acute assessment of the political and tribal situation. First of all, it is suggested, Lumumba took advantage of his membership of the Ba-Tetela tribe successfully to organize a large part of the Ba-Mongo complex of peoples of which the Ba-Tetela are an offshoot. Largely to win Mongo allegiance in this way was of great significance in the spread and organization of the party since the Ba-Mongo and related groups are to be found in every province save Katanga.[1]

Secondly, Lumumba showed great skill in picking out useful allies. Whereas the P.N.P. all too often chose traditional rulers who did not enjoy the confidence of their people, the M.N.C. had a remarkable flair for picking out the influential and the progressive.[2] Related to this was its success in so analysing regional ethnic political rivalries as to make use of them in building up a national party. Thus in Kasai the M.N.C. position was strengthened by alignment with C.O.A.K.A. (*Coalition Kasaienne*), an anti-Ba-Luba party, and with that same Ba-Songe unity party which, we have seen, was eagerly welcomed in the little village of Lupupa, as the defender of Ba-Songe against the Ba-Luba aggression which Independence was expected to unleash. Here evidently is a paradox—the use of tribal affiliations and tribal rivalries to build up a supra-tribal party. Hindsight and the later history of the Congo may suggest that paradox was really contradiction. But at least

[1] Biebuyck and Douglas, *Congo Tribes and Parties*, pp. 24–25.
[2] Hoskyns, *The Congo since Independence*, p. 66.

Lumumba was consistent to the extent of never allying with CONAKAT and A.B.A.K.O., the two parties strongly tinged with separatism.[1]

We have seen the impressive results gained by the M.N.C. in the May elections, but one should not overlook the no less important elements of weakness in the party, and in the whole concept of attaining in any meaningful form the national unity for which the M.N.C. stood. Again we can begin with Lupupa. Merriam makes the important points that the real emotional attachment was to the Ba-Songe ethnic party, and the fact that it was in coalition with the M.N.C. meant little to the Lupupans. Lumumba was supported because he was the most local of the national figures, but when M.N.C. organizers as such came to the village in October 1959, despite a general sympathy with the party, despite the assurance that membership cards would cost nearly three times as much in 1960 and much more again in 1961, and despite stories of the benefits which possession of the card would confer and the penalties which failure to buy would bring, only a handful of people bought them. Similarly, in this whole part of eastern Kasai, participation in voting, both in December and May, varied greatly according to whether or not there was a local candidate. Thus in one near-by village there was, literally, 100 per cent. turn out, because there was a local candidate, whereas in another, which lacked such a candidate, only about 5 per cent. bothered to vote.[2] Turnbull, who was apparently living in a village in north-eastern Congo at much the same time as Merriam, pertinently observed:

The tribal African there had little or no idea of national unity; his horizons were strictly those of the tribe. Stanleyville, Leopoldville, New York, Brussels, London—all were simply 'the great city' to him. Whether they were five hundred miles away or five thousand they were too remote to have any reality.[3]

It is reasonable to infer that attitudes like these were general amongst the rural population.

It could still be argued that this extreme parochialism of the

---

[1] Biebuyck and Douglas, *Congo Tribes and Parties*, pp. 40–41, 45; Merriam, *Congo: Background of Conflict*, pp. 168–8; *Congo 1960*, I, pp. 214–16, 262–3. Ganshof, *Fin de la souveraineté belge*, pp. 107–8.

[2] Merriam, *Congo: Background of Conflict*, pp. 185–8.

[3] Turnbull, *The Lonely African*, p. 78.

man in the bush was not necessarily such as to make it impossible for the M.N.C. to be a national party. After all, the leaders
of the party were instructed, were capable of the broad, national
view, and at the same time enjoyed the confidence of the
untutored masses. But reality had a different face. The party
youth wing, which gave it much of its dynamism and did much
of the work, consisted of young men who were literate, yes—but
not very much more. The provision of primary education on a
large scale, but with the number of secondary-school places on a
scale wholly disproportionate to the demand thus awakened,
had various, and almost uniformly harmful results.

The immediately relevant one was that the party militants,
being in any true sense no better educated than their fellows,
could inject no constructive, national purpose into party
activities. Their principal role seems to have been that of the
strong-arm man. At the level of the party's local officials there
were, no doubt, many men of competence, ideals and integrity.
But in a colony which had not developed any significant
embryonic national institutions, it is not likely that they would
have had much real national consciousness, whilst the education
and jobs open to them were not such as greatly to help them
provide constructive leadership. Much the same might be true
at the top levels of the party. Merriam, in his quite exceptionally valuable grass-roots study, gives a most incisive, yet
sympathetic study of one such party leader, a man who
became a member of the first Lumumba government. As a
Musonge, moreover, his views gained immense credit amongst
the Lupupans. Merriam's picture is worth quoting at length.

Let us call this man M., a young man of about twenty-five, extremely intelligent and quick, a Musongye by birth, and at the time in a
position extremely close to Patrice Lumumba; after independence he
was appointed to a position in the Lumumba government. In the
course of a trip on M.N.C. business he called on me in Lupupa on
the afternoon of May 25. We spoke of many of the Congo's problems
in a lengthy discussion and I shall report his views in no special
order here. Early in the conversation he fell to boasting about the
efficiency of the M.N.C. undercover activities; he said that the
M.N.C. had a 'file' on every administrator and agent in the Congo
and that it had already marked those whom it wished to eject from
the country and those whom it wished to have stay. This, of course,
was before it was known that Lumumba and the M.N.C. would

form the first Congo government. When I asked how he felt he could persuade the 'desirables' to stay and work with the independent Congo, he simply turned the question aside unanswered. Perhaps, more exactly, his response was unbounded confidence that such desirables *would* stay. This attitude was widespread in the Congo. Few plans were ever made by Congolese for a programme after June 30, but with an intense self-confidence it was simply taken for granted that the world would come to the Congo and that, without any effort on the part of the Congolese, help in all its forms would be available. Thus M. was justified in his attitude, at least so far as he was concerned, because the supreme naïveté, the tremendous localization of thought, and the inheritance of paternalism were his as much as any man's: his veneer of sophistication was so thin as to allow him little room for thought.

Although he would deny it, everything for M. was black and white, both figuratively and literally, and thus all Belgians, if not all white-skinned people, were bad, and all Africans, namely the Congolese, were good, and oppressed by colonialism. All the troubles in the Congo at that time, among which the most pressing local problem was the Bena Lulua–Baluba conflict in Luluabourg, were caused by Belgians. Furthermore, in his logic all troubles, for example those in Luluabourg, would stop at the stroke of midnight on independence day, quite literally. If we accept his premise that all problems were being caused by Belgians, then we must accept his conclusion, but we now know, of course, that his premise was only tragically naïve and that independence brought only further outbreaks in that troubled city.

M. was full of generalizations of this sort: 'All whites are armed to the teeth,' he said, and I was unable to convince him of the truth of the fact that I personally carried no arms whatsoever save for a machete. Another generalization which again he would strenuously deny was that everything Western is good and everything Congolese bad, in the sphere, at least, of material culture. When I suggested that perhaps there were things in Congolese life to be valued too, I was hotly accused of being 'like all the other Europeans who want the Congo people to stay as they are, who want to deny us the good things of the West'. I amplified my remarks to say that I personally felt there was much value in Congo art, and the response was: 'Oh, of course we would not forget that. After independence we will have a factory to make masks and we will sell them in America!'

Another subject discussed was cotton, which is Lupupa's cash crop. Citing the price always at 5 francs per kilogram, where in actuality it was 5·85 francs in 1959 and, in the face of a world market drop was *raised* to 6 francs in 1960, he castigated the Belgians, saying that the price was unfair and that they were, in effect, stealing the cotton from the people of Lupupa. 'Look at these poor people. Up at six in the morning and working in the fields until six at night; they suffer terribly.' The fact of the matter is that, quite aside from his misquotations concerning price, almost no one in Lupupa ever worked in the fields from six in the morning until six at night and, in the sense that he was using the word, no one suffered. But these generalizations represented for him a crystallized idea which he used to convince others, and of which he had certainly convinced himself.

I would not suggest for a moment that all his ideas were wrong or that he was a deliberate liar, or that there was not some truth in his charge, but I cite the conversation to illustrate his appalling gener-alizations, his twisting of words, his naïveté, his expediency. I am convinced that he could not, as an ardent nationalist, allow himself the luxury of conceding anything to the other side. All Belgians, if not all whites, are bad; all rival political parties are unspeakable; Lumumba is virtue personified; all Congolese are hard-working slaves to the colonial system; and all would be rosy and calm the day independence dawned.[1]

From the administrator's point of view, this rising tempo of political activity was usually unwelcome and disquieting. The growing hold of the parties over whole areas, the unpleasant activities of their militants, the various degrees of civil dis-obedience which they initiated and the way in which they often took over the functions of government, were all distasteful to the good administrator. Nor, as we have seen, had it been any part of the training even of the younger men to prepare the Congolese for self-government. This was a particularly tactful and demanding job at any time, and they did not even have the time to attempt it—so headlong was the descent to Indepen-dence from the watershed of January 1959. Although relief that something definite had been decided was usually the first reaction of many administrators, as of many other Europeans, to the Round Table Conference, and although the more sanguine hoped that in spite of all they might be able to assist in a smooth transition to Independence, clashes with the political parties all too often brought bitterness or resignation. In such a situation, most just grimly held on, having frequently lost all influence in their territories. At the highest level, in the Government-General in Leopoldville, a general nervelessness and refusal to take decisions appear to have set in.[2] For instance,

[1] Merriam, *Congo: Background of Conflict*, pp. 188–91.
[2] Ganshof, *Fin de le souveraineté belge*, p. 63.

early in April 1960 MM. Saintraint and Ryckmans, the two administrators in the *territoire* of Madimba, took the desperate and unauthorized, but imaginative and promising action of declaring that from the end of April they would hand over their responsibilities to A.B.A.K.O., the effective power in the region. They would be happy to remain as advisers but only if asked to do so. M. Bomans, the Governor of Leopoldville province, endorsed their action. What followed? Bomans was 'promoted' and the action of Saintraint and Ryckmans was countermanded and though the episode did jerk the Government-General into constituting executive colleges in territories where there had been a boycott of the elections for the communal council, both the nominations and the handling of the matter were apparently maladroit.[1]

At no level of the Administration do the transition arrangements seem to have worked at all well. Nothing significant had been done during 1959 to provide accelerated training for Africans, and after the Round Table there was too little time to do very much better. In some quarters the will also was lacking—the Commander-in-Chief of the *Force publique*, for example, was in principle opposed to rapid African advancement into the commissioned ranks,[2] and there were in fact no Congolese officers when Independence broke. Nor in the two months of its effective life, April and May, was the General Executive College much of a success. The six Congolese members had no direct control of specific ministries and there was little chance that effective homogeneity might grow up between men as diverse as Lumumba, Paul Bolya of the P.N.P., Pierre Nyangwile of the M.N.C.–Kalonji and with the Governor-General (the other members were MM. Kashamura, Kasavubu, and Mwamba (BALUBAKAT)). Such chance as there was was fatally prejudiced by the sheer difficulty of the problems which confronted them, and especially by the growing seriousness of ethno-political conflicts in the country, particularly in Kasai and the Maniema district of Kivu.

Disarray at the top was matched by fears and uncertainty amongst both the European and African population. Those Congolese who did not share the apocalyptic optimism of Merriam's friend 'M' were often fearful and apprehensive of

[1] *Congo 1960*, pp. 136–48; 'J.K.', *André Ryckmans*, pp. 263–72.
[2] Hoskyns, *The Congo since Independence*, pp. 59–60.

the unknown. And of course some harboured both the optimism and the fear. Amongst Europeans, anxiety was reflected in a flight of capital from the Congo and a decline in business activity which threatened the colony's solvency. In the spring the Belgian Government took measures which somewhat restored the situation,[1] but another manifestation of the unease of the European population, the dispatch of wives and families to Europe, increased in volume as 30 June approached.[2] Altogether, on the eve of the elections, the immediate herald of Independence, the Congo situation looked more alarming to all who had any responsible part in it than it had in the euphoric atmosphere of the period immediately following the Round Table. Belgium's last major action before 30 June was to supervise the installation of the first Congolese Government, and in the middle of May it appointed a non-political lawyer, M. Ganshof van der Meersch, as Minister without portfolio with responsibility for African Affairs in the Congo.

Ganshof enjoyed in Belgium the reputation of a strong man, having played an important role in the bringing of collaborators to trial at the end of the Second World War. This reputation did not help him as he set out for the Congo, for the Belgian Press portrayed him as the protector of Congo Europeans, and Congolese distrust was heightened by the simultaneous reinforcement of the metropolitan military bases at Kitona and Kamina. It seems that this combination of events re-aroused dormant fears that Belgium did not really mean to let the Congo go after all, that she was resolved to hold it down by force. Both Lumumba and Kashamura left the Executive College in protest.[3] Ganshof's task was in any event one of great difficulty. Following an imprecise decision of the Round Table he was to advise the king upon whom he should call to form the first Congolese Government, in the light of the results of the May elections.

Within days of Ganshof's arrival at Leopoldville on 22 May the election results began to be known. There had been violence in a number of places during the electoral period, numerous irregularities and a good deal of constraint, but the official conclusion, reached in regard to the *Haut Congo* district of

[1] Hoskyns, *The Congo since Independence*, pp. 45–49.
[2] Ganshof, *Fin de la souveraineté belge*, p. 65, cites figures.
[3] Hoskyns, *The Congo since Independence*, p. 63.

Orientale, that abuses did not significantly affect the results, rings true, and is probably of general application.[1] The one clear result of the elections was the failure of the P.N.P. to achieve the overall success which had been expected of it, and the conspicuous success of the M.N.C.–Lumumba. Whereas the former gained only fifteen seats in the central legislative assembly, the M.N.C. with its direct allies took forty-one. The total number of seats was 137. In addition the M.N.C. claimed the support of two allied parties, the P.S.A. with thirteen seats and C.E.R.E.A. with ten. But it was at this juncture that uncertainty began, for it could well be that C.E.R.E.A., having done well in the Kivu provincial elections, would weaken in its support of the M.N.C. at the centre, preferring full power in Bukavu to a share in authority in Leopoldville. The P.S.A., for its part, was divided between the radical and moderate wings of Gizenga and Kamitatu respectively.[2] Moreover, in a situation where no conventions and political habits had been established, where ambition for office was a potent factor, and where everyone more or less distrusted everyone else, there was very great fluidity and uncertainty.

For Ganshof there must also have been the particular need to bear in mind the position of Kasavubu, a nationally respected figure with a party sitting firmly astride the Lower Congo (twelve seats in the central assembly), and of Tshombe and CONAKAT which had emerged as dominant in southern Katanga. Though neither A.B.A.K.O. nor CONAKAT had swept the board in either the provincial elections, or in the national elections in their respective provinces, they had demonstrated anew that the secession of one or both of two strategic areas was still a possibility, if the respective parties were slighted.[3] For Ganshof there was also the problem of whether Lumumba, whose intransigence and anti-Belgian stance had lately been particularly apparent, would be more impossible in office, or more dangerous if excluded from it.

Specifically, Ganshof believed that there were three possible *formateurs* who might obtain the requisite majority in both the Chamber and the Senate—Lumumba, Kasavubu, or a third

[1] Ganshof, *Fin de la souveraineté belge*, pp. 139–46.

[2] *Congo 1960*, I, pp. 260–6, 269–70.

[3] For analyses of the election results, provincial and national, see *Congo 1960*, I, pp. 155–7, 166–7, 171–2, 182–3, 214–16, 240– 3, 260–6; Ganshof, *Fin de la souveraineté belge*, pp. 147–59, 603–30; Hoskyns, *The Congo since Independence*, pp. 68–74.

person who would emerge as a national figure, rallying opinion
in sufficient strength. It may be that Ganshof delayed entrusting
one of the two unquestioned candidates with the task partly in
the hope that such a moderate figure would emerge. But he did
not emerge, and on 13 June Lumumba was entrusted with the
task (technically only of *formateur*—the difference was not
significant). But the assurances of support which he brought
were not sufficient for Ganshof, and Kasavubu was appointed
formateur in his stead. But he likewise failed, Ganshof's withdrawal of confidence from Lumumba having, it seems, rallied
C.E.R.E.A., the P.S.A. and BALUBAKAT to Lumumba.
His enhanced strength was demonstrated in the Chamber's
election of its officers on 21 June, when all the Lumumba bloc
candidates were successful with definite, though not overwhelming majorities. In this new situation Ganshof turned
again to Lumumba and the immediate crisis was passed when
the M.N.C. leader reached a compromise with Kasavubu,
whereby the latter became Head of State and A.B.A.K.O. had
two ministries, and Lumumba became head of a very widely
based coalition. With the requisite parliamentary majorities
obtained on 24 June, all might breathe again.[1] At least the
ship was still afloat and there was a new captain and crew duly
at their posts. Moreover, energetic action by Ganshof and
Schoeller, now back in his position as Governor of Katanga,
nipped in the bud an attempt by CONAKAT—not the first
—to take Katanga out of the Congo on the very eve of
Independence.[2] If this and other secessionist movements, in the
informed perspective of late June, were real possibilities
immediately after Independence, at least Congo unity was
formally inviolate as power was transferred. Finally, the
recently reiterated desire of the Congolese leaders to have King
Baudouin at the formal ceremony for the handing over of power
augured that the last act would be carried out with a proper
decency.

But the Independence ceremony which the king graced on
30 June was a disaster on account of the tirade with which
Lumumba followed the speeches of King Baudouin and

---

[1] For the formation of the first Congo Government, see Ganshof, *Fin de la
souveraineté belge*, pp. 191–299; *Congo 1960*, I, pp. 267–309; Hoskyns, *The Congo since
Independence*, pp. 74–79.
[2] Ganshof, *Fin de la souveraineté belge*, pp. 391, 515–17, 579–86; *Congo 1960*, I,
pp. 243–56.

President Kasavabu. At another level, however, the occasion was one of sheer tragic irony. The King's eulogistic references to Leopold II indicated a failure to realize the true nature of King Leopold's legacy, that Leopold had been the cause of suffering in the Congo at least as much as he had alleviated it, that he had initiated a pattern of colonial development which came to be harmful in certain respects, and that he had bequeathed to his country a colony towards which, because Belgium accepted it only from a sense of reluctant duty, she never displayed an integrated national will and purpose.[1]

King Baudouin's enumeration of subsequent Belgian achievements was no less ironical, not because they were not achievements, for they undoubtedly were, but because Belgium consistently failed to see that a whole series of separate achievements, principally material and mostly related to an un-reflecting economic purpose, was not enough. And she failed to understand that the consequences of those very achievements—especially industrialization, urbanization and the production of an élite—demanded new thought and new attitudes. The scarifying speech of Lumumba which followed[2] was the protest of those for whom Belgian rule, and too many Belgians in the Congo, had not made room.

[1] Text printed in Ganshof, *Fin de la souveraineté belge*, pp. 325–7, and *Congo 1960*, I, pp. 318–20.
[2] Text in Ganshof, op. cit., pp. 332–4, and *Congo 1960*, I, pp. 323–5.

XIV

CONCLUSION

THE recent history of the Congo has been a happy hunting ground both for those who seek evidence of the iniquity of colonial powers, and for those who argue the unreadiness of African states for independence. It has not been the purpose of this book to approach the subject from either of these two directions, but rather to consider why Belgium took over the Congo, what she sought to do there, and what the impact of her presence was. Given such an approach, the notion of a legacy, as incorporated in the title of this book, is not just the adaptation of the title of Dr. Ruth Slade's antecedent volume—*King Leopold's Congo*—but is a useful pointer to the nature of Belgian rule.

It was undoubtedly Leopold II's wish to bequeath his Congo creation to his people. Indeed, we have seen that 'bequeath' and 'will' are terms which can be used in their literal meaning. Even if, in the end, Belgium insisted on her right to take over the Congo in Leopold's lifetime, rather than be the grateful recipient of royal benevolence at his death, the Congo substantially remained the king's legacy to his people. Lacking any interest in colonies herself, Belgium only came to possess the Congo because her king had created the Independent State. It follows from the fact of inheritance that Belgium inherited, not only a colony, but a colony possessed of a certain structure. The elements of that structure were a sparse population and a battered customary society; a vast territory which had not been properly administered; a system of direct economic exploitation, or an unfettered variant of the concessionaire system, and, as a consequence at a further remove, abuse and atrocity. Thirdly, the fact that the Congo was a legacy meant that Belgium had no relevant tradition of policy to invoke, no positive aims regarding it. Finally, this fact that the Congo was a legacy, the nature of that legacy, and the circumstance of its reception, did much to determine the early lines of Belgian conduct in the Congo, especially as there was an urgent need to do something.

What more natural, especially for a country which owed its stature largely to the business and industrial skills of its citizens, than to use the means that were to hand, appropriately purged? Certain companies had agreed to undertake large-scale mineral exploitation in return for the granting of prospecting and development rights: others were exploiting the natural wealth of land over which they had comprehensive rights. Let the extremes and abuses of the last type of concession be checked, otherwise confirm existing rights. Native administration must be put on a truly customary basis, but the chief must still be used primarily as the agent of the Administration. Let civilizing work continue to be the preserve of the missions, especially Catholic missions.

The notion of a legacy is relevant even to subsequent periods of Belgian rule, because there was no major departure from the broad lines of the original Belgian comportment in the Congo which the legacy had done so much to determine, though certainly there was refinement of that comportment. There was the continuation of a privileged position for the big companies and their consequent predominance in the Congo economy, whilst the apparently new departure of the stabilized labour policy from the late twenties onwards is essentially a function of that predominance—which is not to deny that it had impressive results at the human as well as the economic level.

Even the growth of medical work seems to have had as an important impulse the need to develop a healthy *working* population. Customary authorities continued to be too much used as the bottom rung of European authority despite the frequent efforts of a commonly better type of administrator to nurture traditional society and its system of government. The work of Catholic missions is favoured above the Protestant, as under Leopold. And, with the exception of this last, all these characteristics were given an even stronger impulse by the stimuli of World War II and the ensuing boom period.

What was new was the consequences of the fuller working-out of this comportment in a colony of low population density, when at the same time the Colonial Administration did not give to the new society, which the continued operation of these divers pressures was creating, new and different treatment. At one level, and in one period especially, the unbearable pressures of the European impact gave way to messianic movements; at a later period the process of economic growth, urbanization and education, even though the whole emphasis of education policy was at the primary level, gave rise to a self-conscious *élite*, on the margins of European culture and society but denied admittance. And whereas Kimbanguism had worked out ultimately as adaptation and synthesis, rather than as violent reaction, the *évolué*-led political movement of the late fifties was protest and revolt.

Belgium was thus faced with a situation in which the varied excellent things which she had done brought her little credit, and in which she harvested only the fruits of failure to co-ordinate and control the separate activities of divergent interests. Amongst the problems with which this book has failed to deal adequately is that of why Belgium not only had no national will for the initial development of her colony, which, it has been argued, is explicable in historical terms, but why she never developed a national response to what was basically a general African problem, when the existence of the problem was elsewhere generally recognized, and whilst there was still time to give it considered and profitable attention.

One can only mention reasons that are sometimes cited—the lack of awareness of colonial issues amongst a people with no imperial tradition; a pragmatic approach to life which took distrust of theory to the point of refusal to pay attention to those few who argued that change was necessary: a pre-occupation with business and the production of wealth such that the relevance of other goals was obscured; a fear, perhaps, that proposals for change in the Congo would only be a further focus of bitter divisions amongst parties and races in Belgium, as in the case of Buisseret's attempt to extend lay education in the Congo.

It may also be that the people of Belgium, a country which is not a nation (because riven by at least three conflicts: the Roman Catholic Church versus anti-clericals, monarchy versus republicanism and, above all, Walloon versus Fleming), shut themselves up in a conception of the state which is seen only as the arbiter of divergent interests, and which therefore lacks the sense of homogeneity which is a condition of nationhood. If this is so, there would be no disposition to wish upon the Congolese a nationalism which Belgians did not themselves possess, and no real ability to bring it to birth when the Congolese themselves professed to want it. Rather concern oneself with the day-to-day business of making a living. Here, conceivably, are pointers to the nature of Belgium's attitude to her colony and her comportment towards it. But it is essentially a question which only the informed student of Belgian politics and Belgium can answer.

In default of any national purpose for the Congo, the supposed mission and achievement of Leopold II was frequently invoked—finally and unhappily on the very day of Congolese Independence. Perhaps the last legacy of that astute monarch was the received conviction of his people that *he* had had a coherent purpose, even if they had not.

BIBLIOGRAPHICAL NOTE

In dealing with a subject of this kind in a period of recent history, the sources in some measure suggested themselves. Given the non-availability of official documentary evidence for all save the first decade of Belgian rule, primary reliance was on monographs, both books and articles, fortified by recourse, sometimes selective, to published documents and official reports. For an historian a major difficulty was the necessity of consulting work in other disciplines, and his unfamiliarity with those fields. It is probably in what he has failed to consult in disciplines other than his own that he has been most deficient.

A further implication of a study of the contact of colonial rule and African society is that there was profit in simply talking to almost anyone, European or Congolese, with experience of the Belgian Congo, whom one could meet. As with a written source, one did not necessarily believe all one heard but, rather, collated it with other relevant knowledge. My largely haphazard but invaluable sources of this kind are acknowledged in the Foreword.

Written sources which I have found valuable include:

I. *Reports and Documents, mainly published.*

Belgium, *Annales parlementaires* and *Documents parlementaires*—selectively, and mainly to gauge Belgian political attitudes to the Congo in the inter-war years. Reports studied include the *Rapport de la mission sénatoriale au Congo*, 1947, and the Report to the Chamber of Representatives of the Parliamentary Commission of Inquiry into the Leopoldville riots of January 1959.

Belgian Congo (i) Reports of the *Commission Permanente pour la Protection des Indigènes, Bulletin officiel*, 1911, pp. 765–92; 1913, 268–94; 1920, pp. 636–79; 1924, pp. 385–425; 1925, pp. 195–212; 1929, II, pp. 84–120; 1931, pp. 696–718; 1938, I, pp. 980–1185; 1947, I, pp. 816–83; 1952, II, pp. 2994–3045; 1952, I, pp. 880–902; 1956, I, pp. 174–96. (The Reports up to 1952 inclusive were published in full by L. Guébels in the *Bulletin de C.E.P.S.I.*, 1953.) (ii) Annual Reports, up to 1945.—In the post-war years the reports are much less valuable.

Congo Independent State, Report of the Commission of Inquiry, 1905, *Bulletin officiel*, September–October 1905, pp. 135–285.

Congo 1959, Documents belges et africains, Ed. J. Gérard-Libois (Brussels, C.R.I.S.P., 1960).

Congo 1960, I, Ed. J. Gérard-Libois and B. Verhaegen (Brussels, C.R.I.S.P., n.d.).

Parti Solidaire African (P.S.A.), *Documents 1959–60*, Ed. H. Weiss and B. Verhaegen (Brussels, C.R.I.S.P., 1963).

Baptist Missionary Society Archives, Scrivener Box. A. E. Scrivener, 'Notes on a Journey to Lake Leopold II', August 1903.

Casement Report: Enclosure 2 in Casement to Lansdowne, 11 December 1903, printed as a Confidential Print, F.O. 10/806, Public Record Office. Also published in expurgated form as a Parliamentary Paper, *Africa No. 1*, 1904, Cd. 1933.

Books, Articles, Theses, Periodicals.

Andersson, E., *Messianic Popular Movements in the Lower Congo* (Uppsala, 1958).

Anstey, Roger, 'Christianity and Bantu Philosophy', *The International Review of Missions*, July 1963, pp. 316–22.

Artigue, P., *Qui sont les leaders congolais?* (Brussels, Éditions Europe-Afrique, 1961).

Balandier, G., *Sociologie actuelle de l'Afrique noire* (Paris, Presses Universitaires, 1955).

Banton, M., 'African Prophets', *Race*, V, October 1963, pp. 42–55.

Bézy, F., *Problèmes structurels de l'économie congolaise* (Louvain, Nauwelaerts, 1957).

Biebuyck, D., and Douglas, Mary, *Congo Tribes and Parties* (London, Royal Anthropological Institute, 1961).

Boelaert, E., 'Vers un état Congo?', *Bulletin des Séances de l'Académie Royale des Sciences d'Outre-Mer*, VII, 1961, 3, pp. 382–91.

Braekman, E. M., *Histoire du Protestantisme au Congo* (Brussels, Éditions de la Librairie des Éclaireurs Unionistes, 1961).

Brausch, G. E. J-B., 'Communes africaines', *Revue de l'Université de Bruxelles*, January–April 1957, pp. 230–59.

—— 'Le Paternalisme, une doctrine belge de politique indigène (1908–33)', *Revue de l'Institut de Sociologie*, 1957, pp. 191–217.

—— 'Le Groupe social comme synthèse créatrice', *Bulletin de C.E.P.S.I.*, III, 1947, pp. 35–69.

—— *Belgian Administration in the Congo* (London, O.U.P. for the Institute of Race Relations, 1961).

Bustin, E., 'The Congo', being pp. 9–159 of Gwendolen Carter, Ed., *Five African States* (New York, Cornell University Press, 1963).

Capelle, E., *La Cité Indigène de Léopoldville* (Elisabethville, C.E.P.S.I., and Leopoldville, C.E.S.A., 1947).

Carothers, J. C., *The African Mind in Health and Disease* (Geneva, World Health Organization, 1953).

—— *The Psychology of Mau Mau* (Nairobi, Government Printer, 1955).

Cattier, E., *Étude sur la situation de l'État indépendant du Congo* (Brussels, Vve. F. Larcier, 1906).

Coleman, J. S., *Nigeria, Background to Nationalism* (Berkeley, University of California Press, 1958).

Comhaire-Sylvain, S., 'Food and Leisure among the African Youth of Leopoldville', in Daryll Forde, Ed., *Social Implications of Industrialization and Urbanization in Africa south of the Sahara* (Paris, UNESCO, 1956), pp. 113–21.

Cookey, S. J. S., 'Great Britain and the Congo Question, 1892-1913' (Unpublished Ph.D. thesis of the University of London, 1964).

de Cleene, N., *Introduction à l'ethnographie du Congo belge et Ruanda-Urundi* (Antwerp, De Sikkel, 1957).

de Clerq, Mgr., 'L'Attitude du Baluba vis-à-vis de la pénétration Européene', *Bulletin des Séances de l'Institut Royal Colonial Belge*, II, 1, 1931, pp. 46–51.

Dekoster, L., 'Le Rôle de l'administrateur territorial', *Revue générale belge*, March 1949, pp. 772–7.

—— 'La Formation de l'administrateur territorial', ibid., April 1949, pp. 927ff.

Delcommune, A., *L'Avenir du Congo belge menacé* (Brussels, Lebègue & Co., 1919).

de Meeus, and Steenberghen, R., *Les Missions religieuses au Congo belge* (Antwerp, Van Dieren, 1947).

Denis, J., *Le Phénomène urbain en Afrique Centrale* (Brussels, Académie Royale des Sciences Coloniales, 1958).

Denis, L., *Les Jésuites belges au Kwango, 1893–1943* (Brussels, L'Édition Universelle, 1943).

de Vos, P., *Vie et mort de Lumumba* (Paris, Calmann-Levy, 1961)

Dollard, J., Doob, L. W., Miller, N. E., Mowren, O. H., Sears, R. R., *Frustration and Aggression* (New Haven, Yale University Press, 9th printing, 1957).

Doucy, A., 'Politique indigène', *Livre blanc* (Brussels, A.R.S.O.M., 1962), I, pp. 351–69.

Doucy, A., and Feldheim, P., *Problèmes du travail et politique sociale au Congo belge* (Brussels, Les Éditions de la Librairie Encyclopédique, 1952).

Douglas, Mary, *The Lele of the Kasai* (O.U.P. for the International African Institute, 1963).

Drake, A. F., 'Some Contemporary Problems confronting the Protestant Church in the Belgian Congo' (Unpublished S.T.M. thesis, Union Theological Seminary, New York, 1960).

Dugauquier, D. P., *Congo Cauldron* (London, Jarrolds, 1961).

Durieux, A., 'Institutions politiques (1908–60)', *Livre blanc*, I, pp. 255–82.

Forde, Daryll, Ed., *African Worlds. Studies in the Cosmological Ideas and Social Values of African Peoples* (London, O.U.P. for the International African Institute, 1954).

Forthomme, G., *Mariage et Industrialisation: évolution de la Mentalité Indigène dans une cité de travailleurs d'Élisabethville*. Liège, Travaux de l'Institut de Sociologie de la Faculté de Droit, 1957).

Franck, L., 'La Politique indigène, le service territorial et les chefferies', *Congo*, II, 1, 2 February 1921, pp. 189–201.

Ganshof van der Meersch, W. J., *Fin de la souveraineté belge au Congo, Documents et réflexions* (Brussels, Institut Royal des Relations Internationales, and The Hague, Martinus Nijhoff, 1963).

Gille, A., 'La Politique indigène du Congo belge et du Ruanda-Urundi', *Encyclopédie du Congo belge*, III, pp. 709–48.

Gray, R., *The Two Nations: Aspects of the Development of Race Relations in the Rhodesias and Nyasaland* (London, O.U.P., for the Institute of Race Relations, 1960).

Grévisse, F., *La Grande pitié des juridictions indigènes* (Brussels, I.R.C.B., 1949).

—— 'Évolués et formation des élites', *Livre Blanc*, I, pp. 397–407.

—— *Le Centre Extra-Coutumier d'Élisabethville* (Brussels, I.R.C.B., 1951).

Hailey, Lord, *An African Survey*, revised 1956 (London, O.U.P., for the Royal Institute of International Affairs, 1957).

Hoskyns, Catherine, *The Congo since Independence, January 1960–December 1961* (O.U.P. for the R.I.I.A., 1965).

Hostelet, G., *L'Œuvre civilisatrice de la Belgique au Congo de 1885 à 1953* (Brussels, A.R.S.C., 1954), 2 vols.

Jahn, J., *Muntu: An Outline of Neo-African Culture* (London, Faber and Faber, 1961).

Jahoda, Gustav, *White Man: A Study of the Attitudes of Africans to Europeans in Ghana before Independence* (O.U.P., for the Institute of Race Relations, 1961).

Jahoda, Marie, 'Race Relations: A Psycho-analytical Interpretation', in Philip Mason, Ed., *Man, Race and Darwin* (London, O.U.P., for the Royal Anthropological Institute and Institute of Race Relations, 1960).

Joye, P., and Lewin, Rosine, *Les Trusts au Congo* (Brussels, Société Populaire d'Éditions, 1961).

Kalenda, M., 'L'Institution matrimoniale et l'évolution du droit coutumier en milieu urbain', *Publications de l'Université de l'État à Élisabethville*, I, July 1961, pp. 85–97.

K(estergat), J(ean), *André Ryckmans* (Brussels, Charles Dessart, 1961).

Klineberg, O., *Social Psychology* (New York, Henry Holt, 1940).

—— 'Le Kimbangisme', *Courrier africain* (C.R.I.S.P., Leopoldville and Brussels), No. 1, 8 January, 1960, pp. 2–21. (Duplicated.)

Leblanc, Maria, *Personnalité de la femme katangaise* (Louvain, Publications Universitaires, 1960).

Legum, Colin, *Congo Disaster* (London, Penguin Books, 1961).

Lemarchand, R., 'The Bases of Nationalism among the Bakongo', *Africa*, XXXI, 4, October 1961, pp. 344–54.

Lévy-Bruhl, L., *Primitive Mentality* (London, Allen and Unwin, 1923).

Louis, Wm. R., 'Roger Casement and the Congo', *Journal of African History*, V, 1964, pp. 99–120.

—— 'The Triumph of the Movement for Reform in the Congo, 1905–08' (typescript).

Lumumba, Patrice, *Le Congo, Terre d'avenir, est-il menacé?* (Brussels, Office de Publicité, 1961).

Malengreau, G., 'La Politique coloniale de la Belgique', in *Principles and Methods of Colonial Administration* (London, Butterworth, 1950), pp. 35–52.

—— 'La Situation actuelle des indigènes au Congo belge', *Bulletin des Séances de l'I.R.C.B.*, XVIII, 1, 1947, pp. 216–28.

—— *Vers un paysannat indigène. Les Lotissements agricoles au Congo belge* (Brussels, I.R.C.B., 1949).

—— 'Le Congo à la croisée des chemins', *La Revue nouvelle*, January 1947, pp. 3–18 and 1 February 1947, pp. 95–108.

Malengreau, G., and Ugeux, W., 'Recent Developments in Belgian Africa', in C. G. Haines (Ed.), *Africa Today* (Baltimore, John Hopkins, 1955), pp. 337–65.

Malinowski, B., *The Dynamics of Culture Change, An Inquiry into Race Relations in Africa*, paperback edition (New Haven, Yale University Press, 1961).

Mannoni, O., *Prospero and Caliban: A Study of the Psychology of Colonization* (London, Methuen, 1956).

Maquet, J. J., *The Premise of Inequality in Ruanda* (London, International African Institute, 1961).

—— 'Conceptions de vie traditionelles', in *Livre blanc*, I, pp. 177–86.

Maron, A., 'Le Décret du 5 décembre 1933; son esprit et son application', *Bulletin de C.E.P.S.I.*, 1948, VI, pp. 109–29.

Mason, Philip, *Common Sense about Race* (London, Gollancz, 1961).

Merlier, M., *Le Congo de la colonisation belge à l'indépendance* (Paris, Maspero, 1962).

Merriam, A. P., *Congo: Background of Conflict* (Evanston, Northwestern University Press, 1961).

Moeller de Laddersous, A., 'Quelques aspects du Congo en 1952', *Bulletin des Séances de l'I.R.C.B.*, XXIII, 2, 1952, pp. 993–1050.

Mosmans, G., *L'Église à l'heure de l'Afrique* (Brussels, Casterman, 1961).

Mottoulle, L., 'Historique, organisation et résultats obtenus d'une œuvre de protection de l'enfance noire dans la population indigène industrielle de l'Union Minière du Haut-Katanga', *Bulletin des Séances de l'I.R.C.B.*, II, 1, 1931, pp. 530–44.

—— *Politique sociale de l'Union Minière du Haut-Katanga pour sa main-d'œuvre indigène* (Brussels, I.R.C.B., 1946).

Naval Intelligence Division, Admiralty, *The Belgian Congo* (Geographical Handbook Series), 1944.

Nicolai, H., and Jacques, J., *La Transformation des paysages congolais par le chemin de fer: L'Exemple du B.C.K.* (Brussels, A.R.S.C., 1954).

Philippart, L., *Le Bas Congo, état religieux et social* (Louvain, Saint Alphonse, 1929).

Pons, V. G., Xydias, Nelly, and Clément, P., 'Social Effects of Urbanization in Stanleyville, Belgian Congo: Preliminary Report of the Field Research Team of the International African Institute', forming Part III of Daryll Forde, Ed., *Social Implications of Industrialization and Urbanization in Africa South of the Sahara* (Paris, UNESCO, 1956), pp. 229–492.

Pons, V. G., 'The Changing Significance of Ethnic Affiliation and of Westernization in the African Settlement Patterns in Stanleyville (Belgian Congo)' in ibid., pp. 638–69.

Poupart, R., *Première esquisse de l'évolution du syndicalisme au Congo* (Brussels, Éditions de l'Institut de Sociologie Solvay, 1960).

Quinet, P., 'Quelques considérations sur les problèmes du service territorial', *Problèmes d'Afrique Centrale*, 1955, I, pp. 9–15.

Rae, M., 'Note d'histoire et de droit coutumier sur le litige Lulua-Baluba avant le 30 juin 1960', *Bulletin des séances de l'A.R.S.O.M.*, VII, 3, 1961, pp. 366–76.

Richelle, M., *Aspects psychologiques de l'acculturation* (Elisabethville, C.E.P.S.I., 1960).

Rolin, H., 'Les Vices de l'administration du Katanga—les remèdes', *Revue de l'Université de Bruxelles*, December 1911, pp. 177–224.

Rose, A., *The Roots of Prejudice*, 6th impression (Paris, UNESCO, 1960).

Rousseau, P., 'Relations entre chefs d'entreprise blancs et employés autochtones avant et après l'indépendance du Katanga', *Bulletin des séances de l'A.R.S.O.M.*, VII, 4, 1961, pp. 622–42.

Rubbens, A., and others, *Dettes de guerre* (Elisabethville, Éditions de *L'Essor du Congo*, 1945).

Seligman, C. G., *Races of Africa*, 3rd edition (London, O.U.P., 1957).

Slade, Ruth, *English-Speaking Missions in the Congo Independent State (1878–1908)* (Brussels, A.R.S.C., 1959).

—— *The Belgian Congo*, 2nd edition., with an additional chapter by Marjory Taylor (London, O.U.P., for the Institute of Race Relations, 1961).

—— *King Leopold's Congo* (London, O.U.P., for the Institute of Race Relations, 1962).

Smith, E. W., Ed., *African Ideas of God* (London, Edinburgh House Press, 1950).

Southall, A. W. 'Belgian and British Administration in Alurland,' *Zaire*, VIII, 5, 1954, pp. 467–86.

Staner, P., 'Les Paysannats indigènes du Congo belge et du Ruanda-Urundi', *Bulletin agricole du Congo belge*, XLVI, 3, 1955, pp. 468–549.

Stengers, J., *Combien le Congo a-t-il coûté à la Belgique?* (Brussels, A.R.S.C., 1957).

—— 'Note sur trois aspects de l'exercice des pouvoirs au Congo belge (1908–1960)', *Bulletin des séances de l'A.R.S.O.M.*, VII, 4, 1961, pp. 559–80.

—— *Belgique et Congo: l'élaboration de la charte coloniale* (Brussels, La Renaissance du Livre, 1963).

Stenmans, A., *La Reprise du Congo par la Belgique* (Brussels, Éditions Techniques et Scientifiques R. Louis, 1949).

Sundkler, B. G. M., *Bantu Prophets in South Africa*, 2nd edition (O.U.P., for the International African Institute, 1961).

Taylor, J. V., *The Primal Vision; Christian Presence amid African Religion* (London, S.C.M. Press, 1963).

Taylor, J. V., and Lehmann, Dorothea, *Christians of the Copperbelt* (London, S.C.M. Press, 1961).

Tempels, P., *Bantu Philosophy* (Paris, Présence africaine, 1959).

—— Symposium of views on *Bantu Philosophy* in *Présence africaine*, VII, 1949, pp. 252–78.

Turnbull, C. M., *The Lonely African* (London, Chatto and Windus, 1963).

Union Minière du Haut-Katanga, *Notice sur le statut du personnel* (Elisabethville, U.M.H-K., 1961, duplicated).

Van der Kerken, G., *Les Sociétés bantoues du Congo belge* (Brussels, Établissements Emile Bruylant, 1920).

―― *La Politique coloniale belge* (Antwerp, Van Dieren, 1943).

Van der Straeten, E., 'Quelques réflexions à la suite d'un voyage dans la colonie,' *Bulletin des séances de l'I.R.C.B.*, XVIII, 1, 1947, pp. 208–15.

Van Lierde, J., Ed., *La Pensée politique de Patrice Lumumba* (Brussels, Éditions Amis de Présence Africaine, 1963).

Van Lierde, J., 'Patrice Lumumba, leader et ami,' *Présence africaine*, 1st quarter, 1961, pp. 112–19.

Van Riel J., and Janssens, P. G., 'Lutte contre les endémo-epidémies', *Livre blanc*, II, pp. 917–26.

Van Wing, J., 'Une Évolution de la coutume Bakongo (Congo belge)', *Compte rendu de la cinquième semaine missiologique de Louvain 1927* (Louvain, Semaine de Missiologie, n.d.).

―― 'La Situation actuelle des populations congolaises', *Bulletin des séances de l'I.R.C.B.*, XVI, 3, 1945, pp. 584–605.

―― 'Quelques aspects de l'état social des populations indigènes du Congo belge', ibid., XVIII, 2, 1947, pp. 185–201.

―― 'Le Congo déraille', ibid., XXII, 3, 1951, pp. 609–26.

―― 'Impressions du Congo 1955', *Bulletin des séances de l'A.R.S.C.*, II, 1, 1956, pp. 169–86.

―― 'La Formation d'une élite noire au Congo belge', *Bulletin de C.E.P.S.I.*, V, 1947–8, pp. 8–22.

―― 'Le Kibangisme vu par un témoin', *Zaire*, XII, 6, 1958, pp. 563–618.

―― *Études Bakongo, sociologie, religionet magie*, 2nd edition (Brussels, (?) Desclée de Brouwer, 1959).

Vermeulen, V., *Déficiences et dangers de notre politique indigène* (privately published, 1952).

APPENDIX

EVOLUTION OF BA-KONGO CUSTOM

[This article by Father J. Van Wing appeared in 1927[1] and is now virtually unobtainable. Parts of it are here reproduced in translation on account of its succinct and authoritative analysis of Ba-Kongo custom, because the article shows with unusual clarity the tensions which resulted from the coming of European and Christian ideas, and because it relates a most interesting attempt by the author to reduce those tensions by a guided evolution of custom. Van Wing's major work on the Ba-Kongo is, of course, his *Études Bakongo, sociologie, religion et magie*.]

Some years ago a Governor-General of the Belgian Congo adhered loudly to the policy of respect for the integrity of custom; but at the same time he was giving a strong impulse to the industrialization of the colony. Ever since then this policy has progressed according to a rhythm which is certainly not that of Bantu societies. The necessity of an ever-increasing production to remunerate the capital which does not cease to be invested in the colony compels the Government itself to turn native communities upside down, and to allow them to be turned upside down, with an offhandedness and an incomprehension of social necessities and of the long-term interests of colonization which gives food for thought to every attentive observer of Central African affairs. . . .

[It is against this background, Van Wing continues, that methods of evangelism had to be conceived. Ba-Kongo custom was radically opposed to evangelization, and it was necessary to guide its evolution in the interests of missionary work and civilization alike.]

The custom studied is that of the Ba-Kongo. *Mutatis mutandis*, especially in regard to the matriarchate, the study can be applied to all the Bantu, and even to most of the peoples of inferior culture.

What, then, in a general way, is Ba-Kongo custom? It is essentially the very life of the group such as the ancestors have bequeathed it and such as the group lives it in symbiosis with the natural *milieu*, the land of the ancestors. It is this collective life, with its hereditary laws and defences which keep it on an unchanging course, with its social

---

[1] 'Une èvolution de la coutume Bakongo (Congo belge)', *Compte rendu de la cinquième semaine missiologique de Louvain 1927* (Louvain, Semaine de Missiologie, n.d.).

T

and religious organs and its magical forces which protect it against enemies within and without.

Among the Ba-Kongo, the community which lives and which makes the individual live is called *kanda*, that is the clan. For them *kanda* means what the following mean for us: the paternal house, the family, religious and civil society.

The clan is the living organic and mystical whole of all the persons who have descended, by free-born women, from the maternal head of the clan, and who bear the name of the clan. It comprises two classes of persons: the ancestors who live beneath the soil and their descendants who live in the light of the sun. The grave in ancestral soil is the gateway from the second to the first class.

The ancestors constitute the preponderant class. They are the masters of their descendants, masters endowed with a superhuman power. They are the true owners of the soil, their descendants having only the right of use and of usufruct. Their existence is one of superior power [*ils vivent puissament*] and it is from them that the life of the terrestrial clan depends; it is thanks to them that the women conceive and bear children, that the stock prosper, that the lands raise harvests, that the palm trees produce wine, that the forests and bush yield up game, that the streams and lakes provide fish. They both give life to, and contend with, the agents of death, the evil spirits and the *ndoki*-sorcerers whom they prevent from exercising their destructive power. But they accord their protection only on condition that their descendants observe their laws and render the traditional worship.

The second class of the clan consists therefore of the 'terrestrials', those who live in the light of the sun on the ancestral lands. The clan occupies one or several villages, according to the number of lines into which the original clan is divided. Each branch of the clan has its village, its characteristic and independent life; it divides itself into as many compounds as there are lines in the village.

Chiefly authority over the village belongs by right to the most direct descendant of the maternal head of the senior line. The compounds are governed by elders, subordinates of the chief. They make up the council of notables and are present with the chief in all important matters.

The chief is first and foremost the priest of the ancestor cult, essential cult of the Ba-Kongo, on which the prosperity of the clan and of individuals absolutely depends. The chief has custody of the sacred basket which contains relics of all the ancestors who have played a part in the history of the clan. Every four days he offers prayers and libations in their honour; periodically he does the same thing on their graves and, besides this, organizes more solemn festivals in honour of all the dead of the clan.

The chief is, secondly, the judge of the village; he is also the master and in some sense the owner [*possesseur-usufruitier*] of all the members of his line, especially the women. The chief represents the village before men and before the spirits because he is supposed to be the descendant, and therefore the representative, of the original ancestor. In that capacity he in some sense sums up in himself all the interests of the clan.

The clan is established on the basis of the matriarchate or of kinship on the mother's side. The child belongs to the clan of the mother, and the mother to her maternal uncle or to his successor. Succession is from brother to brother, or from uncle to nephew, always in the mother's line.

Children remain with their parents only until the age of about twelve. Then they go to the maternal uncle's village where they are at his service until their marriage. Once married, custom lays down for them the duties which they ought to continue to owe him. The boys used to undergo the rites of puberty and, in many cases, of the *Kimpasi* secret society; they were thus initiated into all the secrets of the social and magico-religious life of the clan.

The girls, towards the age of sixteen, are given in marriage, by means of payment of a dowry, to a man of another clan. The woman, says the proverb, ought to produce riches both material and human. Material riches are the produce of the soil; field-work is the prerogative of the woman, the man scarcely involving himself in it. The woman is therefore only lent to the husband; their union continues to exist only as long as the two parties find advantage in it. Human wealth the woman procures for her clan in bringing to birth new members.

Men or women, whatever their condition, conceive no other ideal than that which they have before them, that which their ancestors have bequeathed to them. With conviction they repeat the proverb: 'What my ancestor said, I say: the way which my ancestor followed, I follow.'

Here is a pale *résumé* of Ba-Kongo custom, of custom in its entirety. It is the clan itself, the extremely complicated social organization which absorbs the individual, but which also protects him first of all against himself and then against other men and against evil spirits.

Into this living whole usages and customs are integrated, that is to say obligatory ways of acting particular to certain circumstances; these are collective or individual practices, religious or magical rites, which tradition has bequeathed and which society imposes on individuals in special circumstances. Such are marriage, birth, illness, death; such again are hunting, fishing and other pursuits. [Van Wing goes on to speak of the developing forms of Catholic missionary work in the Kisantu region (whence stemmed his particular knowledge) in the period up to the beginning of the First World War. By that time nuclei of Christians were well established amongst the Ba-Kongo, and Christians and pagan alike were recovering from the fearful devastation wrought by sleeping-sickness in the preceding fifteen years or so. As both categories again began to envisage a future the tensions between the two conceptions grew.]

Let us spell out the respective positions more precisely. The pagans had the numbers; they had the authority; they had the clan heads, the lineage heads and the chiefs invested by the Government; especially did they possess the forces—living, social and magical [*mânistes* and *fétichistes*]—which act directly on the Ba-Kongo soul.

The Christians were the minority, about one-seventh of the population. But the birth-rate amongst them was higher and their number increased still further each year by the reinforcement of baptized catechumens. As living forces they had their Christian faith, in general firm, the love of their new home, and desire enough to continue their economic ascension. But these three elements were quite contrary to the pagan ideal; so that our neophytes had to struggle against themselves as much as against the environment in which they lived.

Let us briefly enumerate the principal occasions of conflict. In the case of the illness of a child the Christians have to seek natural remedies and, for the rest, trust to Providence. As Ba-Kongo they have to make recourse to fetishes and to the ancestors to discover the author of the malevolent action, the cause of the illness; as members of the clan they have to submit themselves to all the rites which the 'elder' of the clan prescribed. Now not to obey the elder is to provoke the anger of the ancestors, is to expose oneself to the danger of being taken for a '*ndoki*-eater of men', is certainly to attract the hatred of the elders, who would not be able to understand such obstinacy; in a word it is almost to make oneself undesirable.

In the case of the illness of husband or wife the difficulties are of the same kind but still greater because the *corpus delicti* is more important.

At the death of the wife, those who owned her make great difficulties for the husband before proceeding with the burial. The husband has to bury a great quantity of his own goods with the corpse of his wife if he wishes to remain in harmony with her parents; then they will go away taking with them the children and the goods left by the deceased. The husband remains alone, without children, impoverished; he can begin again *ab ovo* to build a home for himself.

At the death of the husband all the goods of the wife are either destroyed or consumed or buried; in the same way the goods of the decreased are consumed or buried with the corpse. The widow, once her very painful period of mourning is finished, returns to her clan.

At every death there is therefore the total dislocation of the family, the stupid destruction of goods.

If the family prospers, if the children reach the age of fourteen or fifteen there are conflicts of authority in regard to them; the clan claims them: the boys, because they are the servants born of the elders, the girls because they work and are worth dowries which become more and more exorbitant in proportion as life returns to normal. In these palavers the understanding between parents very often founders because the mother, harried by those who own her, yields more easily whilst the father holds firm.

All along the line there are conflicts of conscience, complicated by questions of money and other matters.

In this day-to-day struggle the Catholics experienced numerous defeats, but the Christian community was always opposed to the pagan community; it never forsook its principles. From year to year also, since the Christians were increasing in number, their influence in the region caused custom to evolve in their direction.

However, palavers remained numerous. When, on my return to the Congo at the beginning of the year 1921, I was given charge of the Kisantu district, they flowed like water into the valley during a thunderstorm. To obtain respect for the most essential rights of the Christians it was necessary to haggle, to contrive, to negotiate and often to throw into the balance one's personal prestige. From this fact I was able to acquire an absolutely certain and intimate knowledge of the state of custom and of feeling.

In a matter of this kind the Colonial Administration does not, and scarcely can intervene. It would do more harm than good in wishing directly to reform custom in its entirety. But it was that result that it was necessary to obtain. It is impossible to have flourishing and solid *chrétientés* if the social and juridical organization of the people is in direct contradiction with the first principles of religious liberty, paternal authority and domestic economy.

It therefore remained for me to seek a solution myself; I consulted the head catechists, the senior Christians, the [local Church] leaders in the region, and finally some senior pagan chiefs whose confidence I possessed. Meanwhile the movement which brought the pagans to become catechumens grew stronger; the Christians were becoming the majority; the majority of the influential chiefs were Christians or catechumens.

Reform, as I conceived it, had to be based on the principle of the personal right of Christians; it was necessary to ensure that the representatives of custom should work out, in a manner compatible with the indigenous point of view, the personal and family status of our Christians, such as the Congo Civil code laid down for natives who were *immatriculés*. To establish the personal status it sufficed that they should recognize the position of the individual over and against the clan which until then was alone accepted as having civil personality, it was necessary that they should determine the cases where adults could, according to their faith and conscience, act against the laws of the clan—to create the status for the family it was necessary, and was sufficient, that they should recognize certain rights of parents over children, certain preponderant rights which, hitherto, the maternal uncle exercised. In conclusion, as a necessary consequence of this double status, it was necessary to establish the possibility of creating and conserving a family patrimony with a community of goods in the household and the right of succession in direct line.

In 1924, in the month of June, I believed the moment to have come; minds appeared to me to be ripe for reform. The heads of Catholic families of the Kisantu region were summoned to a plenary meeting; 560 responded to the invitation. I set out to them the object of the deliberation: that Catholics should know how to act in the event of illness, death or marriage of one of their family. Then I explained to them the dictates of custom and the ways in which it had accidentally come to be modified on the points indicated, the antinomy of these dictates with Catholic dogma and morality, either with the basic economy of the monogamous family or simply with the most elementary economic laws. The sympathy with which the assembly heard this exposition at once proved to me that the game was won.

I therefore took up again, point by point, the prescriptions of custom and put the question: is it necessary to maintain this prescription or should it be changed? If it is necessary to change it, what ought to be put in its place?

Then the discussion began, but in general only the leaders spoke; the mass listened, approved or disapproved. After three hours of deliberation the essential points had been discussed and modifications generally approved unanimously.

The resolutions taken were then and there committed to writing, copies were sent to the Christian chiefs. They would communicate them to the pagan chiefs and discuss the resolutions with them. Furthermore it was decided that on 15 August following there would be a plenary assembly, also including the pagan chiefs, who would deliberate on the definitive adoption of the new custom in the radius of the Kisantu mission, subject to the at least tacit agreement of the Administration.

The echo of these deliberations spread through all the country round about; everywhere, in the markets and in the village centres people discussed the reforms. On 15 August the plenary assembly approved all the resolutions which had been taken. They were printed and distributed to all the chiefs, to all the Christians.

It remained to supervise the carrying into execution. It was what one expected: on the whole almost perfect; on some ancillary points deficient, especially in some villages where the pagan spirit ruled more strongly.

As the women were directly interested in these affairs it was essential that they should be kept informed and should help in the full execution of the reforms; I got them to hold their meeting in 1925; they were 600. Not having the right of discussion, they listened attentively to the explanation of the question and the justification of the reforms which had been adopted by their husbands.

Because of the immense significance of the modifications introduced, which had repercussions in the whole of family and social life, and because of their complexity, I wished to submit them to a revision in the month of June 1926. The heads of family of Kisantu, to the number of 800, and those of Kimpako, to the number of 450, devoted a long meeting to this examination. Now the two assemblies have unanimously adopted and confirmed the reforms of 1924. Two years' experience has shown them the usefulness of the adaptation of custom to the religious, social and economic progress achieved in their country.

Outside the districts served by the missions of Kisantu and Kimpako, and even among the Protestants, the innovations were warmly welcomed. They are in process of conquering the whole of the Ba-Kongo country.

Here are the principal dispositions of the new custom. In case of illness and death of a child the father alone decides what is to be done. The mother's parents can see to the carrying-out neither of manist nor of fetish rites. They must only contribute to the burial expenses. All the fines laid down for alleged evil spells are suppressed.

When the wife falls ill or dies, the same arrangements. But beyond this the family property is respected. A maximum of what can be buried with the corpse is laid down. The husband can inherit the goods of his wife. The small livestock is shared between him and his parents-in-law; this is a concession to the past, but it has its justification: it is necessary that the parents-in-law remain interested in the smooth running of the household.

At the death of the husband the same rules apply but they are stricter. The widow can inherit everything which entered into the common life but on one condition: it is that she remains with all her children in the clan of the deceased husband. It was the chiefs who wanted this arrangement; I had not dared to propose this degree of emancipation of the widow from the hold of her clan. But the assembly was unanimous in calling for this when it was proposed by one of the most intelligent chiefs in the region. This proves their logical mind and their aptitude in legislation. However, the widow is not required to remain in the village of her brothers-in-law. She can return to her own clan. But then precise rules determine the rights and duties of the respective clans in regard to the widow and the children.

As for the children of Christian families the rights of parents entirely predominate as far as education and setting-up in life are concerned. However, the clan bonds of these children are not broken. The maternal uncle keeps a right of control; he is involved to the extent of a half in the question of the dowry: for the boys he pays half, for the girls he receives half.

Touching the question of adultery, which is of capital importance for the stability of families, the customary fine to be paid by the delinquent was raised by the assembly from 100 to 200 francs, and if there is transmission of venereal disease, to 450 francs.

In all this labour of adaptation of Ba-Kongo custom, we have taken care to be moderate and, whilst being precise, leaving a deliberate flexibility to permit further evolution and adaptation to new social situations. . . .

INDEX

A.B.A.K.O. Party, an ethnic group, 221–2, 233, 242–3, 244; issues manifesto, 221–2, 223; advocates federalism, 221, 232–3, 236; intransigent, 221, 228, 236–7, 238; policy of, 221–2; and elections, 224, 242, 258; exclusive, 226; theoretically dissolved, 229; alliance with other parties, 232, 236–7, 259; and secession, 232, 233, 234, 252, 258; and Round Table Conference, 236–7; and strong central government, 241; has effective power in Leopoldville, 256; is given two ministries, 259: *A.B.A.K.O. 1950–1960,* 222

Aborigines Protection Society, 10

Abyssinian campaign, 143

Accra, 136; Pan-African Conference (1958) at, 226–7

Administrateurs territoriaux, and rubber collection, 5; recruitment of, 9, 87; duties of, 48, 78; and appointment of chiefs, 51; character of, 52–53, 168–9; *-adjoints,* 53, 79, 81; and traditional society, 59, 262; and *chefferies,* 55, 63; and taxes, 56; and *secteurs,* 68; training of, 77; lose touch with Africans, 79–81, 144–5, 150–1, 155, 165; and compulsory work, 82–83, 152; and recruitment of labour, 87; in World War II, 144–7; and Independence, 231, 255–6

Adoula, Cyrille, 219, 220, 226

Africa and Christianity, 96

'Africa for the Africans', 112, 128, 131

African Ideas of God, 96

Africans, and promotion, 198, 204, 207, 222; Europeans' relationship with, 205–6

Agents territoriaux, and rubber collection, 5; inadequacies of, 53–55, 168–9; training of, 53, 77; character of, 81, 86; and compulsory cultivation, 83; attitude to Africans, 168

Agricultural Department, 82–83, 86, 146

Agriculture, needs of, 82, 106–7, 110–11, 114; War increases, 144; sale of crops, 146, 163; low prices for African crops, 161; Ten-Year Plan and, 165

Aketi, 104

Albert I, King, 41, 129

Albertville, 45, 104, 114, 166, 178

All Saints' Day, and ancestor-worship, 135, 141

Alur tribe, 24

Amicales, 219–20

An African Survey, 24, 26, 42, 44, 46, 50, 66–67, 78, 87, 88, 109, 110, 115, 116, 117, 120, 166, 195, 208, 211

Ancestor-worship, 71, 73, 92–93, 98, 135, 141, 274

Andersson, E. (cited), 124, 125, 126, 127, 128, 129, 130–1, 132, 133, 134, 136, 137, 139, 158

Anglo-Belgian India Rubber Company, 9, 11, 38

Ango-Ango, 104

Angola, 126, 222

Anstey, R. (cited), 29, 92

Arabs, 2, 25, 31–32

Argentine, 1

Aruwimi-Lomami region 32

Asamoa, E. A. (cited), 94

Ascherson, N. (cited), 2, 44

Aspects psychologiques de l'acculturation, 97, 157, 181, 182, 184, 189, 192, 209, 212

Association du Personnel Indigène du Congo (A.P.I.C.), 219

Association Internationale du Congo, 1, 29

Association of *Évolués* of Stanleyville, 189

Association of Former Pupils of the Pères de Scheut, 189

Association Progrès Social Rive Gauche, 189

A Ten-Year Plan for the Economic and Social Development of the Belgian Congo, 160

U

S